CHALLENGING TERRITORY

The Writing of Margaret Laurence

the writing of Margaret Laurence

challenging
territory

edited by Christian Riegel

University of Alberta Press

Published by
The University of Alberta Press
141 Athabasca Hall
Edmonton, Alberta, Canada T6G 2E8

Copyright © The University of Alberta Press 1997

ISBN 0—88864—289—X

Canadian Cataloguing in Publication Data

Main entry under title:
Challenging territory

Includes bibliographical references and index.
ISBN 0-88864-289-X

1. Laurence, Margaret, 1926–1987—Criticism and interpretation.
I. Riegel, Christian Erich, 1968–
PS8523.A86Z62 1997   C813'.54   C97-910001-1
PR9199.3.L33C52 1997

Printed and bound in Canada by Friesens, Altona, Manitoba.
Printed on acid-free paper. ∞

The University of Alberta Press gratefully acknowledges the support received for its publishing
program from The Canada Council for the Arts, the Department of Canadian Heritage, and The
Alberta Foundation for the Arts.

COMMITTED TO THE DEVELOPMENT OF CULTURE AND THE ARTS

CONTENTS

CONTRIBUTORS

BRENDA BECKMAN-LONG lives in Regina, Saskatchewan.

GABRIELLE COLLU, holder of a SSHRC postdoctoral award, is working on a study of South Asian writers at York University. She has published on Sara Jeanette Duncan and has guest-edited an issue of *Textual Studies in Canada.*

MÉIRA COOK is a poet, writer and graduate student at the University of Manitoba.

JILL FRANKS is an Assistant Professor of English at Austin Peay State University in Clarksville, Tennessee. She is author of the book *Revisionist Resurrection Mythologies: A Study of D.H. Lawrence's Italian Works.* She is currently editing and introducing the Penguin edition of *Sea and Sardinia,* a travel book by D.H. Lawrence. Besides Lawrence studies, Dr. Franks is a scholar of contemporary Canadian literature by women. She taught at the University of British Columbia from 1992 to 1995.

THOMAS M.F. GERRY is Associate Professor of English at Laurentian University, Sudbury, Ontario, where he teaches Canadian literature and edits the interdisciplinary journal *Arachnē.* Recently he published *Canadian and U.S. Women of Letters: An Annotated Bibliography* (Garland). As guest editor, he is currently preparing a *Journal of Canadian Studies* special issue on interdisciplinarity.

DICK HARRISON is Professor Emeritus at the University of Alberta and is writing a book on "Borders/Frontiers: Fictions of the Canadian and American Wests." His previous books include *Unnamed Country, Crossing Frontiers* (ed.), and *Intimations of Mortality: W.O. Mitchell's Who Has Seen the Wind.*

ANGELIKA MAESER LEMIEUX teaches at Vanier College in Montreal and has published on Laurence, feminist spirituality, multicultural pedagogy, and Native Literature. She is currently completing a longer study: *A Feminist Spirituality: Faith and Politics in the Fiction of Margaret Laurence.*

BARBARA PELL is Professor of English at Trinity Western University. She has recently completed *Face and Fiction: A Theological Critique of the Narrative Stratagies of Hugh MacLennan and Morley Callaghan.*

CHRISTIAN RIEGEL teaches English at the University of Alberta where he is completing his doctoral dissertation entitled, "Death and Mourning in Margaret Laurence's Manawaka Fiction." He publishes on Canadian, American, and postcolonial writing.

MARY RIMMER is Associate Professor of English at the University of New Brunswick. She has recently completed an edition of Thomas Hardy's *Desperate Remedies* for Penguin Books, and is preparing an edition of Hardy's *The Trumpet-Major* for Everyman.

NORA FOSTER STOVEL is Associate Professor of English at the University of Alberta. She has published numerous articles on twentieth-century writers, including D.H. Lawrence, Margaret Drabble, Margaret Atwood, and Laurence. Her books include *Margaret Drabble: Symbolic Moralist, Stacey's Choice: Margaret Laurence's The Fire-Dwellers* and *Rachel's Children: Margaret Laurence's A Jest of God.* She is completing *Wise Heart: A Biography of Margaret Laurence* and *Margaret Laurence, Diviner.* She lives in Edmonton with her husband Bruce Stovel and their two children.

DONEZ XIQUES, a member of the English Department at Brooklyn College, City University of New York, is presently completing a book, *Margaret Laurence: The Development of a Writer,* that treats Laurence's eary literary career. She introduced the ECW edition of Laurence's *A Tree for Poverty.* She has published widely on Canadian and American literature.

ACKNOWLEDGEMENTS

Much of the developmental work on the manuscript would have been infinitely more difficult without the help and advice of Nora Foster Stovel, Jill Manderson, Len Falkenstein, Katherine Robinson, Gwendolyn Davies and Karen Overbye. I also owe thanks to Clara Thomas and Bruce Stovel for their enthusiastic support of the project at its early stages. I have learned much from Mary Mahoney-Robson, editor at the University of Alberta Press, about the job of producing books, and I am grateful for the enthusiasm she has demonstrated for this book.

The University of Alberta Press gratefully acknowledges the Department of Canadian Heritage, The Canada Council for the Arts and The Alberta Foundation for the Arts for their support that made publication of this collection on Margaret Laurence possible.

| CHRISTIAN RIEGEL

INTRODUCTION

Recognizing the Multiplicity of the Oeuvre

Margaret Laurence touched Canadians like no other writer during her celebrated life and career. A nerve was struck in the Canadian psyche with the humanity Laurence displayed in her fictional portrayals of Canada. In her writing she depicted "The theme of survival—survival not just in the physical sense, but the survival of some human dignity and in the end the survival of some human warmth and ability to reach out and touch others" ("Sources" 15). She filled a void in Canadian self-knowledge— what Margaret Atwood described as unknown territory to Canadians: "I'm talking about Canada as a state of mind, as the space you inhabit not just with your body but with your head. It's that kind of space in which we find ourselves lost" (*Survival* 18).[1] Laurence showed Canadian readers and writers that one could legitimately and successfully write about "home," and do so with a voice particularly Canadian.

Dennis Lee remarks upon the effect that Laurence's writing had:

She was the most loved writer in English Canada for a decade or so, about fifteen years from the mid-1960s to 1980. There were people who found that she spoke for them. I remember my parents saying, "God do you know Margaret Laurence?" These were people who'd have roots in small towns, who were intelligent, who were no longer constrained within small-town Puritan Canada....I think they found, reading Margaret, that decency and passion could come together in writing and not be mediocre writing, and be rooted where they lived. (Wainwright III)

As John Lennox notes, Laurence was revered in Canada as a "literary and cultural celebrity" (xii) because her writing spoke to the new sense of cultural nationalism that Canadians were experiencing in the late 1960s and early 1970s (xiii). Laurence did not so much write to a nationalist urge (for she wrote most of her Manawaka work while living abroad), as she provided a body of work that fulfilled a need by a Canadian public eager to explore their own identity—their own psychic space. That Laurence's repute has extended beyond the relatively short period of time when the celebration of Canadian nationalism was yet to be troubled—by the unity debates of the last 15 or 20 years—bespeaks a relevance to her writing that exceeds considerations of Canadian identity and nationalism alone.

Overwhelmingly Laurence is known by the reading public and by scholars for her Canadian work—the Manawaka cycle that comprises five texts set in a fictional Manitoba town is seen as Laurence's culminating artistic achievement. Laurence's publishing history, however, displays a multiplicity that readers familiar with only her Canadian work might not recognize. Laurence possessed a significant corpus of work that pre-dates and post-dates the Manawaka work. While she was not an exceptionally prolific writer, Laurence held a wide range of interests that are mirrored in her oeuvre. She published five novels (*This Side Jordan*, *The Stone Angel*, *A Jest of God*, *The Fire-Dwellers*, and *The Diviners*), two collections of short-stories (*The Tomorrow-Tamer* and *A Bird in the House*), a children's novel (*Jason's Quest*), and three shorter children's books (*The Olden Days Coat*, *Six Darn Cows* and *The Christmas Birthday Story*). Yet, a totalling of her fiction only tells part of the story. She also published five works of nonfiction, displaying her diverse interests. The texts range from the translations of Somali poems and stories (*A Tree for Poverty*), to her critical work on African writers (*Long Drums and Cannons*), to a volume of her own essays (*Heart of a Stranger*), and two memoirs (*The Prophet's Camel Bell* and *Dance on the Earth*). Recent scholarly work has resulted in the posthumous publication of some of Laurence's letters (*Margaret Laurence—Al Purdy: A Friendship in Letters* and *A Very Large Soul: Selected Letters from Margaret Laurence to Canadian Writers*), further adding to the oeuvre. Five of her books deal with African subject matter, the children's novel is set in England, and the remaining five fictional books are set in Canada. The diversity of the essays collected in *Heart of a Stranger* reinforces the image of a multiplicity to Laurence's interests that extends beyond matters Canadian.

Soon after her death in 1987, two volumes of scholarly essays appeared that mark the spirit of response to Laurence's life and work at the time and that mirror the general perception of her in Canada. Both books were offered as tributes or memorials and were meant to honour the writer—as their titles indicate: *Crossing the River: Essays in Honour of Margaret Laurence* and *Margaret Laurence: An Appreciation*. They both reflect Clara Thomas's statement in the afterword to *The Prophet's Camel Bell* that in her lifetime Laurence "became the most beloved woman in Canada" (268). Kristjana Gunnars in *Crossing the River* summed up the sentiment accurately when she wrote:

> It was somehow important to show our appreciation for what she had accomplished in her life. Margaret Laurence has been a founding mother of Canadian literature. She has given voice to the Manitoba prairie. She has raised the value of all sectors of society by showing the full humanity of the most neglected and forgotten among us. From her example we have learned the value of Canadian literature and culture. (viii)

Walter Swayze echoes the feeling of having been touched in a personal way by Laurence's writing: "[We] have read her novels and short stories with gratitude. They have given us a good read, but they have said something important to us, something that has struck home in a significant way" (Swayze 5). W.H. New's words of a decade earlier offer insight into the motivations behind some of the later tributes when he points out that Laurence had a way of writing in the discourses of Canadians—a manner of expression that Canadians could easily identify with. As he writes, "Perhaps more than any other writer of her time, she seemed to have mastered the rhythms and cadences of the Canadian speaking voice. She used them without apology. She celebrated her regional roots" (1).

The critical heritage to this day mirrors the nationalism inherent in those years; the primary focus of the majority of critical responses has been the Manawaka fiction. Within a historical context, the focus on the Canadian work in the criticism is understandable. Canadian literature was just beginning to be recognized as a legitimate subject in universities across the country, and when a writer came along "who wrote about ordinary people and everyday life and who, in the process, powerfully described Canada's historical and cultural geography" (Lennox xiv), then that writer would also naturally be embraced by the fledgling "Canadianists"—scholars, students, and public—who were on a quest for a recognizable Canadian identity.

While the Canadian fiction is the origin of Laurence's reputation in her country of birth, she also had an important impact on other areas of writing. What is less known, and acknowledged, is that she also has had a significant sphere of influence outside her own country of birth. Her first publication, appearing in 1954, *A Tree for Poverty* "is still considered a landmark by scholars of Somali life and literature" (Xiques 7). This early book is notable, in particular, because "the attention paid to the oral tradition out of which the stories and poems grow is a landmark in the study of African literature" (Gunnars 1994, 822). In a larger sense, *A Tree for Poverty* is instructive in indicating "the necessity of probing the oral cultures of Commonwealth countries in order to find the roots of regional literatures" (822–23). Laurence's influence on Nigerian writing, also, is significant: "Chinua Achebe and other Nigerian writers...have repeatedly acknowledged the stimulus and the fostering that she gave to the brilliant literary movement that was so tragically truncated by civil war" (Swayze 3–4).[2] These influences are largely (although not completely) unexplored in the scholarship. The African work in general has had a mixed response from critics and readers; in many ways, the groundwork for assessing these works on a larger scale is yet to be completed.

Recent developments in literary history require that more attention be paid to Laurence's African writing. In the contemporary context, her early work takes on a new importance as Canadians begin to come to terms with the postcolonial condition. The dismantling of colonialism has been described as "one of the most spectacular events or series of events of the twentieth century" (Williams and Chrisman 1). If we stake any validity to that claim in the least[3]—and the growing body of theory that examines postcoloniality seems to support such claims—then we must pay more attention to a writer such as Laurence in that context. This is particularly important since Laurence occupies a singularly interesting and unique position in Canadian writing as both a colonial and postcolonial author.[4] Postcolonial theorists generally would agree that "There is little doubt that matters of colony and empire have moved centre stage in Anglo-American literary and cultural theory over the last fifteen years" (Barker, Hulme, Iverson 1). Yet, there has been a tendency, as Diana Brydon notes, to gloss over the role Canadian writers have in the realms of the colonial and postcolonial: "The history of Canadian contributions to post-colonial studies is now being erased from both Canadian literary history and current accounts of postcolonialism" (2).[5] If we are to avoid what Brydon has termed a "double erasure," then certainly Laurence must figure in the discussion—for her African writings have much to contribute, and should be considered as texts that can signify in their own right and on their own terms.

There is a very real temptation, nonetheless, to write and think of Laurence's work as a homogeneous set of works. In one such narrative, Laurence's writing career is summed up as an "unbroken journey." The African and Canadian work is seen as "a seamless fabric" representing the "growth and maturation" of the author into an individual with a singular "way of seeing" (Morley 33). Another version offers a similar narrative by describing the African work as the "apprenticeship" to the Canadian fiction (Woodcock 5). W.J. Keith, commenting on trends in the scholarship, remarks that "it is a commonplace of Laurence criticism to say that she learned, while in Africa, the complex fate of being a Canadian, and that her presentation of the Manawaka world required the radical distancing of perspective that her stay in Africa provided" (119). Frank Birbalsingh goes one step further than most critics, not only proclaiming the apprentice quality of Laurence's African work but also erasing the possibility of her having been influenced by her experiences at all:

> The African books are rightly regarded as apprentice work, training ground on which the author exercises untried imaginative resources and narrative skills which are later to be deployed on her principle subject....While there is no dispute about the African books representing the initial stages of Laurence's development as a writer, it is not entirely correct to suppose that these books, or her African experiences as a whole, have influenced Laurence's thinking significantly: this early work contributes mainly to her technical development. (108)

The focus is on how the early work leads to the later Canadian work—to how it represents a logical path of development to the texts that have mattered the most to Canadian readers. Birbalsingh signifies the technical development over the possibility that Laurence gained cultural insight into the societies she encountered. Laurence's three nonfictional African books negate his viewpoint to a large extent, since all demonstrate a sophisticated social, cultural and political awareness of her surroundings. Such positions, by their very nature, unwittingly can slide into an elision of multiplicity. I am not arguing that these views are wrong, but I am suggesting that we need to interrogate such readings to be sure that important areas of Laurence's writing are not obscured. These narratives are reflections of the way that histories are frequently written: in the singular and as closed complete narrative. The resulting suggestion is "that history is integral, uniform, and continuous" (McGann 196). If anything, the advent of postmodernist theories has shown us that we must tread carefully in our attempts at finding explanations for the things we encounter in the world.[6] Seeing history from a plural perspective gives renewed relevance to G.D. Killam's assessment in 1976 of Laurence's first novel, set in Africa, *This Side Jordan*. Killam's reading of the novel's importance runs against the grain of the acknowledged narratives of its place in the oeuvre:

> Some critics have suggested that because Margaret Laurence's novel was topical it will prove less interesting and readable, less important as time goes on. I think not, for while the novel carries in itself its own credibility and convincingness, *This Side Jordan* can be taken together with Achebe's book [*Things Fall Apart*] (and now indeed with a spate of African fiction) to illuminate a period in the history and to communicate an understanding gained from contemplating it, which will not lose its relevance. (xii)

The significance of *This Side Jordan* to Killam is of how it relates to other African writing and to a particular social and cultural context. Contrary to later commentators, who limit the importance of social context in favour of formal considerations,[7] Killam prioritizes it. And at the same time, just because the novel's cultural commentary is not aimed particularly at a "Canadian" consciousness, does not mean that it should not be studied along with the more identifiably Canadian texts. Indeed, within the scope of postcolonial theory Killam's assessment takes on a renewed importance. From the perspective of reading history in the plural, however, it does not invalidate the later narrative. Neither is mutually exclusive; rather, the narratives complement each other and help together to gain a fuller understanding of Laurence's career. Jerome McGann commenting on the vagaries of history remarks that "every so-called fact or event in history is imbedded in an indeterminate set of multiple and overlapping networks" (197). E.D. Blodgett calls literary history "the sum of continuous negotiations" (3) and, as Jeanette Lynes and Herb Wyile observed "literary history is hardly a consensual, communal project to which scholars make their contributions, but rather a site of conflict, debate, and revision" (117). Thus, history should be written and read in the plural; frequently, the interplay of the networks that McGann refers to are what allow a fleeting impression of what a life, a career, or a segment of time and space, were really like.

Challenging Territory: The Writing of Margaret Laurence presents the plurality of the life and writing of Margaret Laurence, and signals the plurality and multiplicity of the ouevre. As a collection, the essays stake out a critical territory, charting critical space never before traced, as well as offering a challenge to territory previously mapped by the criticism. The collective offers ways of mapping the territory that do not necessarily invalidate other ways of charting the conceptual space. At the same time, the papers are single pieces, written by different authors and from very different perspectives, and stand alone as statements on specific areas of Laurence's life and work. By "challenging" the territory that has been laid out, critics and readers of Laurence can extend the conceptual space the ouevre occupies.

Mary Rimmer's exploration of the complexities faced by a white writer, working in the English language, in representing the multitude of languages present in Africa, leads the volume. She explores the ways in which Laurence was sensitive to language as a site of cultural conflict and outlines the three-tiered structure of languages that Laurence employs in the African fiction. Central to Rimmer's essay is an emphasis on the importance of identifying Laurence's "sense of verbal communication as a central issue in postcolonial culture." In Laurence's colonial world language is depicted as a commodity, and good English commands the most value within this linguistic economy while Twi and pidgin English are worth the least. Yet, all linguistic interchanges, be they in Twi, pidgin, or English, or a combination of these languages, are fraught with complexities and the linguistic hierarchy is frequently subverted by Laurence to show that true power does not always reside where it at first appears to. Rimmer considers the difficulties—and criticism—that a writer such as Laurence met in trying to represent languages other than English. For there are deeply political implications implicit in the appropriation and representation of another language.

Drawing on a position informed by postcolonial theories of alterity, Gabrielle Collu explores Laurence's attempts at fairly representing the "Other" in "The Drummer of All the World" and *This Side Jordan*. She argues that Laurence approaches the difficulty of representing others from a position of empathy and humility rather than from one of sympathy. The distinctions are integral when one tries to differentiate between exploitative representations of the Other in colonial and postcolonial writing and attempts at narrowing bridges between self and other.

Laurence's vision of colonized peoples challenges typical colonialist representations in large part because of her ability to recognize her own limitations in the project. Collu sees in Laurence's African writing "revisionist, sensitive, and occasionally empowering representations of the Other."

Like Rimmer, Collu recognizes the culturally specific information that can be gained from a closer analysis of Laurence's African writing in light of current postcolonial debates. The first two papers deal with the complexities that a white writer faced in representing a world that was alien to her. Both Rimmer and Collu examine aspects of the relationship between coloniality and postcoloniality in Laurence's work. The authors trace the difficulties that Laurence faced in attempting to come to terms with her experiences in Africa. This theorization of Laurence's tenuous position as a white colonial figure is a necessary and important beginning to further work on the African texts.

Barbara Pell approaches the issue of the African work from another perspective. Rather than examining the texts from a theoretical position mitigated by postcolonial considerations, she argues that Laurence's experiences in Africa, linked with her Canadian background, result in a specific representation of gender and power conflicts. She argues that the Canadian and African works are inter-related in that the Canadian heroines are essentially "born" in Africa—that, in effect, the Canadian writing that was "so crucial in the gender-balanced development of contemporary Canadian writing" grew out of her African experience. She traces this thesis through the African fiction, and nonfiction, to the Canadian work. In all of these texts, matriarchal models are shown to be of particular importance in counteracting phallocentric repression, and Laurence's heroines are seen as victims of social stereotyping constructed by Old Testament and Calvinist archetypes and theology. Laurence uses a pattern of religious imagery that moves from the Old Testament to the New Testament to mirror the heroines' progression from a position of bondage to grace, and Pell demonstrates that on the level of religious imagery the narrative of the inter-relationship of the African and Canadian writing carries a great deal of validity. Combined with Rimmer and Collu's work, Pell's chapter exemplifies how diverse and multiplicitous Laurence's work is. Most importantly, these three papers demonstrate that an approach that prioritizes plurality results in a fuller understanding of the writer.

Shifting to the Manawaka work, Brenda Beckman-Long argues that for *The Stone Angel* to be fully understood, it must be read generically as a feminine fictive confessional. She begins her examination by defining the genre through narratological and life-writing theory. An identification of *The Stone Angel* as confessional fiction reveals a structural and thematic coherence to the novel that is bound by its particular generic traits. Beckman-Long delineates a definition of the genre as it applies to Hagar Shipley's narrative, beginning with Saint Augustine's *Confessions*, extending to Peter Axthelm's attributes of the modern confessional novel, and concluding that *The Stone Angel* is a book of its time in that it appropriates confessional forms with specifically feminine purposes, which are to express feminine experience in new ways. Beckman-Long presents a detailed reading of the novel, drawing on Gérard Genette's writing on narrative time. Implicit in her argument is that with her first Canadian novel, written in 1964, Laurence was in tune with international developments in fiction writing by women.

My own contribution explores death and mourning in *A Bird in the House*, which I argue is structured as a text of mourning, or work of mourning, in the sense of Freud's definition of the term. The term mourning is further theorized in relation to recent sociological work in the field, signalling the cross-disciplinary nature of literary studies that examine the emotions. Such a perspective elucidates the particular social, cultural, and historical, concerns of Laurence's treatment of the phenomenon. My focus is on how *A Bird in the House* functions as a self-conscious text of mourning, and on how the narrator, Vanessa MacLeod, forms and shapes the memories of her formative years into an artistic work.

Méira Cook and Jill Franks offer perspectives on Laurence's fiction that are mediated by highly personal and feminist responses to the work. Cook proposes a way of reading *The Diviners* that is mediated by her own highly personal experiences of reading Julia Kristeva's essay "Stabat Mater" from *Tales of Love*. In doing so, Cook shows us new ways of responding to *The Diviners*, both as private reader and as academic. The two manners of reading and reacting, she demonstrates, are not mutually exclusive but rather are productive means of understanding a text. Cook explores the construction of the maternal in *The Diviners* as both a biological category and as conceptual paradigm that bears upon considerations of identity; she extends this consideration to an investigation of the possibilities of representing the maternal textually—a concern that Cook argues is central to Morag's creative activities in the novel. In "Jesting Within: Voices of Irony and Parody as Expressions of Feminisms," Franks explores the expression of a feminist consciousness in *The Diviners*, *A Jest of God*, and *The Fire-Dwellers*. She presents her readings of these novels from the perspective of a 1990s feminist who sees the central issue in these works as revolving around the shaping of the protagonists' lives. The search for an individual voice, and the attempt at shaping one's own life around the self—as opposed to others—is an assertion of feminism she argues. In Laurence's works, a progression is seen from the first Manawaka novel to the last as each character learns to let her voices speak rather than squelch the inner plurivocality. Franks states that Laurence's protagonists assert their "feminist consciousness through [a] playful plurivocality" that uses parody and irony for various aims—either to maintain control over their lives or to poke fun at the things they encounter in life, for example, literature, God, family and myths of origin, and sex and love. Franks and Cook show that feminist approaches to Laurence reveal much about the artistry. While these approaches to the writer are motivated by highly personal readings of the texts, Franks and Cook demonstrate that their readings are also informed by current theoretical perspectives and that the implications of such reading are wide-ranging.

Nora Foster Stovel brings a different emphasis to bear on the two sister novels *A Jest of God* and *The Fire-Dwellers*. It has been clear from their first publication (1966; 1969) that these are closely linked texts. Nonetheless, apart from acknowledging the sisterhood of the two protagonists, Rachel and Stacey, a thorough examination of the connections between the novels has never been undertaken. Foster Stovel examines the structural, symbolic, and artistic links that bind these novels as closely as real family connections bind people together. Foster Stovel argues that an awareness of the links between these novels enriches a reading of the works. By doing so, she shows that these texts should not be read separately, as they often are. This paper asks readers and scholars to revisit their readings of either *A Jest of God* or *The Fire-Dwellers* to see how already-formed impressions of the novels might be altered by their consideration together.

Laurence's work has been examined in isolation in the criticism to date. Few links have been made between her writing and that of other writers despite the great number of authors who claim to have been directly influenced by Laurence.[8] Dick Harrison begins to rectify the situation by drawing attention to Laurence's ties with Western American writer, Wallace Stegner. Harrison compares the most critically acclaimed novels of the two writers, *The Diviners* and *Angle of Repose*. Arguing that "These are...the best novels of the Canadian and American Wests," Harrison proceeds to show that these works also represent similar developmental paths for the authors from more traditional writing strategies to metafictional narrative approaches. *The Diviners* and *Angle of Repose* share many similarities in basic premise—both are novels about middle-aged writers who create the narrative that we are reading and whose narrativizing is a means for searching the past to glean meaning about the present. While the Canadian and American Wests parallel each other geographically, Harrison demonstrates the "characteristic differences in the cultures of the two Wests that have formed" the narrators. Harrison reminds us that all literature needs to be read in comparison with other literature. As Atwood remarked in *Survival*, to know our own literature on its own is not enough, "to know ourselves accurately, we need to know it as part of literature as a whole."

Proceeding from a different proposition, Angelika Maeser Lemieux examines the underlying significance of the socio-historical context of Laurence's upbringing. Scots Presbyterism has long been recognized as being central to the fiction Laurence produced. Maeser Lemieux offers a detailed examination of three paradigms evident in the longer fiction, moral order, church order, and social order, that are largely informed by Laurence's understanding of Scots Presbyterianism in Canada. Maeser Lemieux draws on numerous theological sources to delineate more precisely the kind of religious influence that Laurence was exposed to and that is manifested in her fiction. The effects of the Federal Theology, Scottish Calvinism, Orthodox Calvinism, the Westminster Confession, the Free Church, European theological trends, and the reaction against them through the Scottish Common Sense philosophy, on Scots Presbyterianism in Canada are traced through the novels and interview material. Maeser Lemieux defines the nature of the God figure in Laurence's work—a figure that is prominent throughout the fiction and that generates frequent references in the criticism. The potential sphere of Laurence's influence is opened up here, from the strictly literary to the larger social and historical arenas.

The final two essays mark a complete shift from Laurence's fictional work to her nonfiction. Donez Xiques presents archival material about Laurence's early newspaper writing that has been overlooked and generally has suffered the fate of being forgotten. Thomas M.F. Gerry writes about Laurence's late nonfiction—work that has languished in the critical spectrum.

In 1947 and 1948 Margaret Laurence (then Wemyss) worked for two different Winnipeg socialist publications—a fact that is mostly not apparent in her memoir, interviews, or in biographical work by Clara Thomas and Patricia Morley. Xiques argues that Laurence's experience working for *The Westerner* and the *Winnipeg Citizen* had far-reaching effects on her later literary career and that a great deal of information about Laurence's formative writing years can be gleaned from an examination of this work. Delving into archival material, Xiques focuses her discussion of the more than 120 contributions by Laurence to these newspapers along four lines: her work for *The Westerner*; her book reviews; analyses of radio dramas; and coverage of the Canadian arts scene done for the *Winnipeg Citizen*. Gerry broadens our conception of Laurence's work in its totality by examining political aspects of her work. Drawing from the fictional and nonfictional work, Gerry argues that throughout her career Laurence implicitly and explicitly wrote with political intentions in mind. The later work has generally been overlooked, he argues, precisely because the politicism was more overt and didactic. This omission in considering the later nonfiction has a dual implication. First, a gender bias is implicit in that Laurence's later writing is sometimes dismissed as the rantings of an aging woman writer (as opposed to the esteem that is paid to the nonfictional writing of figures such as Mordecai Richler); second, the potential that the writing has in the political and social spheres is missed because of the reticence to take her seriously. Gerry's essay is a boisterous call to initiate those readers unfamiliar with Laurence's later writing with the hope that future work will be generated.

| | |

Challenging Territory: The Writings of Margaret Laurence demands of the reader, critic, and scholar, a re-evaluation of the basic assumptions that underlie their understanding of Laurence's life and career. The authors offer new perspectives on the writing that challenge the reader to evaluate and re-assess their impressions of Laurence's place in literary history. The aim is to show ways how one can begin to conceive of, and reconceive, Margaret Laurence. This collection can only draw attention to the many different things that it means to engage in Laurence studies. By attempting to open up Laurence studies to a more pluralistic approach, it is hoped that scholars will be motivated to engage in work on even more of the areas, such as the children's literature, the life writing, and the letters, that can help to gain a greater understanding of the multiplicity of the whole of Laurence's oeuvre.

Notes

1. Atwood was responding to Northrop Frye's famous question from *The Bush Garden*, "Where is here?" about Canadian identity and place in her book of criticism *Survival: A Thematic Guide to Canadian Literature*. Atwood described Canada as an unknown territory to its inhabitants—not geographically but imaginatively. An alternative to the dilemma, she argued, was through gaining an understanding of Canadian literature: "Our literature is our map, if we can learn to read it as *our* literature, as the product of who and where we have been" (19). Atwood's program calls for a Canadian public to understand themselves—have a sense of identity uniquely Canadian—through *their* writing. By the early 1970s numerous Canadian writers had established themselves, and there was an area that could be clearly identified as a Canadian literature. Even though Canadians had been writing in this country for quite some time (Canadian literature certainly was not an invention of the 1960s), only now was local cultural production being seen as pertaining significantly to a sense of a national identity.

2. See also, Craig Tapping: Laurence "had done more than any other person to promote Nigerian writing" (66).

3. Ascroft, Griffiths, and Tiffin state that "More than three-quarters of the people living in the world today have had their lives shaped by the experience of colonialism," lending more weight to the importance of postcolonial studies to the present setting.

4. Her first book was actually a publication of the colonial administration of the Somaliland Protectorate. British Somaliland or Somaliland Protectorate became part of the Republic of Somalia in 1960.

5. Part of the problem of thinking of Laurence as postcolonial has to do with the development of postcolonial studies to date, as Stephen Slemon notes, "it is no secret that the usual orthodoxies of postcolonial critical theory have been developed in other cultural locations, for other purposes, and in relation to other critical problems than those that have troubled Canadian critical readers" (280).

6. See, for example, Hart, "Comparative Poetics, Postmodernism, and the Canon: An Introduction"; and Perkins, "Introduction: The State of the Discussion."

7. See W.J. Keith, for example. Countering the trend is Michael Ondaatje in his anthology of Canadian short fiction, *From Ink Lake*, where he includes the African story "The Rain Child" rather than one from *A Bird in the House*—the more usual choice. While Ondaatje gives no justification for choosing "The Rain Child," the inclusion of this story is an implicit questioning of the master narrative of Laurence's literary history.

8. Wainwright provides ample interview material regarding writers affected by Laurence's large sphere of influence.

1

(MIS) SPEAKING

Laurence Writes Africa

Margaret Laurence had a distinctive perspective as a young Canadian in Africa in the 1950s. As a white expatriate she would inevitably form part of the ruling community in any African colony, but as a Canadian she had grown up in a colonial society where to be fully educated was to learn that colonial experience was peripheral, culturally valid only in so far as it conformed to the norms of the imperial metropolis, and even then less "real" than experience in the metropolis itself. Perhaps most importantly, as an expatriate colonial—especially as an expatriate colonial writer—she was sensitive to the ways in which cultural power was played out in language, and to the gradations of prestige implied in different languages, accents and styles of speech, with their different degrees of connection to the dominant language of the metropolis. Unsurprisingly, then, *This Side Jordan* and the stories in *The Tomorrow-Tamer* set in the Gold Coast/Ghana around the time of independence are concerned with cultural power, and with language as a site of cultural conflict.

Laurence's attitude towards her African works was hyper-critical, but it was so in part because of her sensitivity towards her hybrid roles as a white Canadian in Africa. As she became more aware of African writers she saw the connection between her work and theirs, but saw it primarily as a distinction between their insider perspective and her ineluctable outsider status:

> I became extremely interested in contemporary African writing in English. It had seemed to me, a few years before, that if anything was now going to be written about Africa, it would have to be done from the inside by Africans themselves, and this was one reason I stopped writing anything with that setting. In fact, although I did not realize it then, already many young African writers were exploring their own backgrounds, their own societies and people. ("Ten Years'" 30)

Laurence emphasizes her ignorance of contemporary African writing rather more strongly than she needs to, considering that she had evidently read at least some Ghanaian books before she wrote *This Side Jordan* (Interview 64). Yet in a sense the emphasis is justified as an attempt to underline her inevitable distance from the culture of Ghana, one that no amount of reading and friendship could obliterate.

Similarly, in *The Prophet's Camel Bell* Laurence comments on her early assumption that she was different from British colonialists, and her later discovery that she was more like them than she realized. The book is full of moments of uncomfortable self-recognition, as for instance when the Laurences, initially amused by the Somali conviction that the English are "indifferent where love [is] concerned, and probably inept as well," discover that the Somalis lump them in with the "Ingrese" in this respect and others (106). Finally, Laurence realizes that even her self-chosen outsider's or "stranger's" position is a form of personal imperialism: "For we had all been imperialists, in a sense, but the empire we unknowingly sought was that of Prester John, a mythical kingdom and a private world" (251). To seek a "private world" as a site of self-discovery in a country, which to those who belong there is a crowded, public world of conflict and responsibility, is to exploit just as surely as European governments and businesses do. When Laurence returned to the figure of the stranger in the Foreword to *Heart of a Stranger*, she wrote of the fiction writer's need to remain a stranger; to her, fictional characters, like the members of another culture, are "others" whose autonomy and individual speech must be respected, but who are also part of the writer's "strange lands of the heart and spirit" (viii). Writing itself, as Laurence sees it, is an act both of respect and appropriation, the act of a "stranger" who asks and gives nonoppressive tolerance, but who is also impelled to colonize, to use whatever she encounters in her exploration of her own "inner territories" (viii).

If being a Canadian placed her with what she calls "the well-fed ones of this earth" (*Camel Bell* 35), the ambivalence of Laurence's perspective rescued her African fiction from some of the pitfalls she so clearly saw in the expatriate position by strengthening her "unmistakable contention of the provisional and multiple status of perception" (Richards 19). Her texts reflect a deep awareness of what W.D. Ashcroft has called "the process by which the English language is appropriated and adapted to a use in a new place," a process that occurs in "monoglossic settler cultures" (6) like those of English Canada as well as in polyglossic communities such as Ghana.[1] Ashcroft sees code-switchingwould[2] as an aspect of that appropriation, and uses the Australian Joseph Furphy's *Such is Life* to demonstrate the social contest "for which the language variance is synecdochic" (6), but examples of code-switching also abound in Laurence's Manawaka novels—in *The Diviners* for instance, where the Englishman (and Anglo-Indian) Brooke Skelton corrects Morag's provincial Canadianisms:

> "Shall we have some sherry before you tackle the eggs and bacon, which is all there is here at the moment for dinner?"
> "Please," Morag says, having recently learned to say, simply, *Please*, instead of *Oh yes thanks I'd just love some*, or, worse, *Okay that'd be fine*. (214)

From Laurence's realist perspective, the rendering of speech was central to fiction-writing. In *Long Drums and Cannons*, her study of Nigerian writers, she includes mimetic representation of speech as a crucial factor in the success of fiction: "the main concern of a writer remains that of somehow creating the individual on the printed page, of catching the tones and accents of human speech, of setting down the conflicts of people who are as real to him as himself" (10).[3] In retrospective commentary on her move from African to Canadian settings, she emphasized speech as a primary element of that move: "When I wrote *The Stone Angel*...I kept feeling that I *knew* I was getting the speech *exactly right*! It was *mine*. It was the speech of my grandparents', my parents' generation, and so on. Whereas when I had been writing about Africa I could never be sure" (Interview 68).

Laurence's concern with speech, in her own work and in that of other postcolonial writers, came in part from her sense of verbal communication as a central issue in postcolonial culture. Her chapter on Chinua Achebe in *Long Drums and Cannons*, for instance, emphasizes problems of communication:

> [Achebe] shows the impossibly complicated difficulties of one person speaking to another, attempting to make himself known to another, attempting to hear—really to hear—what another is saying....Yet Achebe's writing also conveys the feeling that we must attempt to communicate, however imperfectly, if we are not to succumb to despair or madness. The words which are spoken are rarely the words which are heard, but we must go on speaking. (124–25)

By the time Laurence wrote the preface to *Long Drums and Cannons* after the Nigerian civil war began in 1968, she knew that the "despair or madness" was more than an individual's existential affliction: its social consequences could be devastating. In *The Prophet's Camel Bell*, Laurence repeatedly stresses the difficulty of merely conveying information among, let alone under-standing, people of disparate languages and cultures. Perhaps one of the most striking examples is the precarious thread of languages linking members of Jack Laurence's work teams:

> When Jack wanted to say something to Ugo, he gave Hersi the message in English. Hersi told Arabetto in Somali, and Arabetto passed the information on to Ugo in Italian. The reply came back in the same way. Considering that Hersi and Arabetto knew nothing about tractors, and that the words for various parts of the machines did not exist in the Somali language, it was little wonder that Jack and Ugo frequently had to make wild guesses about what the other was trying to say. (132)

In a sense Laurence was also making wild guesses about her characters' language and speech in the books she set in Africa, but she elected to "go on speaking," and to make speech and dialogue central elements of those books, especially of *This Side Jordan* and *The Tomorrow-Tamer*. Here the issue is more often cultural dominance than straightforward communication, and much of the dialogue enacts personal and cultural power struggles, particularly for low-status speakers. A case in point is the first conversa-tion between Nathaniel Amegbe and Johnnie and Miranda Kestoe in *This Side Jordan*. Miranda's abrupt appeal to Nathaniel (a complete stranger to her) for his support in her opinion of a painting first elicits unthinking polite agreement with her, and then embarrassment as he wonders whether the Kestoes will think he is "one of those Africans who automatically agree with Europeans" (41). The tide of embarrassment rises as Nathaniel hears himself responding to Miranda's self-introduction, "'We're Johnnie and Miranda Kestoe,'" with the much more formal, "'I am Mr. Amegbe. I am a schoolmaster'" (42). Miranda is effortlessly aggressive in beginning and carrying on the conversation; her fluency and the superior status it registers put Nathaniel at a disadvantage and on the defensive; he feels that Miranda has "tied him here, his hands damply clutching his briefcase" (44). When Miranda turns the subject to African history, Nathaniel realizes despairingly that he cannot find words to express his complex personal and historical knowledge of the past to her because "There [is] too much to say. And so much that could never be said" (42).

Nathaniel, for whom English is a second language acquired through his education, knows that colonial society defines him as a borrower of another's words whenever he speaks English, and he frequently finds himself in situations where those borrowed words betray him. Miranda has recently arrived in Accra from England and—in a phrase Laurence used elsewhere about her own naive younger self—is "collecting African acquaintances as though they were rare postage stamps" (*Heart* 25). Her insistent questions show little respect for Nathaniel; they devalue and silence him as effectively as Johnnie's rudeness does. Although Nathaniel and Miranda both feel dissatisfied with the conversation afterwards, for Nathaniel the memory becomes a festering sore because it connects to his wider feeling of social unease as a person living on the margins of colonial society. Miranda can rationalize her failures by turning them into theoretical encounters with the "whiteman's burden" (54), but Nathaniel remains trapped within his awareness of the things that cannot be said. The linguistic contest, like that between Brooke the "cultured" teacher and Morag the "provincial" student, acts out a wider cultural struggle.

In *This Side Jordan*, the three principal languages are English (the medium of business, trade and colonial power); Twi (the mother tongue of Nathaniel, Nathaniel's wife Aya, and most of the other Ghanaian characters) and pidgin English. Laurence simplifies the situation a good deal by referring to Ghana's other languages very briefly, if at all; she thereby creates a strongly marked binary opposition between Twi and English, one in which the power lies almost wholly on the side of English. Good English is the most important cultural signifier, the one that determines the exchange value of a Ghanaian's labour, and his or her cultural prestige. Despite Victor's sarcasm about the firm's Africanization programme, and Johnnie's dislike of him, Victor's English, which has "more of Oxford than

Accra" (38) in it, forces Johnnie to despise him as something like an equal, rather than simply ignore him, or sneer at him as he does at Nathaniel. Their exchanges bear out Nathaniel's thought: "Victor would have known what to say to Johnnie Kestoe. He always had the right answers" (51).

Jacob Abraham Mensah, the headmaster of the school Nathaniel teaches in, is another skilful manipulator of English, though his goals are simpler and more directly materialistic than Victor's. Like his expensive clothes, his carpeted office, and the never-used textbooks on his shelves, Mensah's English enhances his carefully constructed aura of prestige. Used to his staff, English hints at his economic power, and used to the parents of his students it suggests the status they are supposedly buying for their sons by sending them to Mensah's school.

The decline of Twi is a direct result of the dominance of English and the deculturation inherent in colonial education. Twi is the language we encounter least in *This Side Jordan*, not only because the languages of business and intercultural contact are English or pidgin, but also because apart from isolated words all the Twi speech is rendered as English. In some ways this is simply a necessary convention for a book written in English and directed at an English-speaking audience, but such a translation touches on complex and controversial issues, issues that African writers themselves face. The publishing and linguistic exigencies of the postcolonial situation force many African writers to write in European languages; they are "compelled by historical circumstances to use the language and imitate the literary tradition of an external audience" (Egejuru 14). Writers such as Achebe and Gabriel Okara argue that an African writer can fashion a version of a European language "which is at once universal and able to carry his peculiar experience" (Achebe 29),[4] perhaps by marking that language with syntactical forms and figures of speech literally translated from an African language (Okara 15). Yet others argue that "African literature in English and French is a clear contradiction, and a false proposition, just as 'Italian literature in Hausa' would be" (Wali 14). Moreover, as Ashcroft points out, the "literal translation" technique does not "*reproduce the culture by some process of metaphoric embodiment*" (6); instead, a language variant of the kind used by Okara to convey African speech is metonymic, and underlines rather than collapses cultural distance: "as a contiguous trope it proposes an ability to negotiate that cultural distance of which it is itself a sign" (7).

Laurence stood in a different relation to the issue of speech and language in African novels, since to write in English for her was a matter of neither choice nor coercion. Writers whose mother tongue is English, especially those who use colonial or postcolonial settings, have often used lexical and syntactic variants to convey different languages that they render as English, but the implication of this kind of "translation" have historically been very different from similar techniques used by African writers, such as Gabriel Okara. As J.M. Coetzee points out, white writers' use of translation (or in his terms "transfer") in colonial contexts often encodes a patronizing subtext. Alan Paton's use of it for Zulu in *Cry, The Beloved Country* implies "an archaic quality to the Zulu behind it, as if the Zulu language, Zulu culture, the Zulu frame of mind, belonged to a bygone and heroic age" (Coetzee 128). Laurence generally avoids this technique, for the only stylistic marker she gives Twi is a slightly formal tone, produced chiefly by the absence of contractions, and she confines even this characteristic to the speech of rural people, such as Nathaniel's and Aya's relatives, and to Nathaniel's interior monologues, with their reflections on Ghana's past and future. Here for instance is a conversation between Nathaniel and his uncle Adjei about the job Adjei wants his nephew to take as clerk to a chief:

"Are you well, Nathaniel?"
Nathaniel threw out his hands in despair.
"Yes," he grated through his teeth, "quite well."
The old man's eyes gleamed cruelly.
"I thought you must either be mad or very wise," he said. "Try me again, Nathaniel. You say Nana Kweku is a good man, and yet you refuse to work for him. Why? I am perhaps a little deaf these past years. That part was not quite clear to me——"
"Because I would end by hating him, if I worked for him," Nathaniel snapped. "Oh—many clerks of chiefs despise their masters, make no mistake about it! I'd have to watch him, every day, every day, not able to read or even write his own name, not knowing anything outside his little province, but still able to command, to move people this way and that. I don't want to see it."
The old man looked at him in astonishment.
"Now I know you are mad. Your sisters will grieve. Certainly, they will grieve." (101–2)

Nathaniel's contractions and quick utterance contrast with his uncle's speech, with its more deliberate rhythms, and repetitions that suggest an almost ritual emphasis ("Now I know *you are* mad. Your sisters will grieve. Certainly, *they will grieve*").

The English Laurence uses for Nathaniel's interior monologues, however, resembles Adjei's speech in its formality and "oratorical richness" (Sparrow 131), and the contractions that mark the rendering of his ordinary Twi disappear:

—After the slavers, the soldiers. Our land—overnight, it seemed— became not ours. Oh, it was paid for. Do not say otherwise. We were paid a few bottles of gin for our land. What did you pay us for our souls? —We fought. Our kings were warriors, and our people. Oh yes, we fought. Year after year until it was over. We fought with spears. They fought with Maxim guns. Then it was over. (211)

Yet, even the formal speech in such passages is only lightly marked, and gives a sense of Nathaniel's connection with the past rather than of the language. Ironically, the very ordinariness of the Twi speech as Laurence renders it ensures that Twi as a language has little presence in the novel. Laurence's need to translate it mirrors the need Ghanaians face in *This Side Jordan* either to learn English and weaken their sense of cultural identity by participating in the colonial school system, or to become dependent on those who have learned it.

If Twi is becoming a language that belongs only to the nonliterate and marginalized, pidgin seems already to be just that—to the extent that it is acknowledged as a language at all. More emphatically even than those who live uneasily between worlds as Nathaniel does, speakers of pidgin are labelled as borrowers rather than possessors of culture. In the opening episode in the highlife bar, the British mimic pidgin as they tell anecdotes about their servants' supposed "stupidity." The Cunninghams and the Thayers see their servants' "ignorant" behaviour and "crude" speech as a trail of humorous though exasperating errors, usually involving unorthodox uses of European commodities, from Epsom salts to the word "freedom." The pidgin phrases the anecdotes include are appropriate in the stories because to the British, speaking pidgin means making errors. Just as pidgin, supposedly a debased version of English and thus made up of "mistakes," violates the linguistic codes of standard English, so the servants' "blunders" violate their employers' imported cultural codes.[5] Pidgin is associated with everything that does not conform to the linguistic and cultural "standards" set by the British—begging, bribe-taking, political corruption and illiteracy.[6] Nathaniel is horrified when he hears himself using even the short phrase "I beg you" to Miranda, because this phrase is not only pidgin, but also a begging formula, and one that he was scorned for using as a boy by an English priest.

Yet the interaction between the novel's principal characters demonstrates several cracks in this three-tiered linguistic hierarchy of English, Twi and pidgin. For one thing, the "good" or standard English, which the British characters share, does not stop Johnnie from betraying his colleagues at Allkirk, Moore and Bright to Cameron Sheppard, the envoy sent from the firm's London head office; it also fails to stop Sheppard or the firm from callously dumping those colleagues because it is suddenly expedient to go in for Africanization. Ironically, the cultural pressure to learn English and to compete for scholarships at overseas universities produces people like Victor, who holds a degree from the London School of Economics, and uses his command of English to taunt Johnnie, to write for an opposition newspaper, and ultimately even to get a powerful position within Allkirk, Moore and Bright. Symbolized by his cultured speech, his education ironically gives him a stronger link with Sheppard, his former classmate, than any of the British characters has.

Indeed, even the embattled sense of cultural identity Twi provides is tougher in some ways than the British characters' linguistic and cultural dominance. Though almost always at loggerheads with his own and his wife's relatives, Nathaniel can still face them and the troubling past they remind him of. By contrast, Johnnie steadfastly represses the memories of his slum childhood in a London tenement and his mother's death from trying to self-abort. Nathaniel's relatives visit him, stay in his house, occasionally even joke with him; the language he uses with them is his own, whereas Johnnie now seems to function entirely in the standard English he has learned on his way up the social ladder. Nathaniel's conflicting desires to preserve and to repudiate his cultural and personal past nearly tear him apart, but he refuses to deny his original linguistic identity as strenuously as he refuses to deny his other identity as an educated city dweller.

If English does not automatically create solidarity, pidgin proves more powerful than initially seems possible. Despite its low cultural status, pidgin creates effective bonds—between Nathaniel and his neighbour Yiamoo, for instance. Nathaniel supports Yiamoo, a Togolander, against Ankrah the woodcarver, even though he can only speak to Yiamoo in pidgin, whereas Ankrah comes from Asante, like Nathaniel, and speaks Twi.

The sense of comradeship he feels towards Yiamoo becomes a source of resistance for Nathaniel: resistance to his family's efforts to get him back to his home village, and to Miranda's intrusive overtures on the other. With Yiamoo he communicates not in Twi, with its problematic links to the past, nor in English, which forces him into an inferior's role, but in pidgin, a cross-cultural language that does not belong wholly to any one culture.[7]

Pidgin also serves Nathaniel well in his climactic encounter with Johnnie in the highlife bar. Voiceless to this point, his rage finally finds an outlet in pidgin as he responds to Johnnie's "'Get the hell out of here'" by saying "'No…Get out, you. You go 'way. Who want you here? Go 'way, you'" (222). Johnnie predictably takes the pidgin as evidence that Nathaniel's real level is that of a "stewardboy" (223), but the linguistic and social faux-pas liberates Nathaniel. He responds to Johnnie's taunts by pushing the table over, and Johnnie with it—a suitably ignominious return for his and Aya's various humiliations at the hands of the Kestoes. Earlier that same day, Nathaniel's voice has seemed to him "like a hammer that never succeed[s] in driving a nail" (206) as he tries to respond—in English—to Johnnie's charges of bribery. Nathaniel cannot then answer Johnnie's accusation, because Johnnie's insistence on labelling him a receiver of bribes makes it impossible for Nathaniel to articulate his mixture of motives: compassion for the futureless boys he has tried to help, desire for some relief from his own poverty, and the blurred distinction between bribery and gift-giving as a token of respect. While Johnnie controls the language and the conversation, Nathaniel feels that "To speak would be like straining to make your voice heard across an ocean" (207). In the bar, however, through mis-speaking (in the double sense of speaking in pidgin and defying Johnnie) Nathaniel finally drives the nail home. This time, rather than try to justify himself by Johnnie's standards, he addresses the root of the problem and tells the white man to go.

Some of the stories in *The Tomorrow-Tamer* also explore the potential power of pidgin. Mammii Ama, in "A Gourdful of Glory," often switches into pidgin in her speeches and songs "to captivate a wider audience" (231). Like Nathaniel, she finds herself in an unequal power struggle with an English woman; her usual power of speech deserts her as they argue about whether buses will be free after independence according to Mammii Ama's expectation. When Mammii Ama finally regains her verbal power, the day after independence, she does so in pidgin, in an act that simultaneously rejects the white woman's language and her wealth. Despite her particularly urgent need for money, Mammii Ama makes the white woman return the calabash she has just bought at a wildly inflated price, gives back the money, and asserts her personal independence in the teeth of the other's English taunts:

> She had parted with twelve shillings. She must be going mad. But she would not turn back now. She took another belligerent step, and the yellow menacing skull [the white woman] retreated a little more. She spoke clearly, slowly, emphasizing each word.
> "I no pay bus dis time," she said. "Bus—he—be—free! You hear? Free!" (242)

Though it may seem that Mammii Ama simply lies about the bus to save face, she also asserts her right to speak here, and she points up the political significance of the act in the words with which she follows up her victory: "'Free-Dom he come,' she cried, half in exultation, half in longing. 'Free-Dom be heah now, dis minute'" (242).

As a language that breaks the white man's codes—or rather takes them over and fashions them for local use—pidgin's very outcast status may give it strength.[8] That is perhaps why Johnnie Kestoe reacts so immediately to Nathaniel's use of pidgin, and why Hardcastle in "The Pure Diamond Man" is so upset by the prevalence of pidgin and other appropriated cultural symbols in a modern African city: "'Sleazy nylon shirts. Pidgin English—a depravity, if I may say so. This highlife caper. Signs advertising political meetings and anti-malarial pills. All of it so dreary'" (187). Pidgin does not square with Hardcastle's idea of "'the true Africa'"(187): like political meetings and medicine, it suggests a changing rather than a static society, and so potentially a political threat, even to such a passive exploiter as Hardcastle, more interested in amateur anthropology than in his inherited diamond mines.

In *This Side Jordan*, the imbalance of power between Nathaniel and Johnnie seems to reassert itself quickly; as his rage passes, Nathaniel feels he has to bribe the white man in order to avert the consequences of the confrontation, and the episode nearly leads him to give up his job and admit defeat. Yet as it turns out, the bribe is unnecessary, for Johnnie only wants to frighten Nathaniel with the threat of going to the police, and cannot afford to buy the witnesses he would need. Unlike his earlier encounters with the Kestoes, this one leaves Nathaniel in a position of relative strength; indeed, the bribe seems necessary to him precisely because he has won, and has humiliated Johnnie, reversing the established current of their relationship. What is more, the empowering effect of the incident lasts, even though all Nathaniel can think of on the night itself are the "mistakes" he has made and his desire to retreat from them. The mistakes release him from silence; his continuing conviction that he has doomed himself to leave Accra allows him to speak out again when he announces his resignation to Jacob Abraham Mensah and forces the headmaster to recognize that Futura Academy is selling only dreams to its students. As long as Nathaniel has his tenuous foothold within educated colonial society, he can resist neither Johnnie nor Mensah, because they are part of the power structure that has allowed him that foothold even as it silences him. Only when he breaks the rules and thinks he has lost his foothold for good, can Nathaniel begin to take speech and power for himself. He does not find the "right answers" that have eluded him; rather, he rebels against the power structure by whose standards "right" and "wrong" answers are defined. Significantly, he does not need to draw on pidgin this time, but instead asserts himself to Mensah in English, and for the first time in plain, blunt English that makes no polite or subservient concessions: "'I've worked here long enough. You put your feet on your carpets and you forget a school needs books, teachers. What do you care? The place is no good, you hear?'" (270). In his previous discussion with Mensah about the school's standards, Nathaniel has stammered and hesitated: "the syllabus—perhaps a standard one should be drawn up—you know—" (63). In the later scene however, his emphatic verbs and short, clipped sentences "hammer" Mensah as effectively as his defiant words and acts have put Johnnie down.

The incident in the highlife bar does however have a substantial cost, for the bribe, arranged by Nathaniel's dissolute colleague Lamptey, involves the young prostitute Lamptey has just renamed "Emerald." Johnnie is her first client, and he rapes her, realizing after he has done so that he has also reopened the scars of a clitoridectomy. Yet his encounter with her, as traumatic as it must be for her, does not so much validate Johnnie's status as deliver another blow to it: it destroys his belief that he can control the terms of his experience in Ghana. Seeking a stereotypical erotic encounter with Africa, Johnnie thinks of Emerald as "a continent," and of himself as "an invader, wanting both to possess and to destroy" (231). In the end, however, he is forced to realize that Emerald cannot be his "Africa" any more than he can discover her name or her history:

Had she been sold by her family, or stolen, or had she elected to come here? He would never know. He could not speak to her. They had no language in common.

But it did not really matter who she specifically was. She was herself and no other. She was someone, a woman who belonged somewhere and who for some reason of her own had been forced to seek him here in this evil-smelling cell, and through him, indignity and pain. (233)

Being deprived of language at this point forces Johnnie to step out of the power structure and to recognize powerlessness in himself, in the shape of his inability to communicate with his victim, to use her as the basis for his fantasies, or to do anything to assuage the pain he knows he has inflicted upon her. When he leaves, he can only hold her hand for a moment and then cover her with her cloth, thinking "it [is] all he could do for her, and for himself" (234).

Despite—or perhaps because of—its terrible cost, the evening in the bar thus disables what has been Johnnie's self-assurance by making him aware of the violence inherent in the colonist's power to name and to possess. For most of the rest of the novel he drifts, responding to others' actions rather than acting for himself; everyone, from Cameron Sheppard to the midwife at the hospital where Miranda gives birth, controls events more effectively than he does. In contrast, Nathaniel slowly begins to take control of his life.

Apart from his confrontations with Johnnie and Mensah, Nathaniel's most decisive self-assertion in the novel comes when he renames his son "Joshua." The name's Biblical reference associates it with colonial appropriation, but his gift of it to his son is an act of defiance rather than submission. Nathaniel has received his own Christian name from an Oliver Twist-like alphabetical list kept by his mission school, but here he is taking back the power to name, just as he has taken back the power to speak. He is also making the child heir, not to the Mosaic Promised Land or to the Christian Paradise, which is traditionally its counterpart, but to the emerging nation of Ghana, the country that in Nathaniel's tenuous yet persistent vision will at once be aware of its past and able to survive in the complex future. The gesture is one of *re*-appropriation, in a sense; Nathaniel here begins to use his "borrowed" culture, to make it his own as confidently as the British have appropriated his country (although his understanding of what he takes is deeper than, say, Miranda's is when she collects curios or African acquaintances).[9]

Johnnie also has a child to name, and asks Miranda if they may call their daughter Mary, after his mother. Like Nathaniel's, this baptismal act makes peace with the troubled past, in this case the memory of his mother's death. "Emerald's" bleeding has brought back the memory of his mother's abortion attempt and death, and his disgust at the thought that he can "never be anything more than a clot of blood on a dirty quilt" (59). Nevertheless, Johnnie's exercise of the power of naming seems more tentative than Nathaniel's. Still in flight from the memory of his mother's death, he refuses to consider the significance of the name: "Reasons could be dragged up, no doubt, like the roots of swamp weeds, but he did not want to see them" (267). Whereas Nathaniel "looks over Jordan" and pushes towards a future, even one he knows may never be realized, Johnnie seems still caught in but unwilling to confront the uneasiness of his own past.

The question however remains, just how effective are these realignments of personal linguistic power in cultural or economic terms? Laurence thought of the ending of *This Side Jordan* as a naively hopeful one, in line with the millennial expectations prevalent at the time the book was written, and her own situation as an outsider in Ghana, "young and full of faith" ("Ten Years'"29). Though critics have often followed her lead in seeing that ending as a reflection of her "western liberal convictions" (Thomas 104), *This Side Jordan* reflects those convictions only dubiously and ironically. True, Africanization changes Allkirk, Moore and Bright, and forces Johnnie to work with Victor; Mensah gives Nathaniel a substantial raise so that he will continue to be Futura Academy's resident "honest man" and help it to get on the list of government-accepted schools. Even Aya Amegbe, under the stress of labour pains, uses her limited English to stand up to Miranda's officious goodwill and tell her to go away. But, the London head office clearly still controls Allkirk, Moore and Bright, even if the British government will soon surrender direct political control of Ghana. The British still intend to exploit the resources of Ghana, whoever happens to occupy the desks in Accra. Moreover, almost all the characters who achieve a measure of success by the novel's end have confirmed or accepted compromising positions in the prevailing system. Johnnie never carries through his resolution to confess his treachery to his colleagues and go down with them; Victor has presumably decided to sell himself to Allkirk, Moore and Bright and to stop being a cynical opposition journalist. Still more significantly, Nathaniel uses the freedom gained by his mis-speaking to reinsert himself into the power structure at a higher rate of pay; his honesty has become a marketable commodity.

Bringing the book to an end with Nathaniel's hopeful naming of his son, and with the words "Joshua, Joshua, Joshua. I beg you. Cross Jordan, Joshua"(282), seems to valorize the compromises that have brought

Nathaniel and the novel to this point, and yet these words are also a last echo of the pidgin that has been a vehicle for Nathaniel's resistance and defiance. This final appearance of pidgin is a reminder that more power may reside in acts that transgress conventional codes than in positions of privilege that are bolstered up, and restricted, by those conventional codes. *This Side Jordan* ends with a question mark rather than a statement, suggesting the subversive possibilities of language but also implying the power structure's ability to elude subversion, reconstitute itself, and co-opt its opposition.

W.H. New discusses the ending of "A Gourdful of Glory" in similar terms, suggesting that the moments of "glory" achieved in Laurence's African fiction are shortlived, and somewhat hollow. Mammii Ama's momentary elation fades, though she returns to cautious hope with the help of a song her fellow-traders sing to support and praise her, but her world has changed, and to New the story leaves us asking whether "naive endurance" is "enough of a fulfillment for a person when the world is different" (116). Mammii Ama does not even become more prosperous as Nathaniel does: the bus is not free; she is more than usually short of money because of her daughter's and granddaughter's illness; her daughter must still work in a nightclub, probably as a prostitute, to eke out the family income. Mammii Ama even loses money by her linguistic defiance, and the twelve shillings she returns mean far more to her than losing the argument does to the white woman.

| | |

The books Laurence wrote out of her years in Africa participate in the linguistic tensions that dominate their narratives. *This Side Jordan* and *The Tomorrow-Tamer* stories are Western fiction, written in the realist mode, by a white Canadian writer, and for a largely Western and English-speaking audience: these facts constrain them. The linguistic identity of Laurence and her audience dictates that African languages will be "represented" as English, that even pidgin must be close enough to English to allow readers to follow it,[10] and that Ghana's many indigenous languages will scarcely appear. For that matter, as New points out, the very fact that her "African" books are written sets them apart from the "speech" they seek to represent:

> Traditional African culture…claims at its heart the creative power of
> the spoken word; speaking creates, and hearing enacts; and this dimen-

sion of the culture is one which Laurence (the *un*characteristic Westerner in Africa) does allude to….In traditional terms, however, reducing speech to print robs it of its power to create, for it transforms process into thing; whereas speech had the power to invoke and so re-enact the wisdom of the ancestors (and the gods), and was therefore part of a cyclical process to be enacted anew, written words lodge themselves ineluctably in time and so become part of a linear rather than a cyclical history. (115)

In *The Prophet's Camel Bell*, Laurence refers to her reading of the Pentateuch before her arrival in Somaliland as both accident and appropriate gesture: she read it because she had nothing else to read, and yet also found it the best thing she could have read, since she was going to a desert country, and was going to live there as a stranger. The quotation from Exodus in the first chapter of the book, her first printed reference to the concept of the stranger, is curiously double, both evoking the Israelites' oppressed past, and making it plain that they now have the power to become oppressors themselves: "Thou shalt not oppress a stranger, for ye know the heart of a stranger, seeing ye were strangers in the land of Egypt" (Ex. 23:9). This way of beginning what she later called her "seven years' love affair with a continent" ("Ten Years'" 29) could be seen as one that preconditioned Laurence to interpret Somaliland or the Gold Coast in Western terms. Yet her reference back to the concept of the stranger at the end of *A Prophet's Camel Bell*, and her recognition that strangerhood is neither a neutral nor necessarily a powerless state, underline her awareness that her own cultural framework determined what she saw and wrote of Africa. It is this double perspective that energizes *This Side Jordan*, *The Tomorrow-Tamer* and *The Prophet's Camel-Bell*. All three books are about the fraught and difficult, yet necessary, project of cross-cultural observation and response. One of the last comments Laurence recorded about her African experience, while it does not return to the excessive hopefulness that she and others have seen in *This Side Jordan*, insists on the legitimacy—albeit with qualifications—of her contribution:

We had only a couple of African friends, one of whom taught at Achimsta College, which became the University of Ghana. I learned a great deal from Ofosu. One thing he taught me was that even if I were an anti-colonialist, I need not expect any communication with Africans at that point in history. I learned what it is to be a white liberal. Yet Ofosu and I kept in touch for many years after Jack and I left Ghana, and historical circumstances can change. I have since written one rather amateurish book of literary criticism on contemporary Nigerian writing, *Long Drums and Cannons*, and have met, on several occasions, the Nigerian novelist Chinua Achebe. Knowing that, in our different ways, Achebe and I have been trying to do much the same sort of thing all our writing lives, I recognized that communication could be possible. (*Dance* 153)

No doubt recalling her words about Achebe in *Long Drums and Cannons*, Laurence here asserts that difference, and the power relations that go with it, do not and for her must not preclude the attempt to "go on speaking," even if that means "straining to make your voice heard across an ocean."

Acknowledgement
I am grateful to Dr. Lise Winer for reading an early draft of this article, and for commenting on the linguistic issues raised here. Any blunders where matters linguistic are concerned naturally remain my own.

Notes
1. See also the treatment of the issue in Ashcroft et al. 59–77.
2. "Code-switching" is broadly defined as "the juxtaposition of elements from two (or more) languages or dialects" (McCormick).
3. Commentators on Laurence have also stressed the centrality of speech and language in her works. Mary Renault, even while noting one tiny mis-step in the English characters' speech, praises Laurence's ear as "so good that one cannot wish it less than perfect" (Woodcock 104). Clara Thomas notes that Laurence's ear, "naturally attuned to rhythms and nuances of speech" (33), was further trained by her work on translating the Somali poems and tales that she later published as *A Tree for Poverty*.
4. See also Achebe's and other writers' comments on the language issue in Egejuru 52–134. Laurence also cites Achebe's essay in the Epilogue to *Long Drums and Cannons*.
5. Recent linguistic approaches to pidgin do not support such an attitude; there is now an extensive literature on pidgin and creole languages that examines them not as "wrong versions of other languages but, rather, *new* languages" (Holm 1). (Creoles are usually defined as expanded and elaborated pidgins—most often pidgins that have acquired native speakers.) See also the essays collected in Jones et al. for discussion of the uses African writers have made of pidgin and other language varieties.
6. "Literacy" in British colonies in Africa was generally defined as knowing how to read and write standard English, since the language of education beyond the primary grades was English.
7. Though many pidgins have roots in colonial domination, they also serve a variety of communication needs in multilingual societies. Loreto Todd argues that in West

Africa, among other places, though pidgins at first developed to allow whites to communicate with black servants, "the indigenous people found that the pidgins allowed more extensive inter-group contact than had previously been possible and so they employed it for more and more purposes, and each new purpose for which they used it helped to make the pidgin more adequate and flexible" (14).

8. Rebecca Agheyisi, for instance, notes that in Nigeria, pidgin's "use by the socially uninfluential masses has made it a symbol of solidarity" (230). Cf. the discussion in Ashcroft et al. (59–77) of strategies of appropriation in postcolonial writing; though as New points out writing cannot be equated with speech (115), "written speech" cannot be wholly separated from spoken words.

9. In "A Gourdful of Glory," Mammii Ama thinks of "mission names" as belonging to her society: "Comfort—a decent name. A mission name, true, but it had lived here a long time, until it seemed to have been African always" (226). Significantly, the name Mammii Ama rejects here is her daughter's new name "Marcella," which like "Emerald," is connected to her work as a "club girl" at a highlife bar. To Mammii Ama, it seems, economic and sexual exploitation, and their related linguistic manipulations, are the forces to resist in the Ghana of her time, whereas mission influences can be assimilated and made "African."

10. Laurence restricts the pidgin vocabulary, for instance, to words recognizably derived from English ones, and uses syntactical patterns that are close to English ones.

2

WRITING ABOUT OTHERS

The African Stories

> For the glass wall between colour and colour is not only a barrier against touch, but has become thick and distorted, so that black men, white men, see each other through it, but see—what? (Doris Lessing, "The Antheap," 398)

One of the most frequent criticisms of Western representations of the "Other," particularly from oppressed or marginalized groups themselves, is that the "Other" is really a thinly veiled disguise for the self, the Western man or woman, Western concerns, beliefs, ideals, and desires. For example, Joseph Conrad's Africa represents the darkness of the white man's soul, mind, or origins (it is used, in Chinua Achebe's words, "as a foil to Europe, as a place of negations at once remote and vaguely familiar" (1988, 2)); E.M. Forster's India is, according to Sara Suleri, the setting and backdrop for the story of a white man, as well as the symbol "of something the Western mind must learn about itself" (390); and V.S. Naipaul's India is an excuse to talk about his identity as a successful British writer, in other words, as someone who has escaped the poverty, squalor, and backwardness of India.

Representations like these raise the question of whether it is possible to write about the Other from an external and/or privileged location without appropriating, marginalizing, or misrepresenting the Other. In an article in which he critiques the representation of the Other within his framework of the Manichean allegory, Abdul JanMohamed writes: "Genuine and thorough comprehension of otherness is possible only if the self can somehow negate or at least severely bracket the values, assumptions, and ideology of his [sic] culture…this entails in practice the virtually impossible task of negating one's very being, precisely because one's culture is what formed that being" (65). I agree with JanMohamed on the difficulty of climbing the glass wall, to borrow Lessing's words from the epigraph to my paper, and seeing from another point of view. However, I believe that writing about another's sphere of experience is possible and, as a refreshing alternative to the plethora of criticism (to which I have contributed[1]) on exploitative representations; I would like to read certain revisionist, sensitive, and occasionally empowering representations of the Other in Margaret Laurence's "The Drummer of All The World," with reference to her essay "The Very Best Intentions," and her first novel, *This Side Jordan*.

These texts are focused on because they are interesting in their thematic treatment of colonization, belonging, and identity, their revisionist use of the colonial/imperial trope of land-as-woman ("Drummer" and *This Side Jordan*), and because they illustrate well what I mean by representing the Other, land and people, within an awareness of the power dynamic inevitable in representation, together with an understanding of the cultural differences involved, and particularly with exemplary empathy and humility. I consider empathy more than sympathy or compassion in the sense that it implies an emotional identification that attempts to bridge the distance between the self and the Other. Empathy is the ability to feel for and understand the Other partly because one is attempting to see things through the eyes of the Other. In a way, it means crossing "the glass wall between colour and colour" (Lessing 398). Humility means recognizing one's limitations (biases, prejudices) as non-Other, as white, privileged, and/or male, limitations to the understanding, and therefore representation, of the Other. It also implies an understanding of one's own otherness vis-à-vis the subjectivity one is writing about. To quote Lessing from the preface to the first volume of her African short stories: "Truly to understand, we have to lose the arrogance that is the white man's burden, to stop feeling superior" (10).

Before engaging the texts and looking at the ways Laurence's vision of colonized peoples resists appropriation and offers a refreshing challenge to typical colonialist representations,[2] I would like to briefly review Linda Alcoff's reflections on appropriation in her article aptly entitled "The

Problem of Speaking for Others." In this essay, she discusses some of the issues surrounding the various practices of speaking for Others, their contexts, and the emerging debates. The case, cited by Alcoff, of Anne Cameron, a white Canadian author who writes about native Canadians, is comparable to Laurence's. Although Cameron and Laurence do not proclaim to speak for Others in their works, they speak about Others and often write their native or African characters in the first person, taking on their identity, therefore opening themselves up to potential charges of appropriation. Alcoff recognizes the similarity between speaking for Others and speaking about Others, and argues that it may in fact be impossible to separate the two practices. In both cases, she contends, the speaker participates in "the construction of their subject-positions" (9).

According to Alcoff, the main arguments against speaking for Others have to do with the location of the speaker. For example, some critics have asked whether it is possible to transcend one's social position, and whether we are not always speaking for ourselves, even when we speak for Others? Alcoff suggests that location becomes even more significant when one is speaking from a position of privilege (for example as a Western academic, or in the case of Laurence, as a white middle-class woman in colonial Africa, i.e., the British Protectorate of Somaliland, now Somalia, and the Gold Coast, now Ghana, in the 1950s), because not only are the chances of being heard greater, but the privilege and authority of the speaker are reinforced while the Other is further marginalized and silenced. It is particularly important to raise the question of location in cases such as Naipaul's where the author's authority as a speaker for the Third World[3] appears to jar with his location in the Western world and the Western literary tradition. Gayatri Spivak and Edward Said refer to his ambivalent position as that of a "native informant," while Rob Nixon discusses Naipaul's insider/outsider position, and the tension between the Western public he writes for and the countries he takes his materials from.

Despite the problems inherent in speaking for Others or about Others, Alcoff does not recommend what she calls "retreat," that is to say a refusal or reluctance to speak for or about Others. On the contrary, she criticizes retreat as being disempowering, irresponsible, and apolitical: "An absolute retreat weakens political effectivity, is based on a metaphysical illusion (i.e., the assumption that one can remain within one's own distinct and separate location without crossing other locations [20]), and often effects only an obscuring of the intellectual power" (24). Furthermore, "[e]ven a complete retreat from speech is of course not neutral since it allows the continued dominance of current discourses and acts by omission to reinforce their domination" (20). However, she cautions, "anyone who speaks for others should only do so out of a concrete analysis of the particular power relations and discursive effects involved" (24). Alcoff's stand is, in her words, neither essentialist nor reductionist. In fact, she is careful to qualify that while location bears on meaning, and that it is necessary to question the impulse to speak, to interrogate the bearing of the speaker's location and context on what is said, to analyze the effects of the speech on the discursive and material context, and to be accountable and responsible for speaking, location does not determine meaning. In other words, she suggests that rather than focus exclusively on subject-positions, it is important to also look at the representations themselves to conclude whether they are exploitative or sensitive to the power relations, power inequalities, and cultural differences.

Laurence knows from first-hand experience how difficult it is to see from the other side, and she often refers to this problem in her travel writings on Somaliland, published as *The Prophet's Camel Bell*. To give just one example: "My difficulty was in discovering how the tribesmen actually looked at things, for without a knowledge of basic concepts, communication is impossibly confused" (94). Konrad Groß, comparing Laurence's *The Prophet's Camel Bell* with Mungo Park's *Travels in Africa*, discusses Laurence's awareness of the manner in which her limitations form her writing:

> her distrust of the ideal of objectivity is the outstanding feature of *The Prophet's Camel Bell* in which she constantly reflects on the limitations of her own point of view.... She never assumes the role of the unprejudiced observer and she never pretends to be unbiassed [*sic*]. On the contrary, it is one purpose of her book to show how difficult it is to shed one's cultural skin and to acquire another. In the end she is ready to admit that despite her good intentions and her sympathy with the tribesmen she has not been much different from the white colonials and white travellers who were looking for the mythical kingdom of the legendary Prester John rather than for Africa itself. (77)

In an essay entitled "The Very Best Intentions," where she describes her meeting and ensuing friendship with a man she calls Mensah (she does not reveal the real name of this known opponent of the Nkwame Nkrumah regime in Ghana in the 1960s), Laurence presents the same type of questioning, and awareness of the limitations of her knowledge and perspective, as well as a very critical portrayal of herself as a young, naive white liberal woman in Africa:

At the time I naively imagined that he [Mensah] took us to be sahib-type Europeans, and I was frantic to correct his wrong impression. Later, however—several years later—I came to see that what he really dreaded was an encounter with yet another set of white liberals who went around collecting African acquaintances as though they were rare postage stamps. And now, at this further distance, I am not at all sure that I was not doing precisely that. (25)

Laurence, who came to Africa as a young woman married to a Canadian civil engineer hired by the British colonial office to work on a series of earth dam projects, and remained for approximately seven years (two years in Somaliland and five in Ghana), considered herself a "privileged" outsider, a Canadian who spent several years in Africa. In *The Prophet's Camel Bell* she emphasizes the differences between the English, the Italians, and the Canadians as colonizers, and she implies that the Canadians were, due to their own colonial history, the most anti-imperialistic and sensitive to difference (25, 31), although, "In hindsight," as Debra Martens writes in "Laurence in Africa," "she saw that this [way of thinking] was another form of colonialism" (10).

Laurence's recognition of her limitations as a white woman, her critique of colonialist attitudes whether well-intentioned or not, and her attempts at understanding difference are always present in her travel memoirs, as well as in her African fiction.

Growing Up to Africa

"The Drummer of All the World" can be described as an initiation or coming-of-age story, although not in the traditional sense. It tells the story of a white child who grows up in Africa; however, the initiation is not simply about the passage from innocent childhood to maturity. This child learns or discovers that he—unlike his parents who, as colonizers, felt they belonged in Africa—does not belong. The experience is humbling and painful. It means, for this child, consciously separating himself from his parents but also unwillingly breaking away from Africa, letting go of his childhood, and his past. He must accept that, although he has grown up in Africa alongside Africans, his life, his experience, his expectations, his opportunities are different from those of Africans in Africa because of the colour of his skin and the privileges that are associated with it. In other words, growing up means coming to terms with the fact that he belongs to the group of colonizers, that despite his good intentions and his closeness, occasionally even intimacy with Africans, he is a colonizer, and that is how he is perceived by the Africans. In "The Drummer of All the World," the protagonist is initiated into a different, oppositional (to Western eyes) way of seeing his past, his identity, his place in Africa. And this initiation occurs following the encounter with an African, Kwabena.

Matthew, the narrator of Laurence's story, is born in Ghana to missionary parents. And he is very critical of their "civilizing" mission in Africa, of his mother's hatred of Africa and Africans, and of his father's coercive methods of conversion: "For twenty years he tried to force, frighten or cajole his flock away from drumming and dancing, the accompaniments of the old religion" (4). When his father breaks into the fetish hut and destroys it, he says: "I was ashamed. I still am. Moses broke the idols of his own people" (5). Matthew clearly sees his father's activities in Africa as oppressive and colonizing, and his loyalty resides with the Africans. Although he knows the location of the fetish huts and the identity of the fetish priests, he never tells his father. Furthermore, he believes neither in his father's power to convert Africans, nor in the validity of his father's God in Africa: "When I was with Kwabena, the world of the mission and Band of Jesus did not exist for me. However powerfully my father preached, he could not stop the drums playing in the evenings" (7).

Ironically, while the father tries to "save" African souls, his son is initiated into African beliefs, rituals, traditions. Matthew believes in "the Drummer of all the world, drumming on himself, the Drum of drums" (7), and when his mother is dying he prays to an African God: "I invoked Nyankopon's strong name, Obommubuwafre, not for love of her but as a duty" (10). He also learns to speak Twi better than he can speak English, and feels Africa is his home: "This was my Africa, in the days of my childhood, before I knew how little I knew" (9).[4] As the latter quotation suggests, "Drummer" is told from the point of view of the boy-become-man who knows that Africa never belonged to him, that Africa was never his to take, and this discrepancy between the more mature narrator and the young and naive child he once was contributes to the strong current of irony throughout the story.

Matthew studies in England and returns to Africa as a visitor. His first visit, when he is seventeen, is marked by two events. A discussion with his childhood friend, Kwabena, on the subject of colonialism divides the two young men and reveals to Matthew that, despite their close friendship and shared past, he belongs to "them," to the group of oppressors that his friend wants out of his country:

"We will not always be slaves of the English," Kwabena said.

"That's stupid," I replied. "You're not slaves now."

"If they own us or own our country, where is the difference?"

"So they will have to go?"

"Yes," he answered firmly. "They will have to go."

"Splendid," I said ironically. "And I with them? If I were here in government?" (11)

Following the rendering of the discussion, Matthew recounts his meeting with the beautiful, sensual, "mother-earth" Afua and their subsequent lovemaking. The juxtaposition of these two events puts into relief their connection in the politics of colonization; woman and land are desired and disputed possessions for both colonizer and colonized males. In other words, the political and economic possession of the land and the sexual possession of Afua complement and reinforce each other.

The identification of woman with land is a recurring and particularly revealing image in colonialist texts. In *The Lay of the Land*, Annette Kolodny discusses the discursive tradition of gendering the land as feminine and its strong patriarchal, imperialistic, and economic implications in the context of the conquest and settlement of America: "the initial impulse [is] to experience the New World landscape, not merely as an object of domination and exploitation, but as a maternal 'garden', receiving and nurturing human children" (5). In the imagery Kolodny analyses, America is alternately and, at times simultaneously, virgin, lover, and mother. This trope of land-as-woman can be found in the colonial fiction of writers such as Rudyard Kipling and Conrad, where it serves to reinforce the imperialistic and patriarchal ideologies at work, as well as in the postcolonial texts of writers such as Naipaul and Michael Ondaatje where it signals their identification with the ideologies behind the colonial discursive tradition. Florence Stratton, in *Contemporary African Literature and the Politics of Gender*, contends that there is also an African male literary tradition of using woman as trope for the land (according to her study, African women writers have not employed this "masculinist" trope). She calls it the mother Africa trope and argues that it excludes woman "from authorship and citizenship" (40). However, Stratton also affirms, and here I disagree with the manicheism of her statement, that the use of the trope by contemporary African writers such as Léopold Senghor, David Diop, and Wole Soyinka is revisionist in the sense that, while colonial texts present "a negative image of Africa as savage and treacherous," they offer a positive one "of Africa as warm and sensuous, fruitful and nurturing" (40).

In two articles on the representation and silencing of the African woman in colonial and postcolonial texts, Abena Busia also notes the association of woman and land, and reveals its complexities. Moreover, she underlines the parallel between patriarchal and imperial oppression, and emphasizes the double victimization (racial and sexual) of the African woman. In "Silencing Sycorax: On African Colonial Discourse and the Unvoiced Female," the emphasis is, as the title suggests, on the silencing of African women in colonial and postcolonial texts ranging from *The Tempest*, through *Heart of Darkness*, to David Caute's *At Fever Pitch* and Laurence's *This Side Jordan*. In "Miscegenation as Metonymy: Sexuality and Power in the Colonial Novel," Busia argues that with the arrival of the white woman on the colonial scene, the struggle for domination is translated into terms of sexual behavior and misconduct—miscegenation being the ultimate transgression. And in her innovative reading of Conrad's *Heart of Darkness*, she demonstrates the association between land and African woman with regard to a fear of sexuality and a desire for power:

> In an almost anthropomorphic manner, the continent herself is endowed with a teeming female sexuality which affects everything within her. As in the description of Conrad's gorgeous apparition, the emphasis is on sex and fertility. African vegetation is abundant and luxuriant, African women are tempting, reproductive sex objects, who both allure and repel. The promiscuous nature of the continent in her luscious and uncontrollable fertility affects the Europeans, the men in particular, and they give way to whatever temptations cross their paths, a weakness which always leads to social ostracism and often self-destruction. Even when the landscape is desert, it is the lonely barrenness of that landscape which makes them succumb" (364).

Busia's analysis of the feminization of the land in Conrad reveals the many facets of the trope and contradicts Stratton's blanket statement about the colonial use of the trope. The subject-positions of authors can have a significant impact on their literary representations; however, as Alcoff cautions, location does not determine meaning. Furthermore, the subject-position of most authors, if not all, is never so simple and discrete that it can be reduced to that of a colonizer or a colonized. For example, Naipaul and Ondaatje, two postcolonial writers originally from former British colonies (respectively India via Trinidad and Sri Lanka), have incorporated the imperial/colonial trope of land-as-woman to be penetrated and possessed by the Western male, and they go even further then Conrad because not only do they represent the conquest of the land in terms of rape but they also blame the victim for seducing/provoking/welcoming her rapist. Naipaul argues that India with her great poverty and backwardness was only begging for the British colonization cum civilization cum industrialization, while Ondaatje contends that the seductiveness of Sri Lanka (her richness and fertility, as well as willingness) overwhelmed the colonizers.

Laurence borrows from this trope of land-as-woman/woman-as-land but she uses it in a slightly different manner, and ultimately with a very different meaning for the Other that is being represented. The description of Afua (Africa) in "The Drummer of All the World" suggests the conventional association between land and woman, both fertile and nurturing, sensual and warm, as well as strong and atemporal: "Her body gave the impression of incredible softness and at the same time a maternal strength. She belonged to earth, to her body's love, to toil, to her unborn children" (12). And Matthew says, strengthening the connection between earth and woman: "Possessing her, I possessed all earth" (12). Rather than reinforce the control and dominance of land and woman through the use of this type of imagery, Laurence reveals and criticizes Matthew's inability to let go of the old Africa, his nostalgia for the past, and his present inability to accept that he does not belong in Africa on the same terms as his friend Kwabena. His sexual possession of Afua reveals his location as colonizer and his refusal to let go of Africa. Laurence implies a parallel between Matthew's possession of Afua, his father's proselytizing, and the colonizers' partitioning and exploitation of the continent of Africa. Her use of this imagery exposes the workings of colonialist and patriarchal ideology to the reader and to Matthew who gradually becomes aware of his complicity in the exploitation of Africa.[5]

In her first novel, *This Side Jordan*, Laurence also criticizes the colonialist use of the association between land and woman. Johnny Kestoe, the British accountant for a textile firm in Ghana, sleeps with an African woman he assumes to be a prostitute: "She was a whore—why should she look like that? But he was glad she did. Her slight spasm of fear excited him. She was a continent and he an invader, wanting both to possess and destroy her" (231). Laurence's use of the imagery is not trite or unsubtle as critic Jane Leney has suggested—"Unfortunately, here Laurence has employed the trite symbol of the woman as African continent" (69)—on the contrary, as Busia points out, the trope reveals the brutal and exploitative use of the African woman and by extension the violent colonization of

Africa by white men: "This encounter dramatizes as it satirizes the patriarchal nature of the imperial venture. In making the woman a frightened,
silenced virgin [and infibulated], rather than, as is more common, a
whore, Laurence clearly calls the trope into question" (1989–90, 91–92).
Laurence's use of the trope also explicitly reveals the connection between
the colonizer's/man's desire to possess and his desire to violate, a connection that is implicit and unquestioned in Conrad.

Although, in this case, the African woman is silenced, as Busia indicates, that is not the situation in "The Drummer of All the World," where
Afua is given a voice and a mind that challenge Matthew: "I told her that I
had to go back to England soon. Perhaps I expected her to say she would
be broken-hearted. 'Yes, it is right that you should return to your own
land,' Afua said" (12). The fact that she says this immediately after
Matthew's expression of his desire to possess Africa/woman signals
Laurence's empathy with the African women and her position as anti-
colonialist.

On his second visit to his country of birth, this time as an adult,
Matthew notices changes in the country. He feels the march towards independence, the detribalization and Westernization of Ghana, and he is
nostalgic for the "old Africa," the Africa of his childhood: "The old Africa
was dying, and I felt suddenly rootless, a stranger in the only land I could
call home" (13). This quotation, revealing Matthew's nostalgia for the
"authentic" Africa of his childhood, and implicitly for the colonial Africa,
as well as his fear of displacement and exile, is undercut (as is his use of the
trope of woman-as-land) soon after by a heated discussion with Kwabena
who shows Matthew and the reader the baleful distortion of this nostalgia:
"You would like us to remain forever living in thatch huts, pounding our
drums and telling pretty stories about big spiders. . . . You forget. . . that the
huts were rotten with sickness, and the tales made us forget an empty
belly, and the drums told of our fear" (17).

On this trip, Matthew realizes that Africa was never his home in the
sense that it was never his land; more importantly, he understands his
complicity in the colonial process. He had thought he could distance himself from his father, "the God of [his] fathers" (10), and the colonial
enterprise. Now he realizes the extent of his role as colonizer/oppressor.
When he accidentally meets Kwabena, the contrast between their lives,
their jobs, their beliefs, and their hopes underlines their different racial,
class, and political affiliations and, as Margaret Osachoff puts it, "the
inequality of opportunity" (220). Matthew holds a job in the

Administration, while Kwabena is a medical orderly because he does not have the means or opportunity to become a doctor.

During this second visit to Ghana, Matthew is shocked to learn of the death of Yaa, Kwabena's mother, who was, in his words, "more mother to me than my own mother." Kwabena tells him, "I shared my mother with you, in exchange for your cast-off khaki shorts" (16), exposing another viewpoint to the reader and to Matthew, but more importantly, exposing the unequal power and economic relations between the two men. If we think of the association between land and woman that Laurence has already suggested in her description of Afua, the words "I shared my mother with you" acquire another meaning. Kwabena literally shared his mother with Matthew but he also, figuratively, shared his mother-land. Finally, with Kwabena's help, Matthew comes to this understanding:

> But at last I know, although I shall never be able to admit it to him. It was only I who could afford to love the old Africa. Its enchantment had touched me, its suffering—never. Even my fright had stopped this side of pain. I had always been the dreamer who knew he could waken at will, the tourist who wanted antique quaintness to remain unchanged.
>
> We were conquerors in Africa, we Europeans. Some despised her, that bedraggled queen we had unthroned, and some loved her for her still-raging magnificence, her old wisdom. But all of us sought to force our will upon her. (18)

At this point, the narrator fully understands his involvement in the oppression and exploitation of Africa, and realizes how his nostalgia for the old Africa only keeps the country in fetters, as well as covertly exonerates the colonial enterprise. The "I" of the young boy has become the "we" of the man who knows that, despite his good will towards Africans and his love of Africa, he belongs to the group of oppressors. This passage strikingly resembles one in Laurence's essay, "The Best Intentions":

> I stared at him, seeing for the first time how he must look at the ancient Africa, the Africa of the talking drums and the bizarre figures cast in bronze. I could afford to be fascinated. None of it threatened me. But for Mensah, the time to move on had not only arrived, it was long overdue. What he saw in the old Africa was not the weird beauty of wood carvings or bronze vessels or the exultant pulsings of the drums. What he saw was the fear and the squalor, the superstition, the men still

working the fields in this century with machetes and hoes, the children who still died by the score through lack of medical care. (27)

In the above passage, as in "The Drummer of All the World," there is a contrast between two ways of seeing, two experiences of Africa, and Laurence critiques Matthew's and her own distorted visions of Africa; the African cannot afford the luxury of nostalgia or exoticism.

The image of Africa as "bedraggled queen" in the quotation from "The Drummer of All the World" harkens back to the representation of woman as mother-earth in the scene when Afua and Matthew make love. "Possessing her, I possessed all earth" (12), he says, revealing the colonizer's desire to conquer Africa. The violence of the sexual/colonial act is suggested by the words "force our will upon her" and "bedraggled." The quotation also explicitly problematizes the category of colonizer. Matthew names "the dreamer," "the tourist," "the conqueror," the ones who "loved her" and those who "despised her" but there is no longer any doubt in his mind, as in Laurence's, that "all sought to force [their] will upon her."

The above image of Africa as an old woman also brings to mind the description of the older, ravaged Afua—"in her eyes was the hatred, the mockery of all time" (14). Although Africa is now an old and decrepit woman, she once was a splendid queen, and her splendour and "still-raging magnificence" has not been extinguished despite the colonizers' efficient and forceful attempts. Laurence's narrator tells us, reminding the reader of Afua's sensual dance, that she "will dance again, this time to a new song" (19). While Conrad's and Naipaul's use of the imagery of land-as-woman suggests a nostalgic and desperate desire to possess the unpossessable, the unfathomable "heart of darkness," or to retrieve the lost empire, Laurence's story ends with a forward glance to a future where Africa will be reborn as independent. ("The Drummer of All the World" was published in 1956, the year before the independence of Ghana, the first African nation to obtain independence.) In a similar manner, the theme of the rebirth of an independent Africa is suggested in *This Side Jordan* by the birth of Miranda and Aya's children: respectively a white girl and a black boy who represent the promise of the future. The miscegenationist or neocolonial future that is symbolized by a white girl and a black boy carries certain ideological implications I find troubling (Africa's generative powers are transferred to a white child) and reveals Laurence's desire to see whites and blacks coexist as equals in Africa, a belated wish contradicted by years of white domination, exploitation, and abuse. As Aziz puts it in *A Passage to India*: "'we shall get rid of you, yes, we shall drive every blasted Englishman into the sea, and then'—he rode against him furiously—'and then,' he concluded, half kissing him, 'you and I shall be friends'" (289).

Laurence's "The Drummer of All the World" ends on a sad and bitter note. Matthew leaves Africa, which he loves, and his pain is strong, as is his critique of imperialism: "My father thought he was bringing salvation to Africa. I do not any longer know what salvation is. I only know that one man cannot find it for another man, and one land cannot bring it to another" (18). This conclusion reinforces the nature of Matthew's initiation, i.e., a realization of his complicity in the colonial enterprise, and an awareness of his radically different subject-position in the land from that of Africans. It is significant that the learning process, in "The Drummer of All the World" and in Laurence's autobiographical essay, "The Very Best Intentions," occurs thanks to the encounter or friendship with an African: Mensah in "The Very Best Intentions" and Kwabena in "The Drummer of All the World." Mensah and Kwabena have initiated Laurence and Matthew (and the reader to a certain extent) to a different vision of Africa and of their place as whites in it, an "African" vision; Matthew and Laurence have learned to see Africa and their presence in Africa through the eyes of an African. In other words, the colonial paradigm of the white teacher and carrier of civilization is reversed in another example of how Laurence's African stories challenge the exploitative (colonial and postcolonial) tradition of representing the Other.

Acknowledgement
I would like to dedicate this paper to Craig Smith who read a preliminary version and made helpful suggestions, and thank the *Fondation pour la formation de chercheurs et l'aide à la recherche* for financial support during the writing of this paper.

Notes
1. My doctoral thesis deals mainly with distorted and exploitative representations of the eroticized Other in imperial and colonial contexts. See also my article on Sara Jeannette Duncan, "Portrait of a Colonizer/Colonized," in *Textual Studies in Canada 5* (1994).
2. I have borrowed Achebe's term, "colonialist," that he uses to denounce a certain type of criticism written by Africans "which derives from the same basic attitude and assumption as colonialism itself" (1988, 46). I find the term useful for my purposes because it can apply equally to colonial and postcolonial representations.
3. By "speaker *of* the Third World," I mean to suggest that Naipaul is from the Third World, in the sense that he is of Indian origin—his grandfather came to Trinidad as an

indentured slave—and that he writes about the Third World, that is to say he makes a living out of commodifying and objectifying the Third World for a Western audience. Naipaul is not a speaker for (representative of) the Third World.

4. This scene of the fall into knowledge or "whiteness" is a characteristic moment in white South African writing. See, for example, the fiction of Nadine Gordimer as a whole or Laurens van der Post's *A Story Like the Wind*.

5. Albert Memmi, *Portrait du colonisé*, writes eloquently about the inevitable, albeit unconscious and occasionally unwilling, complicity of the privileged individual with the colonial system. Memmi makes an important distinction between "le colonial, le colonisateur et le colonialiste" (34). The colonial is the European living in a colony who appears to have no economic or social privileges, the colonizer is the one who holds a position in the civil service, administration, or police department of the colony, and the colonialist is the fervent supporter of colonialism as a political system. And he argues that all Europeans in the colonies, whether rich or poor, kind or evil, well-intentioned or not, benefit from the colonial system. In his words: "tous les Européens des colonies sont des privilégiés" (34).

3

THE AFRICAN AND

CANADIAN HEROINES

From Bondage to Grace

Ever since the rib episode, patriarchal religion has defined women by their relationship to men. Moreover, in traditional Judaism and conservative Christianity, the daughters of Eve have been regarded as the authors of evil and the representatives of "the world, the flesh, and the devil," only capable of atoning for their original sin and sexual seductiveness by obedient servitude to man (Gen. 3:16). These attitudes characterized western culture until very recently and were naturally reflected in its male-dominated literature. In these days of women's liberation and prominent female authors, we might easily forget that Margaret Laurence was one of the first Canadian novelists (partly influenced by Ethel Wilson) to probe Adam's exploitation and articulate Eve's search for freedom. The publication of *The Stone Angel* in 1964 liberated the Canadian heroine from being primarily a prisoner of the male imagination and paved the way for the feminist creations of Margaret Atwood, Alice Munro, Marian Engel, Audrey Thomas and of the succeeding generation—Katherine Govier,

Susan Swan, Joan Barfoot, and others—that we take for granted today. Laurence's matriarchal legacy has meant that their creations are no longer confined pejoratively to the ghetto of "women's novels," the female canon for much of our literary history, but can enrich and even dominate the mainstream of Canadian literature.

Laurence experienced patriarchal prejudice in her own Scots Presbyterian upbringing, embodied in her Grandfather Simpson (fictionalized as Grandfather Connor in *A Bird in the House*). But, as she narrates in *Dance on the Earth*, she fortunately had matriarchal models—her mother, her aunt-stepmother, and later her mother-in-law—to counteract the phallocentric repression. With certain autobiographical overtones, she portrays all of her Canadian heroines as victims of social stereotyping constructed by Old Testament archetypes and Calvinist theology, who struggle desperately "to survive with some dignity, toting the load of excess mental baggage that everyone carries, until the moment of death" ("Ten Years" 14). This is their pilgrimage from bondage to grace, often expressed in a transition from Old Testament to New Testament imagery.

Hagar Shipley, in *The Stone Angel*, is the embodiment of Calvinist materialism and patriarchal power ironically trapped in a woman's prison. Her bondage to law and the flesh (the old covenant) has exiled her, like her namesake, in a wilderness of pride (Gen. 16 and Gal. 4:21–31). But she is finally redeemed through sacrificial love accompanied by Christian images of baptism, redemption, and grace, as the stone angel becomes real. In her final experience of love, joy, and freedom, she holds in her hands, perhaps, the cup of salvation.

In the Old Testament, Hagar bore her son as a slave concubine "in bondage" to the first Jewish patriarch. In contrast, Rachel was the favourite wife of the third patriarch and finally bore his favourite son, Joseph (who foreshadowed the Messiah), but only after years of deceitful manipulation by her father and frustrated barrenness with Jacob (Gen. 30). Rachel Cameron in *A Jest of God* is also a frustrated spinster victimized by a manipulative mother (ironically a female counterpart of Laban) who forces her into a sterile Calvinist role of female repression and social respectability. Nor is she ultimately made fruitful by sexual surrender to her self-indulgent male lover, whose reaction to her need, like Jacob's, is: "I'm not God" (154; Gen. 30:2). Only through her final acceptance of "the jests of God" (imperfection, injustice, indignity, and finally death) does she recognize the liberating grace of the Pauline doctrine about the worldly wise and God's fools (141; 202; I Cor. 3:18).

Stacey Cameron MacAindra (*The Fire-Dwellers*) and Morag Gunn (*The Diviners*) do not have symbolic Old Testament names, but they follow the same pilgrimage from the old covenant to the new. Dwelling in the inferno of contemporary society, Stacey attempts to earn salvation through the law (of suburban-housewife perfection) and the prophets (of Polyglam). Her husband, ironically, is a fellow victim of a patriarchal, Calvinist religion-without-God. Stacey's final epiphany comes, not through bondage to the demands of her men, but in acceptance of her own reality: freedom from conformity to the Old Testament ideal of womanhood in which "[her] kids would rise up and call [her] blessed" (272; Prov. 31:28), and a recognition that "the grace isn't given" (280) to put out all the fires of life and death but only to accept love and mercy, giving thanks in all things (Eph. 5:20).

Morag Gunn, exiled from the Garden of Eden (443) by the death of her parents, wanders through a number of wildernesses, conforming to and then rebelling against the bourgeois, patriarchal ideals that she has hoped will bring her, a "stranger" and "sojourner," into the "halls of Sion" (273; Ps. 39). She has treated her adoptive father like a disreputable "Jonah" (390) and attempted to repudiate her past. Finally accepting the redeeming mythology of Christ(ie)'s country, she gains peace within her own Eden, a "wildflower garden" (431), and learns to divine for the truth of life and art by faith through "grace" (477; Rom. 5:1–2).

Laurence's Canadian heroines, in seeking "survival with dignity," so often move from the position of the immature Vanessa MacLeod in *A Bird in the House*, a female Joshua attempting to storm the patriarchal tyranny of "Jericho's Brick Battlements" (184) in order to break her bondage, to an appreciation of the "perpetual grace" of Grandmother Connor whose strength and courage flow from the "acceptance [that] was at the heart of her" (72). This pilgrimage is usually reflected in a transition from Old Testament patriarchal allusions to New Testament images of freedom, grace, hope, peace, and love. Like her heroines, and unlike Grandmother Connor, Laurence was "not really an orthodox Christian," but they shared the same religious "impulses" to "celebrate life" (*Dance* 243).

Laurence's Canadian novels, which have been so crucial in the gender-balanced development of contemporary Canadian literature, did not spring from an autobiographical and fictional void. By 1964 Laurence had spent thirty-eight years experiencing and observing the reality of womanhood on three continents. She was her own first heroine in her juvenilia. And her experiences and observations were focused and fictionalized most acutely during the seven years she spent in Africa—in Somalia from 1950–52 and in Ghana from 1952–57—with her engineer husband. Her awareness of the conflicts of gender and power were intensified in her culture shock. Out of her years in Africa emerged her first publications: *A Tree for Poverty* (1956), a translation of traditional Somali literature; *The Prophet's Camel Bell* (1963), a travel-autobiography; *This Side Jordan* (1960), her first novel; and the collection of short stories, *The Tomorrow-Tamer* (1963). We find in these books the genesis of many of Laurence's later themes, including the pilgrimage of the heroine. Laurence herself articulated these connections:

> My sense of social awareness, my feelings of anti-imperialism, anti-colonialism, anti-authoritarianism, had begun, probably, in embryo form in my own childhood; they had been nurtured during my college years and immediately afterwards, in the North Winnipeg of the old Left; they had developed considerably through my African experience. It was not very difficult to relate this experience to my own land, which had been under the colonial sway of Britain once and was now under the colonial sway of America. But these developing feelings also related very importantly to my growing awareness of the dilemma and powerlessness of women, the tendency of women to accept male definition of ourselves, to be self-depreciating and uncertain, and to rage inwardly. The quest for physical and spiritual freedom, the quest for relationships of equality and communication—these themes run through my fiction and are connected with the theme of survival, not mere physical survival, but a survival of the spirit, with human dignity and the ability to give and receive love. ("Ivory Tower" 24)

During Laurence's sojourn in Africa, the Pentateuch imagery and characterization, which she so often uses for her depiction of patriarchal oppression, became meaningful for her in the nomadic tribes of the Somali desert and especially among the subjugated and victimized African women. In *The Prophet's Camel Bell* she notes how, fortuitously, she read "for the first time in [her] life the five books of Moses" shortly before her arrival in Africa: "Of all the books which I might have chosen to read just then, few would have been more to the point, for the Children of Israel were people of the desert, as the Somalis were, and fragments from those books were to return to me again and again" (17). In the cultural upheaval of the new Africa on the verge of independence, however, Laurence also saw images that she associates with the end of her heroines' pilgrimage out of bondage: freedom, dignity, and spiritual grace.

The Prophet's Camel Bell is an account of Laurence's two years in the Somaliland Protectorate (now Somalia) where her husband Jack was in charge of a reservoir-building project in the Haud desert. Although she kept detailed diaries throughout her time there, she later found many of her impressions were sentimental "bosh" and, in fact, mentally recreated and re-evaluated her experience at a distance of ten years before writing the memoir. Again, Laurence is her own first heroine in publication. The protagonist we meet through her first-person narration dominates the book with her wit, intelligence, energy, and probing mind; she is perhaps the most engaging, exciting character of all her creations. *The Prophet's Camel Bell* is less a travelogue than a story of spiritual growth and emotional maturing: "In your excitement at the trip, the last thing in the world that would occur to you is that the strangest glimpses you may have of any creature in the distant lands will be those you catch of yourself" (10). And in Laurence's personal development we catch glimpses of all her later heroines.

Rejecting the stereotype of imperialist "memsahib," Laurence longed to become involved with the native Somalis through experiencing their lives and translating their literature. But so often their problems appeared totally alien and mysterious and their tragedies meaningless. Finally she was forced to relinquish her fantasies of perfect harmony with Abdi and the other Somalis and admit, as her heroines Rachel and Stacey have since discovered, that perfect human communication is impossible: "My feeling at this time was that I would never understand" (207). However, like her alter-ego Vanessa, in retrospect the author also realized that behind its mask each life has a wholeness and integrity that demands consideration. Laurence devotes four chapters to perceptive, rounded character studies of those Somalis she knew best, and two more chapters to the expatriate groups that were often collectively condemned but actually deserved sympathy, understanding, and often respect. Moreover, she weaves the painful events she witnessed, together with the joys and accomplishments, into a meaningful pattern of education for herself and evolving freedom for Somalia:

Out in the Haud, we felt we had heard the Prophet's camel bell. We had come to know something of these desert people, their pain and their

faith, their anger, their ability to endure. The most prophetic note of
that bell, however, was one we scarcely heard at all, although the
sound was there, if we had had ears for it. In less than ten years, the two
Somalilands that had been under British and Italian administration
had joined and gained their independence as the Somali Republic. (260)

At twenty-four, Laurence bore some similarities to her later characterization of Rachel Cameron, although she was never that paranoid
arrested-adolescent. But, introspective and self-conscious, she felt isolated
from both the conventional "memsahib" community and the native
women in *purdah*. She sometimes felt gauche and insecure with the more
reserved Somalis, and then in recollection was embarrassed by her effron-
tery and air of superiority ("All at once the brash tone of my own voice
was conveyed to my own ears, and I was appalled" [47]).
   She began enthusiastically doctoring the workers with bandaids and
laxatives, then faced with the appalling misery of the Somali nomads,
realized guiltily her own helplessness and the mixed motives of a white
liberal:

> What had I known of life here at all?...It seemed to me that I had been
> like a child, playing doctor with candy pills, not knowing—not really
> knowing—that the people I was treating were not dolls. Had I wanted
> to help them for their sake or for my own? Had I needed their gratitude
> so much? (74)

In the Haud constant suffering and capricious tragedy surrounded
Laurence. Her awareness of death, quest for meaning, and desire for spiritual security have been echoed by all her heroines since:

> So the Qoran gives suffering a meaning and refuses the finality of
> death. I saw the necessity of this belief, without which life for these peo-
> ple would be intolerable. I would have shared such a faith, if it had been
> a matter of choice, but I could not. (95)

But, although she could not share the Somalis' faith and fatalism, she did
learn their lesson of acceptance, preventing them "from wasting themselves in fury and desperation" (64). To accept the reality of death and
make the best of whatever life one is given is the lesson of all of Laurence's
later heroines.

The themes of human suffering and colonial oppression particularly converged, for Laurence, in her shock at the plight of women in Somali society despite their elaborate romanticization in literature. The bondage and subjection of women, usually disguised in Western civilization, were pathetically obvious to Laurence in the Somalis' primitive patriarchal culture of arranged marriages and sexual double standards. She saw child prostitutes; adolescents married off to old men; women scorned, beaten, forced into painful puberty rites, and relegated to long years of menial status, harsh drudgery, agonizing childbirth and an early death, often watching their children die first of thirst or malaria. Life was bitter for all Somali nomads, but the men at least had more freedom, power and independence according to their religious, legal and social mores (101–3). As for their wives: "Women had always lived with pain. Why should it ever be any different?" (76). In the faces of the Somali women we see an exaggerated, primitive portrait of the Laurence heroine, but it was her first graphic realization of the woman as victim.

In *The Prophet's Camel Bell* Laurence acknowledges the psychological insights into colonialism, the master-servant relationship, and the problems of exile, which she gained from O. Mannoni's book, *Prospero and Caliban: A Study of the Psychology of Colonization*. Although she did not read it until 1960, after her African experience but during her work on her African books, this study confirmed most of her personal perceptions:

What the colonial in common with Prospero lacks, is awareness of the world of Others, a world in which Others have to be respected. This is the world from which the colonial has fled because he cannot accept men as they are. Rejection of that world is combined with an urge to dominate. (Mannoni qtd. in *Prophet's* 250)

Laurence recognizes the similarity between the imperialist and the patriarchal oppression of the Other. But she also realizes the "irony" that, although she "started out in righteous disapproval of the empire-builders," she was "forced at last to recognize that I, too, had been of that company" in seeking to impose her own idealism on another culture (*Prophet's* 251).

Laurence began her first novel, *This Side Jordan*, during her five years on the Gold Coast but rewrote half of it after leaving Africa, because she thought she had "been unfair to the European characters" ("Ten Years" 10). The setting of this book is Ghana approaching Independence. It is a country in transition, painfully casting off both the ancestral bonds of tribalism and the European burden of colonialism. We see the tremendous problems of adjustment to Africanization, for both the African and English communities, through the eyes of Nathaniel Amegbe, a black schoolteacher, and Johnnie Kestoe, the accountant for an English import-export company. Confused and frustrated, they stubbornly re-enact the history of Ghana: the frightened, propitiating but resentful African, in conflict with the greedy, white racist and ravisher.

Nathaniel, like his country, is torn between loyalty to the customs and values of his tribal past and the Western, Christian "enlightenment" of the mission school and the city: "You have forgotten your own land. You live in the city of strangers and your god is the god of strangers and strange speech is in your mouth and you have no home" (104). To achieve a sense of freedom and self-worth he must resolve this schizophrenia, identifying himself with the new Ghana, and assimilating "the pride and roots" from the past into the idealism and hope for the future: "its guide in a new land, its ferryman across Jordan" (273). Despite his doubts and humiliations, Nathaniel finally conquers the guilt of yesterday and finds the courage to possess tomorrow, for the sake of his work and his son:

> I have a new chance and I have a new name and I live in a new land with a new name. And I cannot go back.
>
> . . .
>
> My god is the God of my own soul and my own speech is in my mouth, and my home is here, here, here, my home is here at last. (274–75)

In contrast to Nathaniel, Johnnie Kestoe is a ruthless opportunist in the guise of a realist. Through him we meet the white imperialists: actually the pathetic exiles, alcoholics, and incompetents of English society, "the relics of a dead age" (123) desperately trying to preserve their last foothold in Africa. Johnnie has risen from the London slums, haunted by a past as full of brutality and superstition as Nathaniel's. But he adopts the same Western ethic as later characterizes Hagar Shipley, defining freedom as power and status, exploiting enemies and betraying friends in his ambition. Like Hagar, he finally discovers his only true liberation from pride and fear in accepting his kinship with all people. His brief recognition of the humanity of the black virgin (who symbolizes Africa) and his kindness to her are the first evidences of *his* humanity and respect for the Other: "He took her hand and held it closely for an instant. Then he stooped and picked up her crumpled green cloth from the floor. Very gently, he drew it across her body. It was all he could do for her, and for himself" (234). Yet, in the end, he still supports Africanization grudgingly and expediently.

Ultimately both Nathaniel and Johnnie are tarnished heroes; like Moses, their generation will remain "this side Jordan." The final optimism in the novel arises mainly from the character of their wives and the birth—at the same time, in the same place—of their children. For there arises the hope that the symbolically named Mary (named after Johnnie's own tragic mother but also invoked in the novel as the "Mother of God" [60], and "the Mother of all men" [274]) may overcome the fear and hatred in her father's past with a new love. Similarly, Joshua represents the birth of the new African nation, and Nathaniel is confident his son will "cross Jordan" and lead his people into the Promised Land (282).

The women are not the protagonists in this novel, but we can see in Miranda Kestoe and Aya Amegbe a pilgrimage that prefigures the later Laurence heroines. Their development in maturity and self-awareness liberates them from the bondage of their dependent female groups and turns their fears into a sense of freedom and grace.

The English memsahibs are pathetic, frightened mourners at the burial of colonialism, still touting "white supremacy" to bolster their husbands' images and disguise their inadequacies. In contrast, Miranda Kestoe is an intelligent, idealistic, but perceptive liberal who tries to foster communication, understanding, and respect between the two cultures, befriending Nathaniel and encouraging Johnnie in the pursuit of Africanization. But, when constantly rebuffed by English society, repressed by her husband, and misunderstood by the Africans, she becomes fearful and apologetic. She is a re-creation, really, of Laurence herself in Ghana (as portrayed in her essay "The Very Best Intentions") and in Somalia, well-intentioned but, like Miranda, not entirely aware of her own motives as a white, liberal "amateur anthropologist" (53). Laurence describes this type in *The Prophet's Camel Bell*: "[There] are many of those who believe they feel only sympathy towards people of another land, and whose 'sympathy' may lead them to see these people not as they really are but as the beholder feels they ought to be" (251).

This kind of relationship based on projected dreams is not confined to imperialist or patriarchal stereotyping. Laurence examines its female embodiments in Hagar Shipley and Rachel Cameron. And, as Stacey MacAindra's marriage illustrates, "communication" is sometimes only an excuse for manipulation. Therefore, when Johnnie walks out on his wife's inquisition and Aya Amegbe rebuffs her help, Miranda must learn to respect the distance between people, the privacy of their lives and minds: "I don't want to probe any more. Just to accept" (236). She is a Miranda who has learned to curb her aggressive "wonder," for "whether it is Ariel or Caliban who is chosen to populate Prospero's world, there is no basic difference, for both are equally unreal" (*Prophet's* 251). She must finally come to accept the reality and integrity of the Other.

Aya Amegbe is, in many ways, the antithesis of Miranda Kestoe, but she is an equally heroic figure who becomes a bridge between the old and new Africas. At the beginning, she is bound to the superstitious, tribal past more closely than her husband is. Pregnant, lonely, and frightened, she relies on the primitive rites and familiar roles dictated by her female relatives. And Nathaniel bitterly resents her illiteracy and unsophistication, her childish dependence on superstition and fear of modern technology. He constantly attempts to repress her native imagination and exuberance into staid conformity, and isolate her from associations with the past through her family and friends like Charity Donkor.

As Victor Edusei's cynicism contrasts with Nathaniel's idealism, so his mistress' sexual "charity" is a counterpoint to Aya's innocence and integrity. Charity is an illiterate, superstitious bush girl like Aya, who has adopted the seductive sophistications of the city. Her life is dedicated to the enjoyment of serving and gratifying a man and bearing his children: "She would cook for him, sleep with him, bear his child, and be—what she was" (116). His payment to her is scorn and resentful exploitation. To Johnnie, she is only a possible prostitute; to Nathaniel, she means another failure for his friend; to Victor, she represents a bitter consolation prize for defeated dreams and future pessimism: "You wait until after Independence. You'll see such oppression as you never believed possible.... There'll be your Free-Dom for you—the right to be enslaved by your own kind.... You can keep Ghana. I'll take Charity" (118).

Aya and Charity share the same heritage and environment, but Aya is more a soul-sister to Stacey MacAindra than to Charity Donkor; she is not content to accept the age-old stereotype of woman as an ignorant sex-object and inferior domestic possession. She determines to take her place beside her husband: "I think you have forgotten that a woman goes to her mother's people when she reaches the eighth month," she said. "But I will not do it, Nathaniel, even if Adua goes back. I will stay with you" (73). Her act of courage is greater than his when she commits her life and her son to the future in the dreaded hospital. And her independence and strength amaze Nathaniel when she stands up to Miranda as he never would. For

Joshua is her son also; he will need as much guidance from her as from Nathaniel to "cross Jordan" and find the promised land.

Both Miranda and Aya escape the bondage of their stereotyped roles and surprise Nathaniel, the male protagonist, with their humanity:

> Aya was soft-spoken and gentle, but she was strong and vehement, too.... He felt in a way proud of Aya. And yet he had an inexplicable pity for that other woman.... Miranda's eagerness to know, her exaggerated politeness, her anxiety to please, her terrible kindness—none of it had moved him at all. Only, now, the sudden knowledge that she could feel humiliation and anguish like himself. (263)

Laurence's Ghanaian stories, *The Tomorrow-Tamer*, were written contemporaneously with her first novel. Though originally published separately, they are united by one theme also common to Laurence's other African books: the death of the old Africa and the birth of the new, and the conflicts that arise in the transition. Laurence has most often portrayed the essence of Africa in its women, as in this description from "The Drummer of All the World":

> The flame tree whose beauty is suddenly splendid—and short-lived— like the beauty of African women. The little girl dancing with her shadow in the stifling streets. The child sleeping unmindful, while flies caress his eyes and mouth with the small bright wings of decay. The squalor, the exultation, the pain. (19)

However, there are only three stories in *The Tomorrow-Tamer* with female protagonists. Nevertheless, they encapsulate Laurence's themes of bondage and freedom—both colonial and feminist. In "A Fetish for Love" Constance naively experiences, as did Laurence and Miranda Kestoe, the pathetic, subjugated lives of most African women. Her servant, Love, is a teenager married to an old man who beats her in frustration at his own infertility; she survives through submission to his anger and bribes and a "hopeless and enduring hope" in her primitive superstitions (181). But Constance learns that a white woman cannot dictate freedom and fulfilment to a woman of another culture. She grows to acknowledge the cultural distinctiveness of the other ("I don't know.... I—can't know" [180]), and to distrust her own idealistic motives as projections of outraged justice and frustrated power: "Now she was no longer sure of her own reasons" (178).

"The Rain Child" ironically counterpoints two culturally alienated women seeking freedom and fulfilment in a strange land. The narrator, Violet Nedden, pleads for understanding and acceptance, quoting from Exodus 23:9: "Thou shalt not oppress a stranger, for ye know the heart of a stranger, seeing ye were strangers in the land of Egypt" (114). This scriptural reference is frequently invoked by Laurence (and used as the title of her book of essays, *Heart of a Stranger*) to express the theme common to all her heroines' stories: the child or child/adult journeying through the country of experience toward the promised land of inner freedom is always an exile.

Violet was the first female narrator Laurence employed. Her strong, ironic voice ("Pride has so often been my demon" [125]) foreshadows Hagar's. But her lonely, emotionally frustrated, introspective and self-censuring persona, as a teacher loving her students but reminding herself "these were not our children" (115), more closely prefigures Rachel Cameron. Despite her knowledgeable immersion in African culture ("I spoke instead about Akan poetry, and read them the drum prelude *Anyaneanyane* in their own tongue as well as the translation" [107]), distinguishing her so clearly from the other colonialists, she still teaches an "alien speech" (133) to her charges, bears the infirmity of a tropical affliction, and realizes that she cannot ultimately communicate with "the outcast children" of Africa (132). Ironically when she retires to England, she will also be an outcast.

The "child of the rain" and of "tears" (121) is Ruth Quansah, so thoroughly Anglicized by her life with her doctor father in England that she never learned the language of her illiterate mother, who died in exile soon after she was born. Unable to communicate with her black compatriots, but only "almost like" a European (129), she is, like Violet, an exile from both worlds. Ironically named, she cannot say, even of her own homeland: "thy people shall be my people, and thy God my God" (Ruth 1:16). Rather she is appalled at the primitive and sensual exuberance of African women:

> Kwaale threw back her head and laughed. Her hands flicked at her cloth and for an instant she stood there naked.... Ruth, tidy and separate in her frock with its pastel flowers, stared as though unable to believe what she had seen. (127)

Nor can she understand the suffering of the child prostitute, Ayesha, or Kwaale's inevitable destiny: "bearing too many children in too short a span of years, mourning the inevitable deaths of some of them, working bent double at the planting and hoeing until her slim straightness was warped" (113). She remains an outcast without, yet, the maturity to accept her situation and find freedom in a survival with compromises—the lesson learned by Constance, Love, Violet Nedden, and finally by Mammii Ama.

The last story in *The Tomorrow-Tamer*, "A Gourdful of Glory," examines the meaning of freedom for three generations of African women. To four-year-old Comfort, "Independence" is a modern hospital and life (even if one has to wait three days before seeing a doctor) rather than the fetish priest and death. To her mother, who insists on calling herself Marcella, it means prostitution to Western ways and fashions as a club girl in the "Weekend in Wyoming." To Mammii Ami it means free bus rides. When, after the Day of Independence, her pathetic existence continues unchanged, she is temporarily devastated. But an encounter with a white woman who mocks her country's liberation inspires Mammii Ama's pride, imagination, and economic independence: "I no need for you money." She recognizes true freedom means self-respect and courage to accept the realities and responsibilities of life: "Free-Dom he come.... She knew what was what. She knew some things would happen, and others—for no reason apparent to her—would not. And yet, there was a truth in her words, more true than reality" (242). Therefore, the story ends the book with optimism and exaltation for the future of Africa, expressed by a "liberated" woman who foreshadows Laurence's Canadian heroines:

> *"Mammii Ama, she no come rich*
> *Ha—ei! Be so. On'y one penny.*
> *She nevah be shame, she no fear for nothing.*
> *D'time wey come now, like queen she shine."* (244)

In Laurence's African writings, we see her personal development in maturity, self-awareness, and perception of the Other. Themes and personalities from these books are reflected in her later works as are her skilful techniques, convincing characterization, realistic action, and compelling imagery. The main flaw in Laurence's African fiction is an over-emphasis on theme. In *This Side Jordan* the balanced, symmetrical structure is too contrived, the symbolism too obvious, the denouement too fussy in apportioning rewards and tying up loose ends. Even Nathaniel's inner turmoil is displayed tidily, and Johnnie's background is invested with too much "significant" tragedy. In *The Tomorrow-Tamer*, the obvious didactic point to each story sometimes betrays the material, as in the tricky ending to "The Perfume Sea." Yet, the colour and characterization in these books always rise above the critical flaws, and Laurence's later writing demonstrates a growing ability to balance these virtues against her didactic desires.

Margaret Laurence left Ghana in 1957. At that time the prevailing spirit, both of her young self and emerging Africa, was optimism. While her African books faithfully represented the situation there in the late 1950s, they were written by "an outsider who experienced a seven years' love affair with a continent but who in the end had to remain in precisely that relationship" ("Ten Years" 11). In retrospect, she was aware that her well-meaning colonialism had led to some cultural appropriation and naive optimism. Certainly, "if anything was now going to be written about Africa, it would have to be done from the inside by Africans themselves, and this was one reason [she] stopped writing anything with that setting" ("Ten Years" 12).

Certainly, for someone who was "a kind of Method writer, in the same way that some actors become the characters they play" ("Time" 157), Laurence was later amazed that she "ever had the nerve to attempt to go into the mind of an African man" ("Gadgetry" 55). When she assumed the voice of a Canadian woman, it was a homecoming "to the area of writing where I most wanted to be, my own people and background" ("Ten Years" 13). She also felt she had modulated her theme—"the nature of freedom"—to that of "survival...with some dignity," because "perhaps I no longer believed so much in the promised land, even the promised land of one's own inner freedom" ("Ten Years" 14). However, in portraying the women of Africa, at least Laurence is not deceived by false optimism. She realistically portrays their bondage to a patriarchal society, their quest for dignity and freedom, and their compromises for survival. Laurence's Canadian heroines were born in Africa.

4

THE STONE ANGEL

AS A FEMININE

CONFESSIONAL NOVEL

"I'll have a word or two to say, you can depend on that, before my mouth is stopped with dark," (139) says Hagar Shipley, the narrator/protagonist of Margaret Laurence's *The Stone Angel*. The assertion reveals much that is characteristic of the novel's narrating situation. The first-person voice of the narrator dominates the text as she examines and reconstructs her own life story through a sustained retrospective view recounting her suffering, isolation and quest for affirmation. She is motivated by a desire to tell her story and to find self-understanding because as she approaches death she finds, "I'm choked with it now, the incommunicable years, everything that happened and was spoken, or not spoken" (296). Her narrative is an attempt to unify memories of the past and experiences of the present in one account, and it culminates in the attainment of insight into herself. These characteristics indicate that *The Stone Angel* can be read as a confessional novel.[1] But even more specifically, the narrative details the quest of a woman. *The Stone Angel* achieves its fullest meaning if it is read as a fictive confession, and more precisely, as a feminine confessional narrative that gives voice to a peculiarly feminine experience.[2]

Although much has been written about Laurence's use of first-person narration, surprisingly little has been written in the way of extended genre analysis of her works.[3] One critic who has identified the confessional form of Laurence's Canadian fiction is Jamie S. Scott:

> In literary critical terms, the Manawaka narratives are fictional examples of confessional and autobiographical stories. In its emphasis on personal subjectivity, its interest in the meaning of 'I,' and its engagement with some significant problems—each Manawaka narrative assumes the characteristics of confessional fiction. (429)

Scott continues to elaborate on the thematic content but not much on the form. Nevertheless it is, I believe, the confessional form that accounts for the novel's depth of characterization: the protagonist's presence and the reader's sense of privilege in being party to her story.

The identification of the novel's genre can serve to reveal the structural and thematic coherence of the text, and genre can be defined as "a model of narrative structure which organizes events and actors into a signifying field according to repeated and thus familiar conventions of story and characterization" (Cohan and Shires 77). By organizing a signifying field for a story, the genre does more, however, than just give aesthetic unity. Genre is also a valuable tool of interpretation:

> [G]enres can be seen not only in the traditional way as patterns or models that writers follow in constructing texts, but also from the other direction, as different packages of rules that readers apply in construing them, as ready-made strategies for reading. (Rabinowitz 177)

At least in part, genre organizes a reader's response to a text.

Defining genre as a strategy for reading implies that genre is not merely a fixed set of characteristics. Rather, it is a historically produced construction: "a signifying practice as well as a signifying system, for historical conditions determine the actual structures which a given text deploys to emphasize certain values over others" (Cohan and Shires 78). It is therefore reasonable to ask how Laurence modifies the confessional genre by altering the novel's signifying field and extending a general signifying practice to create a woman's confession. To answer such a question, it is first necessary to analyze the confessional novel's traditional form.

In Western literary tradition, confession can be traced to the *Confessions* of Saint Augustine of Hippo written in 397 A.D. (Scholes and Kellogg 216–17). Augustine's work establishes a first-person narrator, a sustained retrospective view of a life story, and a self-transformation, all of which have become characteristic of story development in confessional and autobiographical forms. Typically, the narrator-protagonist begins in the narrative present and proceeds to examine the past, looking back over a lifetime. The retrospection is intermittently interrupted with returns to the present or narrating moment. The narrator's purpose is to write a life story in order to elucidate his progress toward an understanding of himself, which he has gained in the recent present; narrative time or "temporality" consequently becomes an important element of confession.

In the Augustinian model, the narrator's progress toward self-understanding is characterized as a process, and more specifically as a healing process. Healing can be brought about only by some change in the narrator's self; inner change is thus the central movement of confession. The method of the spiritual exercise is to "lay open" the memory in order to awaken and to order self-perception.

Although confession deals primarily with questions of the self, it simultaneously addresses questions about the confessor's historical and social context. For instance, Augustine reflects upon the world in which he lives and he examines the effects of social forces and ideologies upon his life. This concern for subjects beyond the self is retained as a convention of later confessional literature. The scope of confession extends from the examination of one life to an examination of the broader social issues that affect that life.

Confessional literature, both religious and secular, is a subcategory of autobiography, sharing many of the characteristics of that form; nevertheless, confessional literature can be distinguished from the broader category of autobiography. Confession presents a dimension that goes beyond that of a life story: the distinguishing feature of confession could be called a *pacte confessionel,* which "promises to reveal something that is not necessarily verifiable through recourse to the public record" (Whitenack 42–43). Confession also shows a more fundamental concern for exposing errors and weaknesses; it represents a "tearing away" of the "decent drapery" of the confessional persona's public self. Confessional fiction retains the narrating-I's necessary revelation of secrets.

From this early example of confessional literature we can identify these characteristics: it is written in the first-person; it employs a sustained retrospective point of view to construct a life story; and it reveals character development, a change that necessitates an emphasis on temporality. Peter Axthelm's definition of the modern confessional novel is applicable: "The confessional novel presents a hero, at some point in his life, examining his past as well as his innermost thoughts, in an effort to achieve...perception" (8).

Axthelm identifies five characteristics of fictive confessional narrative: (1) the narrating first-person voice of the "confessional hero"; (2) the preoccupation with suffering; (3) testimonial rhetoric; (4) the quest for self-perception; and (5) the sustained retrospective point of view in the handling of time. These five characteristics will form the basis for the ensuing analysis of *The Stone Angel* as a fictional confession.[4]

The first characteristic is the confessional hero who is a narrator/protagonist, and consequently the "I" of the text. The central problem of the confessional novel is the narrator's self-examination. Through a painstaking self-analysis, the narrator shapes the diverse experiences of a lifetime. The first-person voice presents a "self-scrutinizing consciousness," revealing secrets and exposing errors, weaknesses and desires (Axthelm 35). The self-referential voice of *The Stone Angel* belongs to ninety-year-old Hagar Shipley. Hagar acts as a self-confessor who proceeds to tear away the snobbery and puritanical respectability she calls her "pride," which she inherited from her pioneer father.

Secondly, the narrator-protagonist characteristically reveals a preoccupation with suffering. In the present, Hagar suffers physically from the duress of old age and from a deteriorating medical condition, which she never identifies except as "the pain under my ribs" (31). At the same time, she expresses mental anguish. Like many confessional narrators, she finds that consciousness itself is a form of suffering (Axthelm 14). She suffers a lack of privacy and dignity that are "not granted to the aged or to the young" (6). Consequently, her quest for self-affirmation becomes the central conflict in the discursive present. In fact, her quest becomes inextricably linked with her opposition to the proposed sale of her house:

> I can think of only one thing—the house is mine.... My shreds and remnants of years are scattered through it.... I couldn't leave them. If I am not somehow contained in them and in this house, something of all change caught and fixed here, eternal enough for my purposes, then I do not know where I am to be found at all. (36)

Her discourse is motivated by the consuming existential question, "where am I to be found?" Even in the episode of her escape to Shadow Point, she casts her purpose in terms of a quest: "Perhaps I've come here not to hide but to seek" (192). Hagar's narrative illustrates the search for identity: "the spiritual identity of the personality" is sought in "the multiple experiences of a life" as they are "linked reflectively in the consciousness" (Pascal 2).

In the search for self-understanding, the confessional narrator also suffers from isolation. As Axthelm's definition proposes, the confessional hero is at a point in life when she is divided from the world and separated from other characters. Therefore, the confessor is compelled by a secret motive or "plea": "Indeed, the essence of the confession is that the one who feels outcast pleads with humanity to relate [her] isolation to its wholeness" (Spender 119–21). Hagar's confession, then, is not only an examination of her isolated condition, but also a plea for the addressee's empathy.

In isolation, the confessional narrator attempts to understand her condition; and memory becomes the key to self-understanding. Again, age and ill health isolate Hagar. She says she is "humiliated, flustered" (146) in public, eyed "as though I were an escaped convict or a child, someone not meant to be out alone" (148), and "scrutinized" by doctors (116). Most significantly, she is emotionally isolated, a condition that reaches farther into the past. She says Marvin and Doris speak "as though I weren't here" (32). She speaks of herself as "forgotten" (4), and her narrative is often punctuated with the lament, "Oh my lost men" (6). She insists, "Every last one of them has gone away and left me. I never left them. It was the other way around, I swear it" (164). The emphasis on Hagar's isolation is intensified by her proximity to death. But thoughts about her own mortality inspire efforts to assert a heightened consciousness of self:

> They can dump me in a ten-acre field, for all I care, and not waste a single cent on a box of flowers, nor a single breath on prayers to ferry my soul, for I'll be dead as a mackerel. Hard to imagine a world and I not in it. Will everything stop when I do? Stupid old baggage, who do you think you are? *Hagar*. There's no one like me in this world. (250)

Significantly, the novel ends in mid-sentence, "And then——" (308). The breaking off of the text recalls the question, "Will everything stop when I do?" The suspension of the text represents a suspension of consciousness that, in turn, signifies death. The text emphasizes, in both a social and existential sense, the narrator's essential isolation.

The third characteristic the novel displays is the testimonial nature of confession. Stephen Spender argues that the impulse to confess is motivated by a need to state the truth about "this unique and unknown I" (119). A religious confession presupposes audience expectations of truth and the authority of the theological terms that might be used to express the "truth"; but in a secular context, a common standard or understanding of truth is perhaps not as evident. One culturally understood measure of truth is the legal testimony. Therefore, the rhetoric of testimony becomes necessary as a valid means of communicating the authenticity of the narrative. As Hagar asserts that "there's no one like me in this world," the vow, "I swear it," makes explicit her confession's status as a reliable testimony. While her narrative is sometimes a plea for self-justification (for example, she claims she did not leave her men but they left her), it most often expresses a longing to be heard concerning subjects on which she has hitherto been silent. For instance, Hagar reveals a secret pleasure in sex of which she speaks only now in retrospect:

> [Bram's] banner over me was only his own skin, and now I no longer know why it should have shamed me.... I never spoke of it to anyone.
> It was not so very long after we wed, when first I felt my blood and vitals rise to his. He never knew. I never let him know. I never spoke aloud, and I made certain that the trembling was all inner. (81)

The emphasis on the revelation of secrets of which "I never spoke" is unmistakably confessional. Hagar breaks another long-held silence about the pain and guilt of her bereavement after John's death:

> The night my son died I was transformed to stone and never wept at all. When the ministering women handed me the cup of hot coffee, they murmured how well I was taking it, and I could only look at them dry-eyed from a long distance and not say a single word. All the night long, I had only one thought—I'd had so many things to say to him, so many things to put to rights. He hadn't waited to hear. (243)

It is important that Hagar's "testimony" resounds with an authenticity that increases as the narrative progresses. Sincerity is a stance that requires maximal self-disclosure. The narrator's frankness is credible because it finds expression only in the privacy of her thoughts:

> the implied author's choice of this confessionlike form is aesthetically motivated by [her] desire for authenticity or psychological immediacy; but if it were not for the quasi-mimetic reassurance of privacy, [she]

could not with any show of probability make the narrator lay bare [her] innermost thoughts. (Sternberg 277)

Self-disclosure is required of the confessional voice because the whole interest of the story depends on the narrator's degree of consciousness: the narrator's mind must be "acute, imaginative, morally and psychologically sensitive" (Sternberg 292). The voice of Hagar reveals just such a mind. The authenticity of her narrative serves another purpose that is important to the novel's outcome. It gives the narrative the potential for generating self-perception rather than self-delusion.

This attainment of self-perception is the fourth characteristic of the confessional genre. In the present narrative, Hagar's perception comes in increments. Her confession to Lees, in which she recognizes "a kind of mercy," prepares her for a climactic epiphany that occurs in response to a line from the "Old One-Hundredth" hymn, "Come before him and rejoice:"

This knowing comes upon me so forcefully, so shatteringly, and with such a bitterness as I have never felt before. I must always, always have wanted that—simply to rejoice. (292)

This new self-knowledge releases a final speaking of "the heart's truth" about her most profound secret:

Every good joy I might have held, in my man or any child of mine or even in the plain light of morning, of walking the earth, all were forced to a standstill.... Pride was my wilderness and the demon that led me there was fear. I was alone, never anything else, and never free, for I carried my chains within me. (292)

This acknowledgement demonstrates a new vision of self as the climax of the confessional narrative (Axthelm 21).

Hagar's self-perception transforms her relationship with her living son, Marvin, in the discursive present. Until the final chapter, she opposes him, particularly in his wish to admit her to a nursing home. But her new vision permits her to reconstruct her view of him in such a way that he stands not against her, but with her, in opposition to death: "The dead don't bear a grudge nor seek a blessing. The dead don't rest uneasy. Only the living. Marvin, looking at me from anxious elderly eyes, believes me" (304). Here the narrator identifies Marvin with the living and also with the vulnerability of "elderly eyes." Moving from opposition to identification with Marvin, Hagar "lies" in order to "bless" him: "You've been good to me always. A better son than John" (304). Hagar's words display a new understanding of her own motivations and compulsions because "a change of heart is explicable only if the hero's perception has changed" (Axthelm 33). The transformation is confirmed by the narrator's newly found sense of peace: "I feel like it [Marvin's reverence] is more than I could now reasonably have expected out of life" (305).

Hagar's successful achievement of self-perception is further evident in the construction of the self. Eugene Stelzig thinks that, ideally, the confessional form "transcends self-exploration to attain some type of self-transformation" (27). Hagar provides the evidence of change, first, in "lying" to bless Marvin, and, second, in her response to Sandra Wong's crisis. She recognizes a relaxing of the "pride" that once insisted upon correct language. She speaks to Wong with words "I've never used before in my life." These words are accompanied by laughter, which represents a moment of genuine rejoicing. In wondering "if I've done it for her or for myself," the narrator recognizes a moment of self-transformation (30–31). The significance of the transformation of the self is underlined just before the narrative's end:

> I lie here and try to recall something truly free that I've done in ninety years. I can think of only two acts that might be so, both recent. One was a joke—yet not a joke only as all victories are, the paraphernalia being unequal to the event's reach. The other was a lie—yet not a lie, for it was spoken at least and at last with what may perhaps be a kind of love. (307)

The narrator's words attest to the episodes with Marvin and Sandra as unprecedented "free" acts. As such, these episodes represent to Hagar her own self-transformation and the attainment of the freedom that the confessional narrator seeks. Axthelm writes, "freedom holds meaning and perception; but these values are inextricably bound to the 'horror of existence' and to the specter of death. In these equivocal and often paradoxical ways, freedom demands the concern of the sincere confessional hero" (72). The narrator's sincerity and her attainment of self-transformation lead the reader to believe that the text carries the "hope of perception and new meaning" (Axthelm 33–34).

The fifth characteristic of confessional narrative is the sustained retrospective point of view. By definition, the confessional hero is "examining her past as well as her innermost thoughts," implying an interplay of past and present episodes.[5] The text alternates past and present episodes through a series of memories focalized through the narrating consciousness:

> this mind is not merely a chain on which the various episodes are strung but also the center round which the tale is built; the center of interest is located neither in the occurrences themselves nor in the predicament of the other characters but primarily in the [narrator's] reactions to them or the process by which [she] comes to realize their true significance. (Sternberg 291)

An imaginative reconstruction of the past by the narrator is, in fact, the explicit project of the text, and its credibility is determined by the life-story's internal consistency (Stelzig 20, 23). In other words, the confessional narrative represents a mimesis of the narrating consciousness, ranging back and forth through time; this movement through time is achieved partly as a result of embedded points of view because the narrator considers events from various points in the past. Both Stelzig and Spender identify the presence, not of one, but two narrating "selves," and two levels of narrative in confession.

The Stone Angel displays embedded perspectives as the following passage shows: "He made three comments.... None of the three made much sense to me then, but they stuck in my mind. I've since pondered—which was my father?" (19). The narrating voice remains that of ninety-year-old Hagar, but the focalizor—the one who sees the event—shifts from the child Hagar to the adult Hagar, creating an embedded focalization. The purpose of this device in *The Stone Angel* is to engage the narrator in "a coherent shaping of the past by interpreting it from the standpoint of the present" (Stelzig 20). In other words, before she can achieve any self-perception, Hagar must reconstruct her past and reconcile it to her present. The confessional narrative represents the attempt to integrate these past and present perspectives, or levels of narration, into one coherent narrative, effecting a coherent life-story and, ultimately, an integration of the narrating self as well.

Temporality, then, becomes a central component of the narrative structure because of the importance of memory to the construction of the life story and elucidation of the self. Three aspects of time identified by Gerard Genette, order, duration and frequency, require examination. Genette points out the essential temporal duality of any text—that is, the operation of both "story time" (the time spanned by the events in the lives of the characters) and "narrative time"(the space devoted to the representation of various periods of that time, measured in pages). Events in the lives of the characters may or may not be presented chronologically.

Order refers to the comparison of the sequence of events in the text with their supposed order of occurrence: "although the text always unfolds in linear succession, this need not correspond to the chronological succession of events, and most often deviates from it, creating various kinds of discordances" between story time and narrative time (Rimmon-Kenan 45–46). Narrative time in *The Stone Angel* begins only a few weeks before the end of Hagar's life and ends with her death. But the story time spans Hagar's entire life and even probes the lives of her ancestors. The text begins *in medias res* and provides expository returns to earlier periods of time through flashbacks or analepses. The use of analepses "aims at retrieving the whole of the narrative's 'antecedents,'" and "it generally forms an important part of the narrative, and sometimes…even presents the chief part of it, with the first narrative functioning as the denouement in advance" (Genette 62). Analepses comprise the retrospection that is so characteristic of confessional fiction. In *The Stone Angel,* transitions to analepses are usually associative: an object, comment, or situation in the present reminds the narrator of some event from the past.

Most analepses in *The Stone Angel* reach years or decades into the past of the narrator's own life, but analepses in the first chapter reach back an indefinite length of time into the lives of Hagar's father and grandfather, and even into the obscure, distant ancestral past of the Scottish Highlanders. Because analepses reaching into the obscure past usually signify personal myths of origin, Hagar reveals a belief in her inheritance of a warrior-like character. She is a child with "backbone" (10) and a "holy terror" in old age (304). Her myth shapes her life story and affords a sense of closure in the last paragraph. When she says, "I *wrest* from her the glass" before the moment of death (308, emphasis mine), she exercises her autonomy in her last act.

The narrator's retrospection reaches not only backward in time, but also forward through embedded prolepses. Three examples may serve to reveal the importance of the discourse's chronology:

I tried to shut my ears to it, and thought I had, yet years later, when I was rearing my two boys, I found myself saying the same words to them (13);

Hardly ideal accomplishments for the kind of life I'd ultimately find myself leading, but I had no notion of that then (43);

But Jason Currie never saw my second son or knew at all that the sort of boy he'd wanted had waited a generation to appear. (64)

As Genette suggests, "first-person narratives lend themselves to the use of prolepses better than other types, because within the admittedly retrospective character of such narratives it seems more natural for the narrator to allude to a future which has already become a past" (paraphrased in Rimmon-Kenan, 48–49). These prolepses further reinforce the integration of past and present focalizations, again lending coherence to the life story.

The alternation of episodes from the narrative present and analepses from the narrative past is characteristic of the novel's temporal ordering, but within either the past or present narrative level, episodes proceed chronologically. Apart from Hagar's occasional proleptic comment, the past proceeds from childhood to late adulthood. Similarly, the present flows chronologically through the narrator's last weeks of life. The chronological ordering of analepses is the author's conscious choice. Laurence reveals some doubt because

it is not after all the way people actually remember...I am still not sure that I decided the right way when I decided to place Hagar's memories in chronological order.... One can say that the method I chose diminishes the novel's resemblance to life....on the other hand, writing— however consciously ordered its method—is never as disorderly as life. ("Gadgetry" 56–57)

Although she fears some loss of verisimilitude, the chronological order is aesthetically justified because the narrative is apprehended as a fiction. As Spriet states, Hagar rightly "appears as the creation of her own words, or rather those of the wordsmith; the creation of her own past and of the collective past of her family, past and present being inextricably fused in a mutual exchange" (1984, 319, 320). More importantly, the order adheres to the confessional genre that consciously reconstructs the past, unlike the stream-of-consciousness novel that presents the illusion of a random flow of thought (Axthelm 10).

After order, the second aspect of narrative time is duration. Story time is measured by the days, months or years covered, while narrative time is measured spatially by the number of pages written (Genette 87). In a novel of 308 pages, the space or "narrative time" devoted to the past falls only a little short of the space devoted to the narrative present. Hagar's narration of the past occupies some 135 pages while the present occupies some 170 pages. In "story time," however, the past narrative far exceeds the discursive present. The past covers ninety years of Hagar's life and reaches an unspecified number of years into the ancestral past, while the present narrative covers only a few weeks.

The speed or tempo of the two narrative lines also differs significantly. Most episodes in the present are presented as scenes rather than summary. In scenes, story-duration and text-duration are conventionally equated, particularly in dialogue (Genette 87). Some summary and gaps in time occur, but they are minimal and the dominant movement of time is by scenes. The past narrative, however, consists largely of summaries of how life used to be, often leaving gaps or "ellipses." Scenes from the past are sometimes representative or "ritual," such as the child Hagar's recitations of ancestral lore (14–15). In other cases, past scenes are singularly significant, such as the death of a brother. Most frequently, summaries are expressed as interpretations of past events, returning emphasis to the narrating present; what Hagar thinks about the past is of greater significance than a strictly factual account of the past.

This difference of tempo can be illustrated from chapter four by a comparison of two scenes, both about four pages long: a visit to the doctor in the present and a memory that occurs during the medical examination. Hagar summarizes her marriage as "twenty-four years…scoured away like sandbanks under the spate of our wrangle and bicker" (116). Within her past summary are fragments of dialogue that are representative. In the present, she requires almost the same number of pages to describe a medical appointment, a scene covering only two or three hours. As this comparison shows, the tempo of the narrative past is rapid, especially before chapter six because it is dominated more by summary than by scene. In chapters six to eight, the tempo decelerates with the inclusion of a greater number of scenes. Hagar's account of the deaths of Bram and John, in particular, incorporate considerable dialogue and many descriptive details. By the end of chapter eight, the tempos of the past and present narratives are almost identical because both levels of narrative are largely composed of scenes. After chapter eight, the present narrative dominates the text. In fact, chapter nine contains only the narrative present, and chapter ten returns only briefly to the narrative past.

A comparison of the duration of story time and narrative time reveals the relative importance of past and present narratives in the novel. As a rule, the amount of space and detail the author devotes to a segment of time determines its overall significance in the novel (Rimmon-Kenan 56). The present narrative is weighted with a greater number of pages of narrative time. In addition, the present narrative sets the normative tempo of the text; its tempo remains relatively consistent, mostly scenes. The dominance of the present narrative is reinforced by the significance generally assigned to scene before summary: "acceleration and deceleration are often evaluated by the reader as indicators of importance and centrality.... [as] the more important events or conversations are given in detail" (Rimmon-Kenan 56). In contrast, the past narration is rapid, often interpretive, and decelerating until it finally merges with the present that takes over in chapter nine. In chapter ten, Hagar returns to the past for fewer than two pages, only to recall the image of the stone angel and to associate this symbol with her own death, again affording a sense of closure. In fact, the last line "And then—" ends in mid-sentence, effecting an abrupt halt and, paradoxically, a perfect unity of narrative and story time. As a result, the duration of the novel fits the confessional genre. Summarizing much of the past allows maximal retrospection, while the dominance of scenes favours the present narrative. The past is summarized because it has significance only in terms of the present, and past events are cited only if they motivate a change in the present. The present is emphasized in a way that indicates a successful confession: if the confessional text is to produce any insight, that insight must appear in the narrative present in order to signify a transformation of the narrator's present perspective. Favouring the present narrative implies a successful integration of the past, and consequently, a successful construction of a coherent life story.

The third aspect of time, frequency—the "relation between the number of times an event appears in the story and the number of times it is narrated" (Rimmon-Kenan 56)—demonstrates even more clearly the merging of past and present narratives. Most often, a narrator narrates once what happened once, creating a "singulative narrative" (Genette 114). Sometimes the narrator retrospectively describes not what happened once, but what *used to happen*. In other words, the narrator generalizes by narrating representative occurrences of what happened regularly or ritually, creating an "iterative narrative" (Genette 116–17). Both singulative and iterative narratives are employed throughout *The Stone Angel*.

Occasionally, a narrator can narrate more than once an event that happened only once, creating a "repetitive narrative" (Genette 115). The "repetitive" frequency becomes especially important in *The Stone Angel* because it occurs in the text only once, in chapter eight. The events surrounding John's death can occur only once in story time, but Hagar repeats them in narrating time. First, in the cannery she gives Murray Lees a detailed account of her son's death. The first telling is, of course, in analeptic form and in the past tense. Only two pages later, however, Hagar retells the event, narrating in the present tense. In fact, she essentially re-enacts an argument that she traces as the source of John's agitation before his accident. The repetition is plausible because illness induces the delirium in which Hagar mistakes Lees for her son, motivating a second address.

The contrast between the two tellings is significant because the retelling becomes a reconstruction of the memory. In the initial analepsis, Hagar reveals a desire to retract some of her words: "As soon as I'd spoken, I regretted it. But I couldn't humble myself to take back my words" (213). She also reveals her failure to speak out: "I'd had so many things to say to him, so many things to put to rights. He hadn't waited to hear" (243). The confession in delirium adds words that were not spoken in the first telling and revises others, replacing words of disagreement with compliant ones:

> If there's a time to speak, it's surely now.
> "I didn't really mean it, about not bringing her here. A person speaks in haste. I've always had a temper. I wouldn't want you to feel you always had to be going out somewhere. You could come here in the evenings. I wouldn't say a word. I could go into the front room or upstairs, if you liked, I'd not get in your way. Wouldn't that be a good idea?" (247)

Hagar finds the reconstruction cathartic:

> But when he speaks, his voice is not angry at all.
> "It's okay," he says. "I knew all the time you never meant it. Everything is all right. You try to sleep. Everything's quite okay."
> I sigh, content.... I could even beg God's pardon this moment, for thinking ill of Him some time or other. (247–48)

In fact, she endows the reconstruction with the power of absolution and purgation: "I am left with the feeling that it was a kind of mercy I encountered with him" (253). Lees, the man who has "been selling peace of mind since 1934" (224), gives Hagar peace of mind. Having disclosed her darkest secret to Lees, the confessional narrator demonstrates a belief that she is acquitted of faults by sharing them (Spender 122).

Hagar assigns such significance to the confessional reconstruction that it becomes a moment when past and present narratives merge, creating a turning point. J.M. Kertzer recognizes the temporal merging in the narrator's "most bitter memory—the death of her son John—in which past and present are skillfully blended by having Hagar involuntarily recite the episode aloud to Murray Lees" (505–6). By merging past and present narratives, the narrator revises her past. As a result, while revealing the autobiography as a fiction, the confession's temporal patterns nevertheless endow Hagar's life story with structural unity.

This merging of past and present narratives complements the novel's thematic coherence. As some critics have pointed out, throughout the novel Hagar is set in opposition to death, just as the stone angel stands against the grave of her mother who "relinquished her feeble ghost as I gained my stubborn one" (3). But her narration of a series of confrontations with death have the secretive quality of confession. In the past narrative, each account of an important relationship ends with a death, and each ends with a closing reference to an accompanying inability to mourn. For instance, she is "at the time too angry with Father…to mourn his death" (63), and "when we'd buried Bram…it was John who cried, not I" (184), and, again, "The night my son died I…never wept at all" (243). The explicit references to a lack of tears, and by implication, a lack of words, emphasize that a fear of death is Hagar's greatest secret, which she guards because it exposes her vulnerability. Even the profound effect of her mother's untimely death is only intimated in the account of her inability to pose as her mother to comfort her dying brother. The proposition leaves her "crying, shaken by torments he never suspected" (25). In the present narrative, her own mortality is her final secret:

The world is even smaller now [in hospital]. It's shrinking so quickly. The next room will be the smallest of all…. an embarrassing subject, better not mentioned. The way we used to feel, when I was a girl, about undergarments or the two-backed beast of love. But I want to take hold of [the nurse's] arm, force her attention. "Listen. You must listen. It's important. It's—quite an event." (282)

Although she longs to speak of death, only her thoughts broach the subject. The text explicitly compares death to sex as an equally taboo subject, emphasizing the secretive quality of Hagar's reflections on death. It is Hagar's exploration of her fear of death and vulnerability that unites the past and present narratives.

Reading *The Stone Angel* as a confessional narrative, then, illuminates Laurence's means of achieving the novel's depth of characterization of its narrator-protagonist, its effectiveness in ordering past and present narratives into a coherent life story, and its compelling sense of the achievement of identity or self-knowledge. In other words, the novel's genre delineates a powerful signifying field that the author successfully generates for Hagar's fictional autobiography.

However, it is important to recall that genre is a signifying practice as well as a signifying system, and it changes as reading publics change (Cohan and Shires 78). The history of the genre, which traces its roots to the *Confessions* of Saint Augustine and Jean-Jacques Rousseau, and perhaps the novels of Fyodor Dostoyevsky, reveals that both the confessional writer and the confessional narrator are traditionally male. The form in which Laurence writes has historically been a masculine form, but she gives it a feminine voice and subject.[6] This departure from an historical signifying practice suggests that the novel is a hybrid of genres. A literary work may not fit unequivocally into one genre because genres may overlap (Cohan and Shires 78). In addition to being a confessional novel *The Stone Angel*, as a woman's confession, is a feminine narrative that may be defined as follows:

> The genre of feminine narrative is neither just a type of formulaic narrative nor a timeless story but one instance of the way in which all narratives organize a story so as to structure possibilities of cultural meaning. The structure of a story, in short, acquires a social currency that goes beyond the closed system of narrative poetics. (Cohan and Shires 82)

Only a reading that takes into account the overlapping genres of confessional and feminine narrative can resolve the critical debate over whether or not Hagar's rebellion is merely "rebellion for rebellion's sake" (Spriet 1981, 110). It is especially in failing to recognize *The Stone Angel* as a gendered narrative that Pierre Spriet, for example, falls short in an otherwise adept structural analysis: he identifies "opposition" as the "dominant form of

the novel," but one that he claims is "not provided with a uniform semantic content" (1981, III). Spriet recognizes the novel as a story of "opposition,
separation and social failure" but he finds no other purpose for its form:

> The main character in Margaret Laurence's novels is always a rebel and
> a loner. In *The Stone Angel*, rebellion is often difficult to naturalize in psy-
> chological terms, which accounts for the hesitations of the critics. It is
> often ill-motivated because it cannot be adequately motivated. (1984,
> 323)

He astutely characterizes Hagar as an "outcast" who is excluded from "the
dominant group" and "refused peace and the happiness of social integration" (324), but he cannot identify this "dominant group." However, this
group is explicitly represented by the series of men whom Hagar opposes
—father, husband and sons. The "dominant group" from which Hagar is
excluded is "men," and it is this exclusion that motivates her rebellion.
Furthermore, Spriet writes:

> Margaret Laurence did not just write a few novels; she made through
> them an assertion on the world, a proposition on man. I feel entitled to
> read it as a message of resistance whose unmellowed form in *The Stone
> Angel* might be that one lives alone and against. (1984, 325)

Spriet's shortcoming derives from his view of the novel as a "proposition
on man" instead of a proposition on *woman*, who must live "alone and
against" in a patriarchal culture.

While the novel derives a universal resonance from its confessional
genre, it also derives an equally profound resonance from its portrayal of a
female narrator-protagonist. Reading the novel as a woman's confession
can, in fact, naturalize the opposition, separation and social failure experienced by the female confessor. Her opposition is motivated by an attempt
to protect the vulnerability of her position in society as a woman. Precisely
because she is a woman, part of her self-discovery is that she has had to live
"alone and against" in order to preserve her autonomy in a male-dominated
society. She discovers, for instance, that her husband "wanted his dynasty
no less than my father had," and she refuses to be subordinated (101). As
the novel's central symbol, the stone angel that presides over the graves of
father, husband, son, and finally Hagar herself, represents an ultimate
eradication of all social and gender differences in the face of death: the

Curries and the Shipleys, male and female, are "only different sides of the same coin" (184). This is the great truth uncovered by Hagar's reflections upon the secret mystery of death.

It must be pointed out that at the time of the novel's publication, 1964, the confessional genre was being employed not just by Laurence but also by other women writers as a means to voice feminine experience. In "Tell it like it is: Women and Confessional Writing" Elizabeth Wilson shows that as the feminist movement mounted in the 1960s and 1970s, the confessional mode became a genre "in which we could speak our oppression" (Wilson 22). Many women writers appropriated the genre as a "narrative of truth" to "bear witness to the authenticity of their lives, a hidden and neglected truth" (Wilson 28). Much of this writing was autobiographical, but Wilson also traces a related outpouring of autobiographical fiction, including fictive confession. Wilson describes a widespread recognition of the genre's capacity to embody

> the quest for the answer to the question echoing down the century: what does it mean to be a woman? What does Woman want?.... what seemed important…was for women to "find a voice" and to testify to an experience that had been lost, silenced or never even allowed to emerge into consciousness. (27)

With its potential for creating a strong narrating voice, an immediacy of style, and a way of delving into "secret" or taboo subjects, such as female desire and sexuality, the genre lends itself to the representation of female subjectivity.

Hagar's story is certainly an account of the secret anguish of being a self-determining woman in her socio-historical setting. According to Wilson's study, the depiction of such a subject is typical of feminine narratives, as is the closure stressing the female protagonist's self-acceptance as an autonomous woman. Like other women writers of her time, Laurence gives the traditional confessional ending—the achievement of self-perception—a feminist twist. Recognition of the overlapping signifying field generated by a feminine narrative reveals a further interpretive level that can be applied to Hagar's self-discovery. The discovery that she has always wanted "simply to rejoice" can be read in answer to the question, "What does woman want?" The answer is: to rejoice in the freedom to be an autonomous woman. If Wilson's observations are correct, Laurence modifies the confessional genre for the political purpose of creating a gendered narrative. This reading illuminates the social importance or cultural semiotics of the genre, and this level of meaning is particularly important in representations of sexual difference (Cohan and Shires 79).

The genre of *The Stone Angel* serves Laurence's ideological purpose. By adopting a genre that valorizes a solitary quest for self-knowledge, Laurence escapes some of the novel's traditional gender constructions in the depiction of a female protagonist. Confession allows for a self-determining and indeed self-creating narrator-protagonist, and the confessional form permits Hagar to remain alone, with dignity, at the novel's close. In accordance with a developing feminine signifying practice, Margaret Laurence effectively appropriates a literary confessional genre while modifying the form to create a distinctly feminine narrative. Her representation of an autonomous female subjectivity and a strong female voice expand possibilities for characterization that are inherent in the confessional form. Read simultaneously as a feminine narrative, the novel's ending, which culminates in Hagar's self-perception, fulfills both a confessional imperative and a historical imperative for the creation of an autonomous female identity. The convergence of a fictive confessional genre with a feminine narrative results in a literary and cultural generation of meaning and a powerful feminine semiotic for both writer and reader.

Notes

1. According to Cohan and Shires, a literary genre can be identified by the kind of events it organizes in sequence, the principles of combination it follows, the functions that actors perform, and the traits drawn upon to delineate characters.

2. The novel, however, is not aimed at a female audience. The implied reader is not gender specific.

3. Jon Kertzer, in *"That House in Manawaka" Margaret Laurence's* A Bird in the House, discusses the short story cycle as "a woman's confessional memoir," but dwells on questions of unity, development and perspective rather than taking a narratological approach to genre. Two other critics, David Williams and Helen M. Buss, in *Crossing the River: Essays in Honour of Margaret Laurence*, identify confession and autobiography, respectively, as Laurence's dominant form, but Williams goes on to discuss Hagar as storyteller inverting the biblical text, and Buss discusses the identity theme; both essays, while interesting in their own right, do not take the approach of genre study. Pierre Spriet undertakes extended narrative analyses of *The Stone Angel* and *The Diviners* but not from the point of view of confessional genre or gendered confession; I discuss Spriet later in the essay.

4. There is no one paradigm of confession that is generally agreed upon. In attempting to determine whether there is a paradigm that might be applicable to Laurence's work, I will use Axthelm's definition as a point of departure, drawing upon additional ideas as they become necessary. Our ideas of confession may need modification to deal with recent writers, particularly in the case of women's confessions.

5. The narrative's sustained retrospective point of view does not preclude ellipses, or movement between the time of the event and the time of narration. The narrator can return to the narrating moment.

6. I am simply drawing attention here to the relatively recent appearance of the female speaking subject as presented by a female author in the confessional form. I am not attempting to engage in a discussion of a panhistorical "women's language" or "female form," or even to suggest that women necessarily write differently than men. I am indebted to Susan Snaider Lanser's discussion of female voice, "Toward a Feminist Poetics of Narrative Voice," *Fictions of Authority: Women Writers and Narrative Voice.* (Ithaca: Cornell University Press, 1992), 3–24.

5

CHRISTIAN RIEGEL

"REST BEYOND THE RIVER"

Mourning in *A Bird in the House*

Readers of *A Bird in the House* have noted the importance of notions of shaping, ordering, and consciously forming memories—by the narrator and protagonist Vanessa MacLeod—into a carefully structured narrative. Arnold Davidson points out that "Vanessa marks—and retrospectively maps—her course to self-determination. In effect, she frees herself psychologically by remembering a place she earlier left physically and by then restructuring or re-creating those memories into meaningful stories" (100).

While the ordering and structuring aspects of Vanessa's creative activities, in composing her narrative, have been identified and explored to some extent in critical responses, the impulses that drive Vanessa's narrative-creation have received little attention. Vanessa's creative activities in *A Bird in the House* are borne out of a need to come to terms with serious losses in her life. *A Bird in the House* is an exploration of themes of death and mourning, and of the role of representing these themes artistically.

One of the key issues raised by Laurence in *A Bird in the House* is not only of *how* mourning can be represented, in textual form, but also how representation itself—the act of writing—is a process of mourning and is a functional activity. Laurence utilizes structural and formal concerns to implicitly raise notions of how mourning can be an ordering and organizing activity; in essence, she queries issues of what shape the expression of grief through writing can take. Paralleling these functional concerns are the thematics of Vanessa's narrative, for Vanessa explores the deaths of all the important family members in her past and the mourning activities of the surviving members. All of the characters in *A Bird in the House* mourn to some degree, and the book is a wide-ranging exploration of the differences in individual mourning. Vanessa's exploration in her text of these death-related activities can be seen as a means for her to more effectively understand how she herself mourns loss. *A Bird in the House*, then, can be conceived as a text that shows how an individual mourns by writing a narrative and as a text that shows how an individual learns to mourn.

Mourning is an action where the individual, in response to a death or a serious loss, "calls into question the meaningfulness and reality of the social frameworks in which they participate" (Mellor 13). The result of the serious loss is "the shattering of a sense of ontological security." Ontological security, according to Anthony Giddens, refers to an individual's "sense of order and continuity in relation to events in which they participate, and the experiences that they have, in their day-to-day lives" (cited by Mellor 12). Vanessa's mourning activities in *A Bird in the House* represent just such an exploration and querying of the social forces that have shaped her identity. The book is essentially a delineation of the development of Vanessa's formative years—years spent in a small prairie town with its own social restrictions and years spent in a largely patriarchal household (including all the restrictions such an environment places upon individuals).

In his seminal 1917 article "Mourning and Melancholia" Sigmund Freud defines mourning as work—both in the sense of an action and as an object—a dual connotation that the German word for mourning, *Trauerarbeit*, supports even more forcefully than the English term does. Thus, mourning is considered as work that needs completing and, in some cases, mourning work can be the result of the action, such as a literary representation. The textual form that is most readily identified as a "work" of mourning is the elegy. While elegy is most commonly associated with poetic forms, it is, as one theorist points out, "a literary genre that has become increasingly marked by blurred boundaries" (Smythe 4); and fiction that incorporates elements of elegy is, simply enough, termed fiction-elegy. Formally, fiction-elegy is "fundamentally trans-generic in that it brackets other genres in their modal form while retaining elegy as the generic 'dominant'" (6). The dominant genre, then, elegy "is a verbal presentation or staging of emotion wherein the detached speaker engages the audience with the intent of achieving some form of cathartic consolation." In tragedy, for example, where mourning is central, "it is the structure of the text that makes catharsis possible" (3). As a "staged performance of grief-work structure is [also] partially functional" (3) in forms that incorporate elegy. Peter Sacks points out that "the objective of an elegy is…to displace the urgent psychological currents of its work of mourning into the apparently more placid, authentically organized currents of language" (14). Forms that incorporate elements of elegy channel the emotional responses to death into a structure (the creative work) that can more effectively deal with the loss and that offers a means for working through the loss.

In *A Bird in the House*, Vanessa is occupied in constructing a narrative that has the function of offering her a sense of consolation in relation to the deaths that she has faced in her life. The text she writes/composes is a work of mourning—is a working through of feelings of loss that involves engagement between narrator and reader. Jon Kertzer identifies just such an engagement when he discusses the sense of resolution or consolation that reader and character achieve at the end of *A Bird in the House*. While he does not term his view of resolution within the discourses of mourning work, his assessment of the structural significance of this moment in the book is insightful: "the book ends with a feeling of momentary completion rather than of finality, a feeling that depends on the reader as much as on Vanessa. Both character and reader must feel satisfied" (80). Other readers, too, have noticed the importance of structuring actions within Vanessa's activity of narrative-creation. As Michael Darling remarks, Vanessa "is trying to order her past, with the understanding that art can improve upon life in the imposition of order upon chaos" (199). Remarking upon the manner with which the story "To Set Our House in Order" is told, W.J. Keith points out that "Laurence, in making Vanessa tell her story in this particular way, has enabled her to set her house in order" (117).

Formally, *A Bird in the House* is divided into eight separate stories, which, nonetheless have a coherence or unity that approaches that of a novel.[1] Structurally the text makes up a series of intertwined recollections about growing up in Manawaka that are told retrospectively from the perspective of an older and mature narrator. The narrative is framed by six paragraphs that are set off from the text of the final story, "Jericho's Brick Battlements," at the very end of the book. This section has the function of contextualizing the narrative that the reader has just encountered and serves as a self-reflexive commentary on the purpose of the story-telling that the narrator has engaged in. This section is important in identifying Vanessa's narrative as a work of mourning—as a text that is written because an individual needs to mourn and as a text that is the result of the person's mourning actions (in this case creative activities). A work of mourning is defined by Smythe as being "a specific example of the ways in which we use stories to shape our lives, our experiences" (130); by writing her work of mourning, Vanessa orders and structures the experiences that have shaped her in life and thus gains insight into her sense of identity.

Kertzer identifies *A Bird in the House* as a confessional memoir, as a text that "is a sustained act of memory that aims at a totality of vision and judgement." The memoir functions through the process of confession, "that is, honest self-revelation," and allows Vanessa "to see life whole" (23). The form of the confessional memoir is particularly conducive to an examination of identity—one of the basic activities of mourning—and to gaining an understanding of personal development. As a creative endeavour, the memoir form is favourable to self-discovery: "Vanessa discovers that remembrance, confession, and personal identity all depend on story-telling" (24).

Laurence places great importance on the notion of setting things in order in *A Bird in the House*, and acknowledges that such ordering is an entirely artificial means of coming to terms with loss in life. It is, however, the only way for her character to understand her past and to make sense of it in her present-day living. The first and last stories of *A Bird in the House*, "The Sound of the Singing" and "Jericho's Brick Battlements," serve to frame the retrospective narrative that Vanessa constructs and have the function of offering a commentary on the roles of mourning, memory, and the conscious activity of story-telling.

A Bird in the House opens with Vanessa's contemplation, in "The Sound of the Singing," of the significance of her Grandfather Connor's house to her own life. As she asserts, "That house in Manawaka is the one which, more than any other, I carry with me" (11). Later, in concluding the paragraph, Vanessa thinks of the house as a "massive monument" (11). While the rest of "The Sound of the Singing" introduces her Grandfather Connor and the tyrannical influence that he has on his family, the notion of why and how the house becomes a monument—and importantly, to whom and to what—is left for the closing story of the book, "Jericho's Brick Battlements." It is at the very end of this story that Vanessa returns to the notion of monuments, and a larger conception, by the reader, of structure and function in *A Bird in the House* is possible. For, it is here that the narrator comes full circle in her storytelling by paralleling the opening description of the Brick House with another quite different description—a depiction that allows for the superiority of memory as a vessel of memorial over an actual physical object. Since the preceding narrative is entirely made up of memories, Vanessa, at the end of *A Bird in the House,* is avowing a mourning practice that relies not on the real, but on memory rendered fictionally. For Vanessa, it is not the physical presence of the Brick House that exists as the monument to her grandfather; it is the memory of it and the active recollection of the house and all that transpired within its walls that becomes monumental—and the subsequent rendering and organizing of those memories artistically. While Vanessa disavows her Grandfather Connor's grave as his memorial ("I did not look at Grandfather Connor's grave. There was no need. It was not his monument" [191]), she also minimalizes the significance of the physical edifice itself. As Vanessa remarks, the house has passed out of the family's hands and no longer retains the characteristics that defined it as the Brick House of the Connors of old:

> The caragena hedge was unruly. No one had trimmed it properly that summer. The house had been lived in by strangers for a long time. I had not thought it would hurt me to see it in other hands, but it did. I wanted to tell them to trim their hedges, to repaint the windowframes, to pay heed to repairs. I had feared and fought the old man, yet he proclaimed himself in my veins. But it was their house now, whoever they were, not ours, not mine. (191)

The narrator asserts that she only "looked at it for a moment" (191), and yet the house acts as a focalizing agent in the opening story and remains central as an image throughout *A Bird in the House.* The adjectives used to describe the house reflect an artistically refracted vision of the building and not an objective pictorial representation. As Vanessa writes, "[the house] was plain as the winter turnips in its root cellar, sparsely windowed as some crusader's embattled fortress in a heathen wilderness, its rooms in a perpetual gloom except in the brief height of summer" (11). Furthermore, Vanessa's choice of metaphors imbues the description of the house with a symbolism that reflects the characteristics ascribed to her Grandfather Connor later in the story, adding to the impression that the significance of the house lies not in the physical presence of the object, but in the artistic representation—a representation that can imbue the house with some of the life that once was contained within its walls.

The whole last section of "Jericho's Brick Battlements" is a proclamation of the importance of memory, rather than the presence of the actual or physical in mourning and of the role of representing the past artistically. Vanessa makes a key statement here about her mourning since, evidently, lost individuals are always beyond physical recovery; but, for the mourning subject there must be some means for recovering the loss in a meaningful way—which, in Vanessa's case, is through artistic representation. Everything that Vanessa encounters in Manawaka in her visit to the town after a twenty-year absence is without significance in a physical sense—like the Brick House itself. As she points out, without the presence of family members in Manawaka, "there was nothing to take me there any more" (190). Seeing her parents' graves causes Vanessa to reflect not upon them directly, but upon herself and how she has inherited qualities from them: "I realized from the dates on the stone that my father had died when he was the same age as I was now. I remembered saying things to my children that my mother had said to me, the clichés of affection, perhaps inherited from her mother" (190). The references to her parents and the official monuments to them—the graves—are fleeting, just like Vanessa's trip back to Manawaka. It is left up to the artistic representation of her parents' lives, in the stories that make up *A Bird in the House*, to act as true memorials to their existence. The strategic placement of Vanessa's return to Manawaka and her visit to the graves of her parents at the very end of the book underscores the role of mourning—of working through loss— to *A Bird in the House* and serves as an implicit commentary on the function of the preceding narrative in Vanessa's life. Vanessa reflects upon the deaths that have touched her most closely and contextualizes the telling of the stories that the reader has just encountered about these individuals and Vanessa's relationship with them.

In the stories that Vanessa tells in her narrative there are many examples of individuals who are in the process of mourning a loss and she is provided in her young life with numerous occasions for observing others in their grief; the experience of observing grief in others allows her a first-hand experience of how people react to death—an experience that ultimately affects the way she, too, grieves. In this way, *A Bird in the House* has the function of being a narrative about how an individual learns to mourn by seeing how others mourn. Vanessa not only learns how to mourn, but she also gains an understanding about what is most effective within her own needs.

In a sequence dealing with Grandmother MacLeod that begins with "To Set Our House in Order," Vanessa learns about undue attachments to the dead and how such attachments can have harmful effects on those still living. The story opens with the news of the downturn of Vanessa's mother's pregnancy and Vanessa's first realization of mortality. In large part, the story is about how Vanessa comes to learn a little more about the vagaries of life and death and of how tenuous and unpredictable life actually is. Her Grandmother MacLeod's still unrequited grief for her son Roderick, who was killed during the war, gives Vanessa some insight into the difficulties of letting go of a lost individual. As Vanessa attempts to come to terms with the fact that her mother may die in childbirth, her grandmother tries to placate her by citing her perception of her own experience—a rational and ordered vision of dealing with the death of Roderick. She tells, "What happens is God's will. The Lord giveth, and the Lord taketh away" (48). These harsh pragmatic words appal Vanessa, but they make sense within Grandmother MacLeod's own understanding of the world. As she points out, "When your Uncle Roderick got killed...I thought that I would die. But I didn't die, Vanessa" (48). What she preaches is stalwart, stoic acceptance of the tragic and chaotic events of life. However, her own practice refutes the lessons that she hopes to pass along to her grandchild. Grandmother MacLeod's inability to deal with or work through the memories of Roderick result in a stultifying atmosphere in her life and house—an atmosphere that seriously affects her relationship with her other son, Vanessa's father—and stands in stark counterpoint to her feeling that "God loves Order.... God loves Order—he wants each one of us to set our house in order" (49).

Grandmother MacLeod's bedroom is an example of the manner with which she has kept her life, essentially, devoid of reality. It is a stultifying place that is out of bounds for Vanessa and that has been kept sterile and clear of the disorder that having a healthy daily life would incur:

[My] presence, if not actually forbidden, was not encouraged.... [in] Grandmother MacLeod's bedroom, with its stale and old-smelling air, the dim reek of medicines and lavender sachets. Here resided her monogrammed dresser silver, brush and mirror, nail-buffer and button hook and scissors, none of which must even be fingered by me now, for she meant to leave them to me in her will and intended to hand them over in the same flawless and unused condition in which they had always been kept. (47)

This same stale room is where the memories of Roderick are kept alive and somehow never let go: "Here, too, were the silver-framed photographs of Uncle Roderick—as a child, as a boy, as a man in his Army uniform" (47). And later, in the title story, Vanessa thinks of her grandmother as "sleeping with her mouth open in her enormous spool bed surrounded by half a dozen framed photos of Uncle Roderick and only one of my father" (103). It is almost as if, with the death of Roderick, that Grandmother MacLeod's life too has become inert. The sense of stasis and lifelessness extends to the house as a whole. The house has an atmosphere that is stopped in time and that denies both progress and the effects of the currents of daily life. Vanessa remembers the house as being "like a museum, full of dead and meaningless objects, vases and gilt-framed pictures and looming furniture, all of which had to be dusted and catered to for reasons which everyone had forgotten" (78). In another memory, Vanessa thinks of the house in terms of death, as opposed to the lives that the dead people lived:

> The unseen presences…I knew to be those of every person, young or old, who had ever belonged to the house and had died, including Uncle Roderick who got killed on the Somme, and the baby who would have been my sister if only she had managed to come to life. (46)

While Grandmother MacLeod's sensibility imposes order on the deaths in her life, the order is not one that necessarily provides needed consolation; nor is it particularly effective. Essentially, Grandmother MacLeod's order is one that unwittingly occludes anyone outside herself. For example, when Beth's baby is finally born, Grandmother MacLeod's sense of order dictates that the boy be called Roderick to ensure that her son's memory is passed on. While her wishes seem reasonable enough, she does not ever consider that Ewen too has suffered because of the loss of his brother. For her, there is only one appropriate action, one sanctioned response to death, and it is an order that does not fit everyone equally. Vanessa can appreciate the grief that her grandmother feels—"All at once, her feelings for that unknown dead man became a reality for me" (57)—but she also realizes that grief can be harmful if it is allowed to consume those that remain alive.

At the conclusion of "To Set Our House in Order," Vanessa contemplates order and disorder, for she has seen that order does not necessarily represent the best solution to events, and she has seen that unpredictable events are a part of daily life. She ruminates: "I thought of the accidents that might easily happen to a person—or, of course, might not happen, might happen to somebody else" (60). And she concludes, later, "I felt that whatever God might love in this world, it was certainly not order" (61). And yet, these words are tinged with the thoughts of the young Vanessa, and not the older narrating person. Michael Darling points out that "In giving order to her own life by retelling the events of her childhood, Vanessa learns that seemingly obvious differences conceal deeper affinities, and that an apparently rigid order may be only a flimsy structure hiding a chaotic turmoil" (192). Indeed, it is the kind of order that is imposed on events that is important here for Vanessa, and the implicit rejection of the kind of order that her grandmother represents is an important step in gaining an awareness of what will work for herself in her specific frame of reference.

Vanessa's exploration of her father's death in "A Bird in the House" offers insight into another mode of mourning loss—a mode that is informed by religion. Like her Grandmother MacLeod's stoic form of ordering death-related experience, this religious form of response (which is, after all, another form of ordering experience) is found to be antipathetic to Vanessa too. Running through the story are notions of what sort of afterlife the deceased can expect to encounter. One version of the afterlife is rendered by Noreen, the hired girl. Noreen's vision of life after death includes both heaven and hell, places that she

> had an intimate and detailed knowledge of.... She not only knew what they looked like—she even knew how big they were. Heaven was seventy-seven thousand miles square and it had four gates, each one made out of a different kind of precious jewel. The Pearl Gate, the Topaz Gate, the Amethyst Gate, the Ruby Gate—Noreen could reel them all off.
> ...
> Hell was one hundred and ninety million miles deep and was in perpetual darkness, like a cave or under the sea. Even the flames (this was the awful thing) *did not give off any light.* (96)

Yet this version of the afterlife is one that is alien to Vanessa's own religious upbringing, and it is one that offers her no conceptual possibility. Rather, it is the more familiar words of a church hymn that seem to offer Vanessa the possibility of an afterlife at this point in the story. The words to the hymn include the phrase "Rest beyond the river," that seems to Vanessa more appropriate for Grandmother Connor than Noreen's version of Heaven. Vanessa asserts, "She had believed in Heaven, but I did not think that rest beyond the river was quite what she had in mind. To think of her in Noreen's flashy Heaven, though—that was even worse" (100). Indeed, Vanessa's conception of a heaven where her grandmother could rest in peace mirrors her conception of her grandmother's character:

Someplace where nobody ever got annoyed or had to be smoothed down and placated, someplace where there were never any family scenes—that would have suited my Grandmother Connor. Maybe she wouldn't have minded a certain amount of rest beyond the river, at that. (100)

When Vanessa's father dies, however, she finds that a response to death guided by religion offers her no consolation. When Vanessa remembers the visits by the local church minister to her mother after the death, her memory is formulated in language that reflects upon the negative aspects of the experience and not on any potential good that might have resulted:

> What I thought chiefly was that he would speak of the healing power of prayer, and all that, and it would be bound to make my mother cry again. And in fact, it happened in just that way, but when it actually came, I could not protect her from this assault. I could only sit there and pray my own prayer, which was that he would go away quickly. (103–4)

Vanessa rejects the ordered means of grieving—prayer—that Reverend McKee offers; and indeed, her choice of the word "assault" to describe his advice effectively represents her view of his coping strategies. After her experiences with how organized religion deals with death, Vanessa rejects outright the notion of an afterlife. She feels that her father "is not in Heaven, because there is no Heaven" (105). And the words from the hymn, "Rest beyond the river," no longer have the influence on her that they originally had: "I knew now what that meant. It meant Nothing. It meant only silence, forever" (105).

In "The Mask of the Bear" Vanessa experiences for the first time the grief of someone close to her, and she sees here that mourning in an individual does not always manifest itself as one would necessarily expect. Not only does Vanessa have her own first experiences of losing a close family member, she also is in the position of witnessing her Grandfather Connor's deep grief at the death of his wife. Early in "The Mask of the Bear" the narrator remembers her young image of death and mourning as it is represented in the stories she writes. In her stories, death is romanticized and depicted as an event that is closer to glory than misery. Vanessa comments that "the death scenes had an undeniable appeal, a sombre splendour, with (as it said in Ecclesiastes) the mourners going about the streets and all the daughters of music brought low" (66). For Vanessa, "death and love seemed regrettably far from Manawaka," but, as she finds out soon enough in the events that transpire in her life, these categories of experience are not at all as she has envisioned them. Later in the story, the focus shifts to the death of Grandmother Connor. When her grandfather explains to her what has happened, Vanessa at first is more shocked by Grandfather Connor's reaction to the death than to the loss itself—for Vanessa has never seen this kind of emotion in him before: "As I gazed at him, unable to take in the significance of what he has said, he did a horrifying thing. He gathered me into the relentless grip of his arms. He bent low over me, and sobbed against the cold skin of my face" (79). At this stage, Vanessa is still unsure of exactly what the loss of a family member represents, and a feeling of incredulity reigns in her mind: "I still could not believe that anyone I cared about could really die," she thinks; and, "I did not fully realize yet that Grandmother Connor would never move around this house again, preserving its uncertain peace somehow" (80). What she does gain, however, is an insight into the nature of death and into the pain that accompanies loss: "I had not known at all that a death would be like this, not only one's own pain, but the almost unbearable knowledge of that other pain which could not be reached or lessened" (80).

An examination of the funerals represented in the text reveals much about Vanessa's relationship to both recreating the past and to coming to terms with the dead in her life. Similar to her opinion of Grandmother MacLeod's reliance on rigid notions of order, which represent a kind of tradition, Vanessa has little regard for the effect of the ordered forms of mourning ritual—namely the funeral.

In "Jericho's Brick Battlements" Vanessa comments on funerals by remarking on the "Bizarre cruelty of such rituals" (188). While a number of people died during her formative years, Vanessa actually never attended a funeral until her Grandfather Connor's when she was twenty. This is in large part due to the prevailing notion that children should not be exposed to such rituals but should be protected from death. Vanessa reflects upon how her grandfather's funeral service shapes and orders the memory of his life, but also imposes a legitimized version of events:

What funeral could my grandfather have been given except the one he got? The sombre hymns were sung, and he was sent to his Maker by the United Church minister, who spoke, as expected, of the fact that Timothy Connor had been one of Manawaka's pioneers. He had come from Ontario to Manitoba by Red River steamer, and he had walked from Winnipeg to Manawaka, earning his way by shoeing horses. After some years as a blacksmith, he had enough money to go into the hardware business. Then he had built his house. It had been the first brick house in Manawaka. (189)

What is particularly striking about this telling is that it is a sparing account of a man's life and resembles most closely the form of the newspaper obituary. The bare essentials give all the important details, but do not give much in terms of what the man was actually like. The conventional summary of the man's life does little, in fact, to tell about what kind of person he was. In telling her own stories, Vanessa rewrites these conventional forms of summing up a person's life, and, through artistry, she shows how another way can be more effective in getting at the true essence of a life.

Contrasting the passage about Grandfather Connor's funeral is an imagined reconstruction of his brother Dan's funeral. While Vanessa knows that the funeral could not have been as she envisions it, she decides that the imagined version is more appropriate and does greater justice to the man's life—which in the end does not amount to much in terms of a conventional summation:

> Dan had never ceased being a no-good, a natural-born stage Irishman, who continued even when he was senile to sing rebel songs. For years Grandfather Connor had virtually supported him. His funeral must have been quiet and impoverished, but in my head I had always imagined the funeral he ought to have had. His coffin should have been borne by a hayrack festooned with green ribbons and drawn by six snorting black stallions, and all the cornets and drums of the town band should have broken loose with "Glory O, Glory O, to the Bold Fenian Men." (188)

Anything but conventional, this imagined funeral does justice to the soul of the man, rather than the quantifiable life. Such an approach informs Vanessa's own practice in remembering the dead.

A Bird in the House is very much focussed on Vanessa's memories of her grandfather, and her narrative can be seen as a rewriting of the spare account of his life that she encountered at his funeral. This account was one that did not bring Vanessa to an emotional response to Grandfather Connor's death: "I could not cry. I wanted to, but I could not" (189). Later, when Vanessa observes his body—"after the accepted custom"—the sense that she is not emotionally engaged in the funeral service is underscored: "I was not sorry that he was dead. I was only surprised" (189). It is only many years later that Vanessa can begin to explore the relationship that she had with her grandfather, and the first step is to acknowledge that his influence was integral in forming the person that she has now become.

Vanessa reflects at the end of the book that "I had feared and fought the old man, yet he proclaimed himself in my veins" (191). Her narrative, then, seeks to find a way that allows her to understand—and accept—how her Grandfather "proclaims" himself in her veins. As such, Vanessa's narrative in *A Bird in the House* becomes a text that mourns her grandfather's life and death, as well as a text that mourns the other important losses of her life. Mourning is a process that implicitly involves the questioning of social structures and shaping forces, and Vanessa's practice in the text mirrors the definition. She questions and rejects traditional forms of mourning because they have not fulfilled her emotional needs, but she also constructs her own manner of grieving from the experiences that she has had and she finds that through creative means she is able to mourn the losses of her life effectively.

Acknowledgement

I would like to thank Nora Foster Stovel for her insightful reading of an earlier draft of this paper.

Notes

1. Criticism of *A Bird in the House* has frequently concerned itself with structure and form. As a series of eight linked stories, but as not quite definitely a novel like the other texts in the Manawaka series, the book has confounded precise generic definition. *A Bird in the House* cannot accurately be defined as a collection of stories because of the interrelationship of the individual pieces; as Bruce Stovel points out, "the artistry in each story lies in the interconnected, cumulative resonances that bind the stories together into a single, coherent whole" (130). And yet, at the same time, *A Bird in the House* is consciously *not* a novel as Richard Davies has demonstrated. Jon Kertzer perhaps best expresses some of these concerns when he argues that "it does not matter whether we treat...[Vanessa's recollections] as a collection of stories or novel with eight chapters. In either case the book aspires to a special kind of unity" (22).

6

BECOMING THE MOTHER

Constructions of the Maternal in *The Diviners*

"I am the mother now."
  A Jest of God

The Standing Mother

Morag Gunn's coming of age in Laurence's *The Diviners* traditionally has been constructed as a search for the lost father since this is a text that (with the dubious exception of Catharine Parr Traill) has no textual matrilinearity and so must produce its own feminine genealogy. In my study of *The Diviners*, I want to suggest ways in which the maternal is constructed both as corpus—as body reconceived as text; and as incorporation—the means by which a series of embedded fictions are included in a host-text.

In the construction of her subjectivity, Morag assumes a position as speaking subject in which her authority is alternately appropriated and authenticated. By this means, the texts she produces (both writing and visual media) become the icons that accommodate her emergent subjectivity. Since it is the incidence of maternal loss that precipitates this narrative, in much the same way that the loss of her parents signals the beginning of Morag's construction, I would like to suggest a reading of *The Diviners* that takes into account a maternal function that both authorizes and resists power.

Julia Kristeva'a 1976 essay, "Stabat Mater" offers a treatise of the (im)possible positions of maternal representation in so far as she invokes the maternal body as the unimaginable site of signification. In her refusal to confine representation to signification, Kristeva's split discourse imagines the disallowed maternal text that brings the body to writing in a trope that implies Laurence's construction of Morag as writing subject. Through reading Kristeva's maternal text, I hope to provide a re-ending of Laurence's textual maternal in Morag's fictional discourse that is written as a means of grieving and surviving the deaths that women as subject cannot achieve.

Laurence's last novel, conceivably read as a temporal narrative of loss and absence leading to recuperation, is more accurately the story of the "standing mother," the maternal body constructed spatially as textual fold, the body that cannot signify for itself and yet that generates meaning in the place of the speaking subject. In much the same way, Kristeva's construction of this figure approximates a spatial narrative of the inclusiveness of the maternal signifier.

In "Stabat Mater," Kristeva isolates the condition of motherhood as the variable that functionally defines the female integer. In this way she privileges reproduction as the means by which the woman inscribes her difference, at the same time implicating the female body as locus of subjectivity and writing. The paradox of her position is that while maternity constitutes a consecrated representation of femininity, at least in the western world, it cannot escape its illusory status, what she calls "a fantasy of a lost continent" (133) because of a prevailing idealisation of primary narcissism, that being the belief in an unbroken dyad of infant and mother. Kristeva's point is that in resisting this image, feminists have become immune to the experience that the fantasy obscures. "Stabat Mater" is a poetic and analytic attempt to represent this experience and to propose a new discourse of motherhood—and is appropriate to Laurence's ambiguous constitution of the maternal in *The Diviners*.

The maternal, defined simultaneously as biological category and as attribute of identity, largely situates the female as symbolic construct in the context of Christianity, which in turn sanctifies the female body by constituting it as maternal body. Kristeva asks what it is about the representation of the virginal maternal that satisfies both male and female, supplies what it is the male lacks and hides from the woman what it is she provides to complete his lack. In an examination of the history of the Marian doctrine situated on the right-hand side of the margin, site of reason and teleology, Kristeva examines the potency of the constructions of virginity while at the same time providing an imaginative left-hand gloss on the experience of maternity.[1]

According to Kristeva, the paradox of the Maternal Virgin is that her body, intact and complete, is the site of a simultaneous denial and participation in death. Significantly, Kristeva sees Mary's anguish at the foot of the cross as a desire to participate in that from which she as the origin of life is excluded in death. This gives rise to a resurrective mythology, providing the aspect of biological and maternal immortality to the symbolic Name of the Father, while at the same time assuming the paranoid fantasy of being excluded from sin, time, flesh and death.

Kristeva concludes her analytic argument by invoking the mother's body as a "strange fold which turns nature into culture, and the speaking subject into biology" (149). The implication for this fold of nature is that no signifier can represent it completely; it is a body located on the periphery of nature and culture, a body that explodes with pregnancy, a body both unique and anonymous, masochistic and jubilant, profligate and ethical; it is a body that represents desire as desire for continuity, and it is a body that finally encodes perversion in the transaction of a patriarchal law in which the mother's share is the offering up of her own masochism.

If the maternal body cannot be represented entirely or in its entirety by the signifier, a position that is particularly relevant to Laurence's text, then we must read Kristeva's split text as a refusal to confine representation to signification. On the contrary, the left-hand margin that speaks allusively of conception, gestation, childbirth, caretaking and separation, of the relationship of the mother to the child she has produced and the child once reproduced by her own mother, this site of memory and desire, expresses Kristeva's need to construct an ethics appropriate to women, to bring to the Law the resonance of a feminine discourse, a *jouissance* of and beyond the flesh. In this way the left-hand margin contains the other text, the maternal text that has been disallowed in the academic/paternal/critical narrative of the right-hand margin, the acoustic text that brings the body to sound, to writing.[2]

The implications of the split text are that in it the maternal body is conceived of as geography rather than identity. Dawne McCance makes the point that Kristeva's subject is one who asks *where* am I, rather than *who* am I, again emphasising her function as a threshold/wound/scar, something about which narrative arranges itself (29).

The Acoustic Mirror

There are, however, limitations of Kristeva's theory of representation. In *The Acoustic Mirror*, Kaja Silverman is critical of "Stabat Mater" both as a genealogy of the body and as a poetical representation of maternity. She sees Kristeva's exaggerated desire to distance the maternal from the symbolic order in the development of the Kristevan *chora*, the fantasy of a pre-oedipal existence, a scene of subjectivity that is maternally connoted, a utopian figure in which the integration of mother and child is symbolised by the pregnant body of the mother. In this reading, the mother becomes both receptacle and inhabitant of the receptacle, as Silverman says, "simultaneously the container and its contents" (107).

What is the desire, asks Silverman, behind Kristeva's desire to enclose the mother within the womb? In answer to this, she proposes a Kristevan fantasy: the desire to fuse daughter with mother and mother with her own mother, to relegate all mothers to the interior of the chora/womb. For Silverman this position silences the mother, all the mothers who have rejoined their own mothers in the act of birth, because as mother she is constituted through the mediation of father and infant so that to speak is necessarily to occupy a male position. And if, as she maintains, the *choric* fantasy excludes both mother and daughter from language, then it is not therefore possible to occupy this or any other semantic position in the articulation of a new discourse. For Silverman, Kristeva's semiotic discourse is aligned with the maternal, her *chora* becomes the womb that encloses the female space, space of writing and desire, an acoustic envelope that seals her off from the other. This argument of essentialism is one that Kristeva's text is peculiarly prone to since in stressing the maternal body as the site of the pre-oedipal, Kristeva would appear to insist on the primacy of the mother's language, thus destabilising the Lacanian argument that the subject comes into language through the Law of the Father. What then is the alternative to the phallic narrative, the absurd fantasy of virginal birth, asks Silverman, but an equally absurd fantasy of the woman made word, the babble of womanspeak for and of itself, indecipherable to anybody beyond its own body:[3]

> The strained eardrum wresting
> sound from the headless silence. (Kristeva, 138)

The Speaking Subject

> All this is crazy, of course, and quite untrue. Or maybe true and maybe not. I am remembering myself composing this interpretation, in Christie and Prin's house (16).

Like the Kristevan subject, Morag Gunn is constructed through a dissemination of plural selves in a variety of speech and writing acts; memorybank movie, innerfilm, photographs, letters, tales, telephone conversations, dialogue, excerpts from *The Canadian Settler's Guide* and *The 60th Canadian Field Artillery Book*, recipes and epitaphs, songs, musical notations and the retelling of legend as revisionist history. This sliding of genre together with a constant slippage between first and third person subjectivity, doubles the "I" in the act of remembering and invention. The result is the destruction of self-possession through a plurality of what Foucault has called "author functions" (270) where the dispersion of subjectivity in discourse results in the production of multiple subjective sites. By this means the received fact of authority/authorship is problematised; the author is no longer fully in possession of her story, indeed, story exists only in mediated relation to various discursive sites.

The assumed position that Morag occupies at the beginning of *The Diviners* as owner and producer of discourse, breaks down at the moment of the unknown reader's phone call and her own outrage that is a response not to the pragmatism of the query ("what did you *do*?" [32]) but to the disbelief in her own authority. From this point onwards, the text progressively interrogates the logistics of story—who gets to speak and who to listen, and most importantly, which stories are told. When Christie narrates Morag into subjectivity by conferring upon her the other story, the myth of appropriation, he authenticates her in a way that she fails to do for Jules whose marginal position in text and in history must necessarily conform to the unauthorised version. Much of the resulting narrative is an attempt to find a textual space for Jules, a search that is continued in the dispossession of his daughter who, unlike Morag, does not yet know that she cannot tell a story that is true, but can only tell a true story:

> "But some of those stories you used to tell me when I was a kid—I never knew if they happened like that or not."
> "Some did and some didn't, I guess. It doesn't matter a damn. Don't you see?"

"No," Pique said, "I don't see. I want to know what really happened." (373)

When Morag marries Brooke she accedes to him in all matters of authority, occupying at this moment, the position of the split subject, the lover, who like Donne's beloved, strains to see and be seen in the same transaction:

> I mean, two people who love each other are separate individuals, but they're both seeing everything, including themselves, through the other person's eyes. At least, I think that's what it means, partly. (207)

Her tentative challenge to the authority of Donne, via Brooke, is a confirmation of the position of narcissism that the split subject is forced to occupy in a narrative of appropriation, as in the later scene with Chas, when she is described as being "her own voyeur" (348). Watched and watcher, the image of a woman imagining her seduction, she must become her own author in order to accommodate this subjectivity.

When she leaves Brooke she becomes a writer by virtue of her transgression, and her ensuing individuation is dramatised as a struggle for ownership of discourse until, years later, after the publication of *Shadow of Eden*, she is referred to in reviews as "an established and older writer" (445). At the moment that she enters the canon, becoming herself the perceived source of truth and authenticity, she must break the staff and burn the books, relinquishing her own authenticity in the interests of narrative. In the last part of the novel, Morag tells stories of "real" characters, Christie Logan and Lazarus Tonnerre, rather than their stories. In this way the focus is displaced from tale to teller as the agent of authority. Hers is not the predicament of Lilac Stonehouse, the protagonist who is "virtually inchoate" (244); in her appropriation of the various subjective positions available to her as "standing woman," Morag Gunn speaks and is spoken through a gendered body. By the end she is constructed, in the words of one critic, as a woman situated "aslant the patriarchal discourses of her day" (Hjartarson, 44).

Constructions of the Maternal

> Pique had gone away. She must have left during the night. She had left a note on the kitchen table...(11).

The novel that Morag is writing, as yet unnamed, begins with her daughter's absence. In the place of the daughter she has lost, Morag finds the writing that is itself a substitute for another, and presumably more authentic version. "Slightly derivative, perhaps, but let it pass" (11), she thinks on reading the note Pique has left her. Yet it is this writing constructed as passage, as "blood-hyphen"[4] between mother and daughter that constitutes what Linda Hutcheon has called the "authorised transgression" of parody. Barbara Godard reads *The Diviners* as an attempt, alternately revealed and resisted by the subject, to revise patriarchy by substituting in its place, a communal text, "that endless feminine text according to Cixous" (213). Parody as a form of discourse that frees the (female) subject from formal discourse is the structural device of a narrative that recalls for Godard the great tradition of Shakespeare, Milton, Donne, Hopkins, Wordsworth and Joyce with Louis Riel and Ossian as cultural attachés and comic relief courtesy of Hilaire Belloc and Tarzan. Apart from the female pioneer Catharine Parr Traill, *The Diviners* evades its textual matriliniary and must produce its own feminine acoustic.[5]

What is interesting is that the incidence of maternal loss precipitates this narrative in much the same way that the loss of her parents signals the beginning of Morag's subjectivity. What she mourns initially is not the fact of their deaths but the loss of an iconography, signalled by an absence in the scopic field of any appropriate referent:

> "I want to see my mother," Morag says. "I am going up to see her right now. I won't stay long, Mrs. Pearl. I promise."
> "No, you don't," Mrs. Pearl says sharply. "They're too sick to see you, just now, Morag. They don't want to see you." (23)

Morag is prevented from seeing or hearing her mother before she dies: "(t)here is no sound of her mother's voice, no sound at all" (24); she does not witness her parent's burial, so that later she can read nothing but the failure of signification, in place of their memory: "Now I would like to see that grave, only once, although I know quite well it couldn't tell me anything" (27).

Deprived in this way of the iconography of her parentage, Morag reads into the photographs an anticipation of herself as subject: "Morag Gunn is in this picture, concealed behind the ugliness of Luisa's cheap housedress, concealed in her mother's flesh, invisible. Morag is still buried alive, the first burial" (15). Morag will spend much of the ensuing narrative in search of a progenitor, yet the mother herself is absent to the point of redundancy. She is so far beyond the possibility of signification that she is barely represented in the text except through the parody of pregnancy that we perceive in the body of the rapidly expanding Prin: "Morag is crying. Holding only Prin's awful fat belly wrapped around in a brown wraparound, Prin's good good good. Prin wipes Morag's eyes with fat warm hands. 'The Lord knows I care about you. I lost my only one'" (53). This grotesque Pieta ends with Prin's retraction: "'I shouldn't have said,' Prin says 'never you mind' while Morag's reaction is one of emphatic non-signification: Morag doesn't say. Doesn't say. Doesn't say. Doesn't say" (53). Later, when Prin lies in her hospital bed, her eyes are open but unseeing and her face "is as blank as a sheet of white paper upon which nothing will ever now be written" (270). The mother is monumentally silent, unregenerate in her refusal to signify, so that the child must seek, in other transactions, the maternal gift whose only value is in its structure as transference.

In this circulating text, all gifts are eventually lost; Christie the storyteller who at the end can barely croak out his blessing, Jules the singer who dies of throat cancer, Dan McRaith, Royland, Fan and Morag all lose, or are in imminent danger of losing, their various talents. The Diviners is a story composed of stories and stories about stories, so that it is in the metaphor of storytelling itself that we may understand the significance of the gift that (like the knife/plaid pin) spans books and lives and whose only imperative is to be passed on.[6] Even Pique, who, in a repetition of the scene of Morag's abandonment, does not get to see her father before he dies, receives the assurance that he has seen the song by means of which she has fictionalised him and in this manner has fulfilled her responsibility as receiver of the gift.

The other way that the maternal is constructed in this narrative is through the metaphor of the host-text. Warwick uses the word "incorporation" (44) to describe the means by which a series of embedded fictions take root in the body of the host-text. The various plots of Morag's novels are offered to us as alternatives by which to read the body of the absent mother or alternately the absence of the mother's body. She writes into the character of Lilac Stonehouse, in Spear of Innocence, the dangerous naïvete that has allowed her to marry Brooke. At the moment when Brooke refuses to father her child, Lilac aborts herself, so that we read Morag's act of writing as the beginning of a slow process towards incorporating the maternal body that is eventually subverted in her last named novel, Jonah, the myth of male rebirth.

Language and Representation

"Och aye. Only showing them what they thought they would be expecting to see, then, do you see?"

She does not see (47).

Christie crosses his eyes, his mouth dribbles with spit, he twists his face into many "different crazy masks" (47) for the benefit of the onlookers. Unlike the inscrutable face of the mother, his is crazily graphic, articulate to the point of self-parody, a repetition in the body of the language act that is constructed both as transgression and transference:

> Since Prin's death, and the last sight of Christie, Morag has experienced increasingly the mad and potentially releasing desire to speak sometimes as Christie used to speak, the loony oratory, salt-beefed with oaths, the stringy lean oaths with some proteins in them, the Protean oaths upon which she was reared. But of course does no such thing. (276)

From the crazy rhetoric of Christie's speech in which simile turns metaphor in a single elision ("the sky was *like* fire. Like fire, did I say? It *was* fire"(101)), to the strange tropes of Dan McRaith's vernacular, which sounds, Morag tells him, "as though it's being translated from another language" (395), Morag is inserted into the patrimony by virtue of a language that names her as non-sense: "In this last book she looks up…the word for black. It says *dubh, dhubh, dhuibh, duibhe, dubha,* but omits to say under what circumstances each of these should be used. Morag Dhu. Ambiguity is everywhere" (427).

In an attempt to escape this world in which "words have lost meaning…babble babble" (300), in an attempt to become "unhaunted now, forevermore" (219), Morag begins to question the linguistic basis of the patriarchal discourse: "What means *Law*" (38), "What means *Strap*?" (40).[7] What she learns is that language is opaque, words have their own power to resist and that it is necessary to use them even beyond the subject's understanding of their quotidian content.[8] She wakes up with the enigmatic word "Jerusalem" in her head (185), strenuously disputes Brooke's use of the name "little one" (277), and is distracted by the call of the bird, "prespres-pres-pres-Presbyterian" (108). The name Culloden is not merely the reference to a geographical place but her recognition of the arbitrariness of the linguistic act:

A station flashes by. The train does not stop, but Morag reads the sign.
CULLODEN
There is such a place. It really exists, in the external world.
Morag feels like crying. (408) [9]

It is at the moment that she first mis-reads the signs that Morag begins to write.

The Unrepresentable

"I'm twenty," Morag says. "Or nearly. I don't feel—I don't know, I just feel as though I don't have a past. As though it was more or less blank." (211)

Morag, unable to write. (471)

In order to avoid Silverman's essentialist bias in her reading of Kristeva's text, we must attempt to read the unrepresentable narrative. The other-text, the one Morag cannot write even while writing the substance of *The Diviners*, is nevertheless present in the various acts of amnesia and erasure that she undergoes at moments of crisis. After the unwitnessed deaths of her parents, she experiences one of these absences: "And after that, for one entire year, my memories do not exist at all. A blank. Nothing of what happened then remains accessible" (38). Yet these moments are always recouped, since for Morag the tale-teller, story is her only consolation against death, a constructed presence that stands in for inconsolable absence.

Another construction of the silences in this text is yielded by Kristeva's reading of "the abject" in her essay on abjection, *Powers of Horror*. For Kristeva, the abject is that unrepresentable, inexpressible site at which object and subject converge.[10] In Laurence's text, this would appear to occur at the scene of the erasure of the female body, most noticeably in the episode when Piquette and her children are burned alive in the Tonnerre shack. In the same way that "Stabat Mater" performs, that is both represents and reports, the woman's body, this episode is performed textually by silences, omissions and an averting of the gaze: "Morag looks, too, and then realises what is still in there. She can see only smokened metal and burnt wood, but there is something else in there as well" (175).

What is in there is so unspeakable that it cannot be referred to again, except by omission and so Pique tries to become the inheritor not only of her mother's stories but of her silences as well:

> Well, I never knew him that well myself, but I remember the last time I ever saw him. It was at the time of the fire.
> (I don't like that part. Don't tell it again.)
> Okay. I won't, then. (393)

Later, when Jules repeats this story to his daughter, her response is similar: "do you have to tell me again, I don't want to hear it" (454). Of course it is precisely by articulating the horror of this sight that Morag and her daughter can be released from their specular identity as subjects of a female body that is alternately inchoate (bois-brulés) and startlingly graphic: "I guess I vomited, as they brought the stretcher out. I realised then that the air didn't only smell of smoke and burned wood. It smelled of—well, like roasted meat, and for a minute I wondered what it was, and then—" (296).

At any rate, it is the sight of this inexpressible body that so traumatises Morag that she loses touch with Manawaka, cannot write, and marries Brooke. Conversely it is only when she "confesses" to Jules what it is she has seen, that she is freed from the circumstances of her oppression. For his part, Jules too must perform a language act in order to redeem the abject body of his sister: by being brought to language, even (especially) a language that cannot signify to itself, the body is re-membered:

> My sister's eyes
> Fire and snow—
> What they'd be saying
> You couldn't know. (487)[11]

In the maternal story, the standing woman cannot die. Her condition is one of perpetual mourning because she cannot experience a death of the body, her death in the body, as Christ could. For Morag, writing the unrepresentable body/story is a way of experiencing her death as a woman.

In Jules's case, the problem of signification is similar, since although he is a man and therefore apparently capable of language/death/representation, he is, by virtue of his marginal status, also outside the denotations of the patrimony. Renamed because of his trade as skinner, his real name is mispronounced even by his lover. The places that he inhabits and in which he meets Morag are located outside of culture: the nuisance grounds, the middle of the river, the Tonnerre family shack.[12] Although he is able to bring his sister's body to language in the end, he is unable to do the same for himself as subject: "Some guys can make songs like that, out of what's with them, but I can't. Don't know why. Made some for Billy Joe, and even for some women, but not for me. Maybe somebody will do it for me someday" (293). Jules, who cannot compose songs about himself, resists representation whether acoustic or visual. In a narrative impelled largely by the photographic mnemonic, Jules is the person behind the camera "who has just refused to have his own picture taken" (360). By this means he is the erased subject, taking up the self-conscious position of surplus. It is of him that we must say, like Nietzsche, "always too soon, too late." In his failure to be represented as subject, he is always beyond the frame, the one represented only by omission. What Morag calls "the things which the snapshot doesn't show" (347). In so far as this is a redemptive text, Jules (like Lear) is rescued from this impossible subject-position by his daughter, or at least the promise of regeneration and inheritance that her existence promises: "Would Pique create a fiction out of Jules, something both more and less true than himself, when she finally made a song for him, as she would one day, the song he had never brought himself to make for himself?" (474).

The Female Body

> On the walls, pin-ups of movie stars, women with big breasts and carmine mouths. Also the pelt of a skunk, black and white (151).

The image of the female body is positioned in this narrative somewhere between pin-up and pelt. The reproduction of the Botticelli Venus that Morag fails to recognize is, ironically, one of the few expressive female images. Unlike Prin, she at least meets the viewers' gaze:

> The picture is of the head of a girl, features so finely cut, so entirely beautiful that you know all at once this would be how an angel or the Mother of Christ would have looked if ever such had existed. The eyes met yours, looked into yours, without flinching or avoiding. (171)

In the process of bringing this ideal to language in her newspaper report, Morag translates her into icon: angel and virgin, queen of the old poems, the beloved of men. Yet when she finds that she is indeed precisely that, a reproduction of a detail from a Renaissance painting, she discards her and all that she signifies. Instead the image of the female is figured in a variety of ungainly metaphors. She is gutless like Eva "as a cleaned whitefish" (71) who later achieves this state in a more literal manner when she aborts herself with a clothes hanger, or Prin, "that whalewoman, unwholewoman, unwholesome flesh" (226) alone in her lost mind. She is the sequinned costume burned in the garden by Fan, the bottle that Lazarus holds up in defiance—"this here is my woman, now"(155)—and the faulty reproductive system that must be adequately reinforced before marriage: "get yourself fixed up, won't you?" asks Brooke (220). When seen through the eyes of the male artist, she is always radically dispossessed, echoing the title of McRaith's painting: "A grotesquerie of a woman, ragged plaid-shawled, eyes only unbelieving empty sockets, mouth open in a soundless cry that might never end" (402).

The female body in this text constitutes a final erasure of the source, a kind of mise-en-abyme that refers the reader back to itself as the final referent. So that in order to find an image of herself as body, the female protagonist must return to her own body, recognised in the present because framed in the past tense. Morag looking at Pique: "How could any woman's belly be that flat and breasts upstanding and unsagging? Morag's once were" (372). The image in which she recognises herself is a misrecognition,[13] but it is the only recognition she permits herself and one in which she is in any case irretrievably split.

Becoming the Mother

"Hey, Morag, here's a riddle for you—who buries the undertaker? Give up? Whoever'll undertake it." (127)

In his critique of écriture feminine, Christian Bök (1992) via the French feminists, defines parler-femme as a subversive language, an alternative to phallocentric discourse that interrogates traditional forms of narrative structure and establishes a direct connection with the unconscious. Arguably, Kristeva in "Stabat Mater" establishes herself as oneiric voice in one of her subject positions, a "semiotic" communication with a maternal function that both authorises and resists power.[14] In this sense, the maternal can be perceived as a conduit through which marginal or unincorporated voices may speak, as we have seen in the case of dispossessed males like Jules and Christie.

Morag's search for a reference, a mentor, a place from which she can speak significantly, is the search for the father she has lost and continues to lose, through the stories of Christie. That she achieves this inheritance is indicated by her entry into the canon, the gift she has claimed of writing/divining. The loss of this gift is always imminent and it is to achieve its permanence that she sets out to find the source, a journey home that is also implicitly figured as a search for the mother.

The construction of writing home, going west, making pilgrimages, returning to the source, of each person going back "to the place where he'd begun" (369), is emphatic. Morag flees Manawaka, travelling to Winnipeg, west to Vancouver and east to London, only to find that the town inhabits her: "I found the whole town was inside my head, for as long as I live" (376). What she learns apparently is that redundancy is a condition of life, we always end up at the place where we have begun. When she touches Dan on the wrist to indicate to him the way in which past and heredity flow through the blood, she places herself as a subject speaking from the position of the body, rather than from an Archimedian point projected beyond it (Europe—Britain—Scotland—Sutherland).

It is for this reason that *The Diviners* ends where it has begun: "Morag returned to the house, to write the remaining private and fictional words, and to set down her title" (477). Morag as writer has completed the book that we have been in the process of reading. Yet at the moment of completion, the source is appropriated. Because she cannot simultaneously be and have the mother, Morag ends from the place where she has begun, and begins again as origin.

Acknowledgement
I would like to acknowledge Professor Dawne McCance of St. John's College and Professor David Williams of St. Paul's College, both of the University of Manitoba. Their insights and rigorous scholarship have influenced this paper.

Notes

1. The genealogy of the body of the Maternal Virgin has, according to Kristeva, under-
   gone three main transformations. The first is the analogous status erected between
   mother and son so that as both the mother and wife of God, Mary is freed from the
   twin sins of the flesh—conception and death. Because she avoids mortality, her own
   death included, she has no need for resurrection and so becomes the unique reposito-
   ry of a feminine power that excludes all other women and which is in turn excluded
   by the severity of the father. Secondly, as the declared Mother of the Church, she is
   proclaimed queen and awarded the attributes of royalty in the form of terrestrial
   power and through the external signs of opulence. She is coded both as the heavenly
   queen and as the noble lady of the feudal courts, and as such becomes the focal point
   for male fantasy, combining desirability with inaccessibility in the tradition of the
   courtly love ideal. Finally the relationship between Christ and Mother becomes the
   matrix within which all other types of love relations—romantic, parental, courtly,
   sacred and profane—are constructed.

   There is a further aspect to the body of the Virginal Maternal that Kristeva isolates
   in *Nativity* by Pietro della Francesca, a mother kneeling before her son, which she
   describes as a position tinged with masochism and ecstasy. It is at this praxis that
   Kristeva locates the humanisation of love in the context of Christianity through the
   cult of the mother represented here as tender, devout, modest and humble. As privileged object of art, music and literature, the virginal body is represented
   metonymically as breast, milk or tears, established in space as a nonverbal semiotic.
   Sexuality is reduced to implication and the maternal virgin is transformed into a
   receiver of sounds, the acoustic site by means of which man surmounts death through
   perfect maternal love, or at least through the memory of its perfection.

2. For Kristeva, the Menippean discourse of the left-hand side approximates what she
   calls the semiotic, the mark or trace in language of the unconscious other. This is the
   language of the pre-oedipal, where maternal rhythms, anarchic meaning, parapraxis
   and silence, all the oral and instinctual aspects of language, precede the symbolic
   order, the language of signification. In this way the maternal body is situated at the
   intersection of nature and culture; hers is the threshold that resists the paternal order.
   In an interview, Kristeva confirms this image: "I didn't want to give an impression of
   coherence, on the contrary I wanted to give an impression of a sort of wound, a scar"
   (Jacobus, 167). In this reading, the text of "Stabat Mater" itself presents as scar, divided
   like the maternal body at conception and parturition, a metaphor for original division,
   the split between her participation in the paternal discourse and the *jouissance* of her
   position as mother:

   > I desire the Law. And since it is not made for me alone, I run the risk of desiring
   > outside the law. (Kristeva, 143)

So that what she, the mother, gives birth to in this language event is herself as other, the subject in and of language, the I interrogated by a discourse dissembled from another discourse. This narrative of the subject-in-process defines what Dawne McCance calls the space of the outcast, the excluded, the abjected (McCance, 29), a place both catastrophic and divided because it writes the primal repression, the precarious casting out that marks the signifying subject.

3. Where this argument fails is in its assumption that in refusing one form of representation Kristeva is substituting another, in reading the left-hand margin as a subversive narrative of woman, she is nevertheless presenting a realised and alternative narrative of representation. My reading of "Stabat Mater" is that, far from trying to represent an alternative female image as an antidote to the masculine fantasy of the Maternal Virgin, Kristeva is, in the left-hand margin of her text, inscribing the not-woman, the impossibility of representing woman, indeed the impossibilities given the essential reductiveness of signification, of any adequate representation. In this way the split text is presented as a fiction by which we must learn to read the semiotics of significance. The implicit chronological assumptions in Silverman's view, of the continuum from semiotic to symbolic language, is thereby questioned because for Kristeva the "Stabat Mater" constitutes a treatise on the possible positions by which we may read texts formulated in a spatial rather than temporal dimension.

What is the desire, we must now ask, behind Silverman's desire to read Kristeva's desire as approximation/substitution/metonymy, the means by which representation represents itself as Other? For whatever else it is, "Stabat Mater" is a text that includes its own Other and, in ignoring this reading by insisting on the monologic either/or position, Silverman indicts the consciously split text in a text that is unaware of its own split, that excludes its Other and that neurotically insists on the apparently seamless surface of the right-hand margin.

Since Kristeva's text privileges the personal, I feel justified in recording my own more visceral response to the "Stabat Mater," my own inscription of desire as it were. For a long time after first reading the text I was resistant to it, a resistance that translated itself into physical symptoms—lassitude and nausea. I felt blocked by the dichotomy it set up between the spoken and the speaking subject, between the woman as image and woman imagined. What I came to realise in the course of painfully working through the text was what this phantom pregnancy signified—the desire behind the desire to refuse signification both as subject and object of a discourse that too narrowly defined me. As a woman writing an academic paper about the possible positions that language can occupy in the body, I felt divided, inhibited. What allowed me to continue, to see the choice as continuum and not confinement, was a dream I had about reading. After an evening of working drearily and apparently fruitlessly on the text I fell asleep and dreamt that I was reading Kristeva's "Stabat Mater" very carefully, so carefully that my lips moved as I read each line.

Slowly it became clear to me that I was not holding the book in my hands but in my body and what was moving were my vaginal lips. I would like to say that when I woke that morning the text had tumbled miraculously out of my head and into my body, but that is perhaps an exaggeration. Nevertheless I was able to overcome my resistance to it and I offer this dream as a possible reading strategy—the position occupied by language in the body, not only of the writer but of the reader.

4. This phrase is taken from the novel *Swann: A Mystery* by Carol Shields, where it also describes the apparently indissoluble relationship between a mother and daughter.

5. When Morag interrupts Brooke's class, she does so in the interests of the silent female subject: "Well, like 'For God's sake hold your tongue and let me love.' That's a very cruel line. Supposing the lady had been able to write poetry—I mean, you wonder what she might have said to him" (208). In this sense, the text she writes may be read as a response by the literate female reader/writer to the poet.

6. By this means a heroic discourse is narrated by an anonymous oral teller who does not claim ownership/authorship. The narrative in which Morag is perceived to have descended from valorous ancestors is a means, via the knife as talisman, of inserting her into the patrimony and in this way establishing generation.

7. In contrast to these acts of naming a discourse that repeats in its insistence on discipline and punishment, the Name of the Father, the act of naming for women is creative, fertile, as evidenced in the Edenic gesture of Catharine Parr Traill: "Imagine naming flowers which have never been named before. Like the Garden of Eden. Power! Ecstasy! I christen thee Butter-and-Eggs!" (186). The other moment of feminine renaming is in Morag's self-christening as Princess Eureka—both are conceived of as acts of generosity and surplus.

8. In response to Morag's iteration "what means," critic Lynette Hunter speaks of the compulsion of words that "speak to an experience beyond the private"(150).

9. Her recognition of language from her position outside of discourse, that is, as a subject passing a sign in a moving train, is reminiscent of Lacan's scene of (mis)recognition in "The agency of the letter in the unconscious or reason since Freud" (1957), where he speaks of passing two doors marked alternately "ladies" and "gentlemen" from his vantage point in a moving train.

10. Kristeva speaks of the abject as inhabiting the binary properties of taboo; it is both sacred and consecrated, as well as potentially dangerous, forbidden and unclean. The category functions through a "logic of exclusion" (65) that negotiates the transference of the object from filth to defilement. Kristeva sees abjection, in part, as an encoded performance of social taboo, so that defilement, for example, may be read as incest—a transgression of the boundaries of what is considered clean and proper. In *The Diviners*, the nuisance grounds with its collection of refuse, rotting food and buried corpses is a striking instance of the place of the abject.

11. Faces are curiously unresponsive in this narrative; they refuse to signify. When Morag looks for the face of her father in the group photograph, she cannot find him because "they all look the same" (100). When Christie tries to assist her, he finds that far from being able to recognize Gunn, he cannot even find his own image: "Morag looks at the long-ago picture. One of these men is Colin Gunn, her father. But it could be anyone of them. She says nothing" (101).

12. The lists that Morag includes in her narrative are many and varied: what she sees in the nuisance grounds, the merchandise in the lingerie department, the lists of the dead at the battle of Dieppe where she looks for Jules Tonnerre's name. Morag's com-

pulsion to make lists may be read as her need to make language representative—the collection of nouns that make up the list, each stands in for the object that is absent and in this way provides startling evidence of the failure of language to signify.

13. In the sense that Lacan named the image in which we first recognize ourself as *méconnaissance* referring to the inability of the child to see himself as anything but cohesive and constructed, despite his status as fragmented body. "The mirror stage as formative of the function of the I as revealed in the psychoanalytic experience"(1987).

14. This is Kaja Silverman's point and the main issue upon which her critique of French feminism stands. I hope I have pointed out Kristeva's somewhat more complex awareness of the subject as being spoken for/produced by the discursive system within which she speaks.

7

JESTING WITHIN

Voices of Irony and Parody as

Expressions of Feminisms

Margaret Laurence's protagonists in the Manawaka novels do not, on preliminary consideration, seem feminist.[1] Rachel and Stacey, the main characters of *A Jest of God* and *The Fire-Dwellers*, are trapped within socially-conditioned roles and behaviors; they take care of men, children and parents while neglecting their own self-development. Their relationships with men are characterized by communication barriers and pain; they lack control and ultimately have no rewards in these relationships. Morag, the protagonist of *The Diviners*, is more self-defined than Rachel and Stacey, as she is a writer and a single mother, but she still suffers from her need for sexual connection, her vulnerability towards men, and her desire to fulfill men's needs. She suffers because she initially puts men's needs before her own, and perhaps even understands them better than her own, although she moves away from this behavior towards the end of the book.

Although Rachel and Stacey do not engage in specifically feminist activity—a real, material displacement of male dominance in the spheres of their own and other women's lives—they do exhibit a budding feminist consciousness that is easy to overlook when a 1990s reader focuses on their enmeshment in patriarchal domestic arrangements and mindsets. Reading carefully, however, a contemporary feminist will notice a progression in consciousness from Rachel to Stacey to Morag. Morag's feminism is active: she rejects her domineering husband, bears and raises a child without male support, and pursues the activity of writing despite heavy social strictures that make this profession more difficult for women than for men.

Morag's achievements, much though she undervalues them, are at the extreme end of the scale for feminist "success" in her time (I hedge the term with quotation marks because Morag's life does not proclaim its happiness with bugles and trumpets, but limps and straggles towards enlightenment like most people's). Stacey's and Rachel's lives are more typical of the lives of most women of the sixties. Their feminisms lie within their own brains, and it is only through hearing their voices in the act of novel-reading that we may know of their qualified liberation. This liberation is portrayed via their many-voiced internal conversations, in which it is possible to identify two particularly strong strands: one, the voice-of-conformity to societal (hence, male-dominated) standards for women's behavior and roles; the other, the voice-of-rebellion that is ironical, cynical and often parodic of the other voice and the culture it represents.

These voices can be said to assert a feminist consciousness through playful plurivocality.[2] The voice-of-rebellion grows stronger through the progression of the three novels. By comparing the voices of the three protagonists as they "play" with specific topoi—literature, God, family romance, and sexual love—I am able to chart this progress. First, the characters' use and abuse of literary themes, sources and conventions is a key to their level of control regarding the dominant discourse of phallocentric culture: the more educated the character, the more she flaunts her awareness that canonical works are by, about, and in service of patriarchy. Second, the ways in which each character envisions and interacts with her personal God figure adumbrates the degree of self-awareness and acceptance that she possesses: the stronger the self-image of the character, the more her God resembles herself. Third, the characters' relative degrees of psychic separation from their families of origin reflect their relative stages of individuation. Finally, the degree to which each is capable of maintaining autonomy in her relationships with men, despite each one's deep need for sexual intimacy, influences her ability to hear and heed her own voice(s).

Playing with Literature

Linda Hutcheon has described parody in contemporary women's fiction as "one way of deconstructing male-dominated culture; its simultaneous use and abuse of conventions that have been deemed 'universal' works to reveal the hidden gender encoding" (110). Hutcheon sees women writers using parody for at least three functions: broadly, to contest the post-romantic notion of uniqueness and single meaning by questioning the authority of male law and literature; secondly, to critique culture directly instead of silently; and thirdly, to work against marginalization, by incorporating the very body of work that they critique (121).

Laurence's protagonists use parody and irony insistently, although with varying aims: sometimes playfully and at other times as a desperate attempt to maintain control of their despair. Rachel, Stacey, and Morag's literariness is both a crutch (living in a dream-world) and a weapon against this despair; it enables them to play games with phallocentric culture in their minds (and in Morag's case, in her work). Each character is more educated than her predecessor and each one's level of literary curiosity is proportional to the level of parodic intensity in her internal conversations. While Rachel has curtailed her education early in order to care for her mother, Stacey continues hers by taking night classes in topics that give her a broad grasp of (phallocentric) culture: anthropology, literature, psychology and philosophy. She attempts to make these discourses relevant to her life by applying their queries to her own condition, while at the same time mocking the impracticality of their intellectual, depersonalized approach: "*Pre-mourning is a form of self-indulgence*" was her "brainy…aloof" female professor's answer to Stacey's practical question, "I asked her if she didn't worry." (15).

Morag embraces a world of linguistic and intellectual exploration early in life (like James Joyce's Stephen Daedalus, she remembers her childhood awareness as a struggle to conjoin words with meanings), and immerses herself in the literary realm through a university major in English and a career in fiction-writing. Not only does Morag possess the highest level of formal education of the three characters; she is also the most intensely engaged by literary questions, the most prominent one being the question of meaning that she expresses in child-like phrases beginning "What means…?" As a function of this engagement with literary matters, Morag is also, of the three, the most in control of the parodies, puns, and other games that run through her head.

While Rachel is at an embryonic stage of feminist consciousness, she does finally, at the end of the novel, attempt to shape her existence around herself rather than Nick or her mother. Rachel's visions of a new life in Vancouver are focused on self, not other. She imagines that she may marry, but that the chances are against it. In describing her new life to herself, she echoes J. Alfred Prufrock, a timid, repressed character with whom she identifies: Rachel's "I may begin to wear outlandish hats, feathered and sequinned and rosetted" (209) recalls Prufrock's "I grow old...I grow old/ I shall wear the bottoms of my trousers rolled." But this self-prognosis of her future, eccentric state of mind is cheerier than Prufrock's, who does not think the mermaids will sing to him. Rachel thinks the kids will laugh at her, but that she will laugh, too, in time. Like Prufrock, she is afraid of becoming fussy: "I will grow too orderly, plumping up the chesterfield cushions just-so before I go to bed" (209). But alternative fantasies suggest an opposite type, a Cassandra: "I will rage in my insomnia like a prophetess" and "I will ask myself if I am going mad, but if I do, I won't know it" (209), immediately answered by an ironic, real-life voice saying that she will carefully remember to take a vitamin pill each morning with her breakfast.

Rachel's sense of play suggests a freedom that allows her feminist consciousness to develop. She parodies her literary flights of fancy, answering them with realistic and practical alternatives for what may happen. She certainly does not ally herself with male literary figures, although by incorporating them in her thoughts she acknowledges their influence. Scripture is another male, authoritative text that occupies her thoughts on her westward bus-ride, but she does not cite the psalms as a direct balm to her spirit; rather, she ironizes them to indicate how much unnecessary martyrdom may have occurred in her life lived by Christian principles: "I do not know how many bones need be broken before I can walk. And I do not know, either, how many need not have been broken at all" (208). Has she paid too high a price to achieve social acceptance, she seems to ask, by trying to comply with her mother's standards and with her own selfless approach to love? As Rachel contemplates the future, which inevitably entails an evaluation of the recent past, she continues the internal debate that characterizes her consciousness: her "should do" voice, which is the internalized patriarchy, is answered by a voice of irony, skeptical of all things rigid, universal and patriarchal. The play between these internal positions is in itself her liberation from a perceived entrapment by the dominant discourse of her society. The subsequent texts, *The Fire-Dwellers* and *The Diviners*, show this play becoming more prominent in the consciousness of the female protagonists; they show, as well, the voice of irony gaining prominence in the internal discussion.

Playing with God

In the opening pages of *The Fire-Dwellers*, we immediately notice that Stacey's voice is tougher and more cynical than Rachel's. While she is saying "nice" things to her "ultra-feminine" neighbor, Tess, her internal voice is contradicting them and expressing all the anger, envy and distrust that she feels towards Tess and the society that creates Tesses (women who are super-conscious and careful of their appearance, but who, as a consequence, seem only to adorn men's existences rather than to live for themselves). On the next pages we encounter Stacey's existential alienation that she projects onto the city; what she sees is a group of broken images reflecting her guilt, anxiety and dread (again recalling T.S. Eliot, and also Dante). These culminate in an apocalyptic vision of Vancouver, that "jewel of the Pacific Northwest," whose buildings are "charred, open to the impersonal winds, glass and steel broken like vulnerable live bones, shadows of people frog-splayed on the stone like in that other city" (14–15). In the private Hell that the city represents to her, people are not real, but only shadows (Stacey has no real friends whom she can talk to), and everywhere people (especially children) are vulnerable to the "impersonal" winds of the horrible events that Stacey hears about on the news and imagines in her mind. Stacey's world view is darker than Rachel's but she asserts herself more strongly.

Part of Stacey's assertiveness, and thus, of her particular version of feminism, is the dialogue of voices within her mind, a dialogue that is more engaged and self-conscious than Rachel's. Stacey, in fact, seems to talk to herself more often than Rachel, and to consider her dilemmas from more angles. She is aware that her "games" (her internal dialogues) are necessary because her husband Mac will not talk to her. One of the characters to whom she talks in her head is a being she only half-believes in, whom she calls God, but addresses ironically as "Sir." He is not God-the-Christian-patriarch; he is a manifestation of one aspect of Stacey's consciousness, which does not hold a religious view of life at all. When asking God why Mac should sleep soundly while Stacey suffers insomnia, she plays His voice, and responds assertively: "You are suggesting that if I am expecting justice I am a bird-brain? You have a point there, Lord" (27). Her "Lord" is neither the benevolent, merciful, otherworldly being that the Bible promised her when she was a child, nor is he the respectable, secular, patriarchal authority figure that the title "Sir" suggests. He is an aspect of Stacey that allows her to make fun of the idea that any knowable entity is there to protect her and her children. But it is an important aspect of her that has some kind of faith, although she is unsure whether or not it is related to another being: "We've brought our own selves up and precious little help we've had from you. If you're there. Which probably you aren't, although I'm never convinced totally, one way or another" (156). This God is one that Stacey is allowed to talk back to when her faith is low: "Listen here, God, don't talk to me like that. You have no right. *You* try bringing up four kids" (156). While He figures as an internalized parental authority or superego, Stacey tires of his insistence that everything would be all right if she would just be better: thinner, smarter and cooler, less emotional and needy of human contact. As such, He also represents the voice of society that says a woman (any woman) with working husband (any husband) and children (any children) should consider herself blessed and graciously perform her "duties." Stacey struggles against this facile and very repressive view of a woman's place in the world. Her ironies, her "games" (her word for the puns and stories in her head), her memories of her childhood strengths such as swimming, dancing, and creative self-expression, and her fantasies (taking the children to live in the Cariboo where she will have a log cabin and be a teacher) all contribute to an active mental life that sustains Stacey through the banalities of her existence. Only when her frustration peaks does she seek to externalize this creative activity in an affair; otherwise, the voices themselves provide the company that she needs to survive.

Playing with Family and Myths of Origin

Stacey's greater assertiveness relative to Rachel is perhaps connected to the fact that she has already found the courage to break the primary attachments to mother and father that Rachel only partially lessens by the end of her book. In the beginning of *A Jest of God*, Rachel is still bound to the original patriarchal figure of her life: her father. She is fascinated by his morbid fascination with death and she has internalized his needs for solitude and his melancholy temperament. Her visit to the funeral parlor and her conversation with Hector Jonas give her insight into her likeness to her father, when she is asked to consider that this was "the kind of life he wanted most" (131). She easily identifies herself-before-Nick with her father: "Did he ever try to alter it [his life]? Did I, with mine? Was what he needed most, after all, not ever to have to touch any living thing?" (131).

Rachel's affair with Nick, although existentially painful in its feelings of loss and lack of communication, does provide her the energy and will to make a change—to move to Vancouver. It helps to free her of the guilty association she had unconsciously made between herself and her mother as oppressors of her father. It is also in her unconscious mind, the realm of dreams, that she reads this beyond-the-grave message from her father: "He says run away Rachel run away run away (25)." In this nightmare, Rachel runs away from her mother, who is "singing in a falsetto voice, the stylish tremolo, the ladies' choir voice" (25). This dream-mother is emblematic of all that is false, stylish and lady-like (prudish) in her real mother and of the very qualities that Rachel needs to escape in herself, for, if she has internalized her father's moodiness, she has also strongly internalized her mother's voice, to the detriment of vital parts of her, such as her libido and self-love. Rachel's primary attachments to father and mother are being worked out, in the course of the novel, through her affair with Nick, while Stacey, her sister, has already found the courage to break those attachments before her book begins.

In the beginning of Morag's book, we see her struggling with the opposite problem regarding her origins: orphaned at an early age and brought up by an alcoholic, war-scarred garbage-collector and his obese, sedentary wife, Morag longs to discover some redeeming truths about her unknown "real parents" to give her a sense of identity and pride. Morag yearns for the very attachments that Rachel and Stacey need to break. As a consequence of her relatively unsheltered youth, Morag gains a verbal and intellectual toughness, as early as the first day of school, when she sums up the moral lesson of the day: "Hang onto your shit and never let them know you are ascared" (42). Young Morag inspires confidence in the reader that she will be able to fight later battles, by using a voice adopted from Christie, that is tough, knowing, and cynical. This voice recedes during high school and university days, once she is trying to impress boys and get dates. But it returns in force when she needs it to tell Brooke off for calling her "little one" for eight years:

> *Little one.* Brooke, I am twenty-eight years old, and I am five feet eight inches tall, which has always seemed too bloody christly tall to me but there it is, and by judas priest and all the sodden saints in fucking Beulah Land, I am stuck with it and I do not *mind* like I did once, in fact the goddamn reverse if you really want to know, for I've gone against it

long enough, and I'm no actress at heart, and that's the everlasting christly truth of it. (277)

This is Christie's voice, brought back to Morag by her recent visit to Manawaka to attend Prin's funeral. The diction is colorful, the rhythm is poetic, and the swear words are inoffensive ones, or are in any case used inoffensively; it is a voice to be proud of, especially for a writer who will discover that her material and her identity comes from those early voices and places. But although this is Christie's voice in its diction, rhythm and sentence structure, it is Morag's in its thoughts and feelings; it is Morag standing up for herself against all the bloody-minded patronizing bastards of the world, whom Brooke in the moment represents to her, though she does not dare to say so directly, either to him or herself. It is the voice of a feminist who is beginning to knock against the walls that attempt to contain her within a gender role; Brooke projects a demeaning, undermining, "feminine" image on her that does not reflect her true self at all. It is with this rediscovered voice and self-assertion that Morag is able to find the courage to leave Brooke and resume life on her own terms.

On the first pages of *The Diviners* we are introduced to Morag's plurivo-cality. After the third-person narration of Morag's waking to a going-away note that Pique has left on the typewriter, Morag's internal conversations begin, with one voice commenting critically and ironically about the liter-ariness of Pique's writing. Another voice chides her for being humorous at a time when anxiety would be the more appropriate response. Anger sur-faces as she recalls her recent living situation in which she had been taking care, not only of Pique, but also of Maudie, A-Okay and other "hangers-on." But anger fades to nostalgia for the company and hominess of those days. The tone and rhythms of Morag's interior conversation are much calmer than Stacey's; sources of strength and faith that Stacey did not have are immediately revealed as Morag gazes meditatively at the river outside her window and the swallows dancing over it. The sight of the river occasions reveries of her childhood, her other source of inspiration. By the time the series of SNAPSHOTS segue into the first MEMORY BANK MOVIE, we know that Morag's search for her childhood is not only a search for solace and understanding about Pique's departure, but also the topic of her writing.

In the first chapter, Morag's two main sources of strength are revealed: nature and writing. The anxieties that distinguished Stacey's voice are still present in Morag's; we recognize traces of Stacey's cynicism when one of Morag's inner voices rises in mysticism ("Perhaps they're my totems [the saved snapshots of herself and her biological parents], or contain a portion of my spirit" [14]), only to be cut off by another ironic, practical and economic consciousness remonstrating her with the fact that the photos are just what they seem to be—"a jumbled mess of old snapshots which I'll still be lugging along with me when I'm an old lady, clutching them as I enter or am shoved into the Salvation Army Old People's Home or wherever it is that I'll find my death" (14). This cynical voice with its concern about economic matters reminds us of a very major difference between Morag and Stacey: Morag earns her own living. This task both strengthens her and separates her from others, since her trade is the solitary one of writing. The concern about supporting oneself not only makes Morag's a more difficult life, in one sense, than Stacey's, but it also makes her a more independent person whose feminism is more successful than Stacey's because she defines the nature of her existence without reference to a controlling male figure. Although male figures—Royland, Dan McRaith, Jules—are still important to Morag, she no longer allows them to control her existence, as Brooke once did and as Stacey to some extent allows Mac to do.

Even from early childhood, Morag is a stronger character than either Rachel or Stacey. Her early role models, as her later ones, are female: Rose Picardy, her alter ego in youth, was a tough rider who slew polar bears: "not for her the martyr's death," nor pining away for an absent cowboy. Morag also identifies with the female pioneer Morag Gunn rather than her husband Piper. As an adult writer, Morag idolizes Catharine Parr Traill, a nineteenth-century Canadian pioneer, mother of nine, and writer of gardening books, for similar qualities that the legendary Morag Gunn had, according to Christie: "the wisdom and the good eye and the warmth of a home and the determination of quietness" (96). But Morag especially envies Traill's practicality and refusal to indulge depression and melancholy. The very simplicity of her advice appeals to Morag, who sometimes becomes mired in the plurivocality that is a natural response to the more complex era she lives in. The last words that Morag hears Catharine say in their imaginary conversation are: "In cases of emergency, it is folly to fold one's hand[s] and sit down to bewail in abject terror: it is better to be up and doing" (431). These words are Morag's parody of Catharine's voice; they ironize its simplicity. In this final conversation with Traill's ghost, Morag bids her farewell, hoping that she will not need a role model any longer. With characteristic honesty and humility, Morag recognizes and accepts the differences between her own energy level and that of Traill, Maudie and Pique, whose entrepreneurial, pioneering, and constructive energies enable them to take on large projects. Morag finally is able to consider her writing a "large project" in its own way, and her own garden, albeit wild, nonetheless a garden.

Morag's relationship to this imaginary figure, Catharine Parr Traill's ghost, is similar to Stacey's relationship to her god, "Sir," in that both figures are created to provide solace and authority in the two character's lives. But both the nature of the figures and the relationships that each woman has with them indicate the progression of feminism from one character to the next. Stacey's God is modelled on the Christian patriarch, though he is quite unlike that god in his salty, witty, and cynical attitude towards the world. Morag's conjured ghost of Catharine Parr Traill is a pagan spirit-of-the-prairies, a "natural woman" who made everything all right for her nine children and wrote books to disperse her wisdom in perpetuity, ensuring that even future generations would benefit from her rational, practical, caretaking abilities. The differences in these two powerful figures represents the difference in their conjurors' levels of feminism: Stacey's god is male, Morag's is female; Stacey's term of address, "Sir," is respectful, if ironic, while Morag's—sweet Catharine, Saint C. (which mocks her martyrdom), and Mrs. Traill—are variously familiar and sardonic, indicating that she has a closer relationship with her role model than Stacey has. Finally, while Stacey's God is a guy who sometimes just sits up there and laughs at it all, Morag's is a woman who is "up and doing," and, importantly, her activities are the same as Morag's: maintaining her garden (or Morag's country home in a broader sense), writing, and bringing up children. Morag's discovery of a real-life (though deceased) role model is also an affirmation of her own lifestyle choices, whereas Stacey's adoption and perversion of the myth most central to patriarchal Western culture reflect the painful lack of female models and human contacts in her life.

Playing at Sex and Love

All three of these female protagonists crave human contact in the form of erotic connections. Characteristic of all of the connections they achieve is a painful gap between themselves and their partners, which may be described as a different level of availability or awareness between the genders. Each of the female characters deals with this pain through an intensification of the competing voices within their consciousness. In this raised level of discourse, the characters are able to process some of the pain that they feel. The victorious voice is always critical of the romantic expectations of the others and is able to ironize the neediness indicated by the sex act. Irony is the voice of victory and the voice of feminism; it validates and reaffirms the centrality of the female perception, as threatened as that is by the strong voices of the patriarchal culture, both external and internal. Those voices chide the female for not offering a fuller love to the male, an unconditional love that is not contingent upon the male's generosity of spirit. The voice of irony recognizes the difference between social expectations for male and female behavior. Although irony may seem like a small "victory" over patriarchal expectations, it is the only resistance available to some women (like Stacey) who have decided to live with men on men's terms.

Sexual Relations

One of Margaret Laurence's strongest skills is writing convincingly about sex, rendering characters' pain in response to feeling trapped within their individual consciousness at a moment when they wish to be merged with the other. All of the protagonists' sexual experiences are "strange" but perhaps that is because all of them figure the unequal power relationships that form their social contexts. Rachel's first sex with Nick is awkward, as she is a virgin. But Nick's uncaring attitude about pregnancy, pain, and feelings accentuates the awkwardness of the situation. He is angry that Rachel has no birth control device, while she is angry that *he* has none. Promising that he will not ejaculate inside of her, he does so nevertheless, then does not apologize for it. Nick's awareness of her physical pain is suggested by Rachel's interior monologue (in which she apologizes to him for the shudder that is not desire), but he does not respond to this pain. His receptiveness to her emotional pain is no greater, but, rather than confront him with it, Rachel promises herself that she will get used to it, "this practicality, these necessities, this coldness" (99). A cold irony of her own puts Rachel's prospects back into perspective: "What do I expect? To have him say he loves me? That he'll never say. He doesn't like people telling lies" (99). She does at least become "used to" the sex act, as she deeply enjoys it on their third and final date. But her sexuality is almost purely receptive; furthermore, her perception of herself in the sex act is completely defined by his needs:

> Nothing is complicated. He inhabits whatever core of me there is. I can move outward to him, knowing he wants what I am, and I can receive him, whatever he is, whatever. (153)

Rachel's choice of words imply that she is uncertain of the nature or even existence of her core (a metaphor for self) in this passage. But she can offer it to him as long as she knows he wants it. Although I do not want to read this passage too one-sidedly (we are not given Nick's point of view),[3] it suggests, taken together with the verbal exchange that follows, that Rachel is offering much more of herself than Nick offers back. When Rachel feels empowered to "speak from faith, not logic" after the "tender cruelty" of lovemaking and tells Nick she would like to have his child, Nick's response—"Darling...I'm not God. I can't solve anything" (154)—suggests a marked detachment from her and a fear of assuming responsibility for what he perceives as her problems. She has expressed her love and he has regarded it as a problem to be solved by someone else.

Stacey's sexuality is also characterized by receptivity rather than assertiveness, but her knowledge and acceptance of her sexual nature is greater than Rachel's. Mac's violence against her in bed—he half-strangles her while demanding she say it doesn't hurt—this makes him climax—elicits only the vaguest response from Stacey. She attempts to understand his motives and acknowledges her fault in causing his frustration; she deals with the horror of this situation only in her nightmare that immediately follows, in which her children's lives are threatened by forest fire. She may be turning the violence she has just experienced outwards, by projecting it onto the environment; she also may identify with the helpless children in the dream, one of whom must be abandoned though he does not understand why. Their helplessness and lack of understanding are equivalent to Stacey's feelings about her husband.

Her next lover is domineering in a different way: he likes to tell Stacey what she wants. When Luke and Stacey are caressing on the rug, Luke interprets the situation for Stacey:

> Merwoman   you're trembling
> Am I? I guess it's because I want
> What you want is this
> Then she takes his sex in her hands and guides it into her. (187)

Luke has interrupted Stacey's speech, when she may have been intending to express a feeling that surpassed the plainly sexual. But Luke supplies his own interpretation of her needs in the light most flattering to his pride. Afterwards, he continues to characterize her as sex-starved, which she resents ("maybe it gives him something, to imagine he's like the rain in a dry year?" (187)), though she never corrects his assumption. In fact, it is a foregone conclusion for Stacey that she cannot know what Luke thinks: "What does he think? I'll never know" (187). She does not permit herself a conversation with Luke that might jeopardize her pride, for she is afraid that he may have had sex out of kindness alone (187). Her relations with Mac and Luke, like Rachel's with Nick, are encumbered by her fear of judgment and rejection and an uncertainty about her value.

Morag is initially somewhat like Rachel and Stacey in her verbal reticence with Brooke (she abstains from criticism), but she is better able to verbalize the power imbalance between men and women, at least from a theoretical standpoint. In Brooke Skelton's English class, Morag condemns the poet John Donne for his cruelty, asking, "how is it he can know so much about people's feelings and then write so many cruel lines?" and citing as proof the line, "For God's sake hold your tongue and let me love" (208). But she allows Brooke to cow her then, in class, as she does later, in bed. After some years of marriage, Brooke's jealousy and possessiveness have not lessened, and he incorporates what she calls a "joke" into their sex routine: "Have you been a good girl, love?" he always asks before "permitting his arousal or hers" (264). Brooke assumes authority over Morag, even with regard to her sexuality, deciding when she may and when she may not get aroused. He assumes that she is childlike about sex, as he assumes that she is childlike about everything else. In fact, for Brooke, the success of the marriage rests on his infantilization of Morag and his assumption of the role of authority.

With Jules, Morag takes more control, sexually, though not verbally. In their brief time together in Vancouver, their sex, at least, is good. In the narrator's mind, the partners are "equal to each other's body in this urgent meeting and grappling" (365), suggesting that their respective levels of need and desire are commensurate and are equally expressed. Indeed, they make love twice in this passage, the second time on Morag's initiative, and they take turns crying out loud. Helen Buss finds the image of Morag "riding Jules's stallion" significant as a reversal of muse figures because the artist, traditionally male, usually finds himself a female muse, whereas Morag finds a muse in Jules, who is the projection of her own creative power insofar as he expresses the rebellious spirit that she also has, though she often represses it (365). Morag's sexual relations with Dan McRaith are perhaps more positive than what she has with Jules, however, as they share artistic interests that Jules, even though he is a song-writer, does not discuss with Morag. Dan is more of an intellectual equal to Morag, and an aspect of that parity carries over into their lovemaking, which is "the continuation of their talking" (401).

Romantic Relationships

Of the three characters, Rachel struggles across the greatest distance to come to an ironic acceptance of life in a sexist, patriarchal world. The title of her tale, *A Jest of God*, suggests the cruel jokes that she thinks are played upon her (loving a man who does not love her back) by God, while at the same time making fun of the idea of God by endowing Him with the human quality of having a sense of humor. Assigning the agency of cruel jokes on her life to another, however, is a symptom of her lack of identity and control; she feels that "all of my life seems a chance encounter, and everything [bad] that happens to me is permanent" (156). The need to have Nick love her is so strong that she willingly creates a fantasy world around him. But when she becomes convinced that Nick is married and a father, she has to deconstruct her fantasy and acknowledge that she has created a Nick who does not exist:

> The layers of dream are so many, so many false membranes grown around the mind, that I don't even know they are there until some knifing reality cuts through, and I see the sight of my other eyes for what it has been, distorted, bizarre, grotesque, unbearably a joke if viewed from the outside. (157)

Rachel's dissociation from herself continues to the enigmatic ending of the book, in which she exhorts an impersonal God for "mercy on reluctant jesters, God's grace on fools, and God's pity on God" (209). But the last phrase, "God's pity on God" suggests that she, like Stacey, is identifying herself with her god and closing up the gap between self and God. Compared to Stacey and Morag, Rachel is distanced and detached from the "voice of God" within her, which is not only her judging, critical conscience, but also her source of self-acceptance. The fact that Stacey's and Morag's gods resemble themselves more than Rachel's resembles herself suggests that they have internalized their authority figure, and seek guidance from within rather than from an external, male figure. In the last line of the book, however, Rachel asks God's pity on God, and this God seems to be herself. There is an identity between herself and the two categories of "sinners" she has prayed for: "reluctant jesters" (playing at love was reluctant play, as she would have liked it to be "the real thing") and "fools" (she fears nothing so much as to be a fool— "Am I unbalanced? Or only laughable? That's worse, much worse" (25)). Just as she identifies with reluctant jesters and fools, so the grammatical trinity suggests that she identifies with the third "sinner" as well, which is God Himself. When she asks for God's pity on God, she asks for self-forgiveness and that all-too-rare quality in Rachel, self-love. She has perceived her affair with Nick as a jest of God, because she now understands that her belief that there was love and commitment between them was just a fantasy.

The words "joke" and "game" come up repeatedly in the three characters' reflections on how their various internal voices interact. These word choices are ironic, because another way to look at their lives is as tragedies rather than comedies. In all three cases, however, the characters' self-deprecating irony saves them from being victims of both their circumstances and their particular psychological make-ups, for with irony they take intellectual control of these forces and, by naming, take the first step towards understanding and controlling them.

Morag is already well beyond this threshold of control when she encounters the first person who is a real challenge to her self-definition: Brooke. Even on their first romantic date, she is strong and clear in saying "I am far from a child, Brooke—you know that" (212). Furthermore, she is courageous in asking Brooke what he likes about her, asserting her right to know something personal, and leaving herself vulnerable to what might have been a painful response. Of course what Brooke likes about her, "her lack of a past," is not a real characteristic, but only one which they both like to imagine, and while Morag recognizes this, she believes at the same time that she can "conceal everything about herself which he might not like" (213). It is significant that the first thing she feels the need to hide about herself is "Christie's swearing," because her later recourse to that voice and to the pride and courage it expresses is the first active assertion of her feminism. Using Christie's swearing voice to tell Brooke off, Morag asserts her pride in herself as a tall woman and an honest one ("I'm no actress at heart" (277)). The sound of this voice surprises her, and Laurence writes in italics, which is the format she reserves for characters' deepest, truest revelations: "*I do not know the sound of my own voice. Not yet, anyhow*" (277). This revelation positively claims that Christie's voice *is* her own, and that she intends to know it in future. Her "outburst" is accompanied by the realization that she is "very, very angry, and at the same time doubtful about her right to be angry, at him or at the composition of her own composite self "(277).

These doubts about her own "composition" (insecurities about her origins and her right, as a woman, to be self-defined) are what cause her to remain inside her unhappy marriage for another year. Jules arrives fortuitously to propel Morag quite suddenly out of her lethargy. As soon as she is with Jules again, Morag is hearing another voice, like Christie's, that is honest and proud, even though it is sometimes filled with hate. Brooke's voice had never been like that, never a spontaneous expression of his thoughts and feelings, but always low, quiet and intellectual. His repressions absolutely barricaded Morag from his inner life; she often felt sorry for him, but never close to him.

Morag's next sexual encounters are brief and painful, but when she finally becomes involved more deeply with a man, in London, the voice that expresses her true self is no longer stifled. On their first date, Morag finds herself telling Dan McRaith about Christie, Manawaka, Brooke, Jules and Pique. She asks herself if this is "really her," revealing her once-embarrassing origins and divorce story to a stranger. But she feels comfortable doing it. Her relationship with Dan is marked by several occurrences of self-assertion: when she tells him she does not want to monitor his drinking (396), when she warns him that she is not on call for him (399), when they "talk interminably" and their love-making is a continuation of their talking in a different form (401). The last is very different from her relations with Brooke, in which, at the end, love-making was not the "unworded conversation and connection" that it once was, but rather "An attempt at mutual reassurance, against all odds" (282). It is very important that Morag continue to talk with her lover; Dan's wife Bridie is the frightening example of what it would be like for her to accept Dan's sarcasm and anger without words. Seeing his family, however, Morag is no longer able to see him as her lover.

The trip to Scotland frees Morag of two misconceptions that have plagued her for a long time: first, her idealization of Dan as a man who wanted an equal partner, and second, her myth that Scotland was where she belonged because of the Gunn legend that had provided her with enough pride to tolerate Manawaka, Christie and Prin as a youth. Once again, her affirmation of her real self contains an identification with Christie, this time not with his voice, but with his roots. She tells Dan, "It's a deep land here, all right [Crombruach].... But it's not mine, except a long way back. I always thought it was the land of my ancestors, but it is not." When Dan asks, "What is, then?" Morag responds, "Christie's real country. Where I was born" (415). This embracing of her humble origins enables her to accept yet more parts of that "composite self" that had so embarrassed her while she was with aristocratic Brooke, and guides her to a place, McConnell's Landing, that will become a true home. Although she says that the myths of Piper Gunn are her reality, she is learning to dispel other myths that have proven false and caused pain, such as the belief that the writers of London would create "home" for her, and the idea that she could share Dan, or any man, with his wife.

The last man with whom Morag identifies strongly is Royland, a seventy-year-old diviner. Although they have wonderful conversations, her connection to him is mostly mysterious, as she compares his divining powers to her own power, finally acknowledged, to create the magic that is her fiction. The day on which Royland tells her that his divining powers are gone, but that they were not as magical as everybody seemed to think, is the day that Morag believes she has understood what she had wanted to learn from Royland all along: that she, too, is blessed (with the gift of writing), but that the gift can be taken away and "inherited" by someone else. Not only does she thus prepare herself for a dry spell in her own creativity, but more importantly, she finds a message of hope and a sense of power, which is usually so difficult for her to feel. Pique is *her* "inheritor" who has gone to discover her Métis identity in Galloping Mountain. Implied in Morag's musings about the inheritance of power are the hope and belief that she has passed along something good, some deep vision, to her daughter.

Morag's cynical voice recedes as her life moves along, and in its place comes a surer but less embittered one. All Laurence's protagonists are anxious people, and important changes or ruptures continue to happen to Morag and give her reason to lose faith, such as Pique's third departure to live at Galloping Mountain with her uncle Jacques. But, at forty-seven, Morag has developed a greater faith in both Pique and herself, believing what she says when she tells Pique that she is "okay"—"And in a profound sense, this was true" (475). Her whole life has propelled her towards an ability to speak her profounder truths (find her own voice) and, although she still experiences fear before doing so, her honest speaking gains her better relationships. For instance, her ability to reveal to Pique and Dan that their lovemaking in the house makes her jealous results in Pique offering her love and support as well as moving out of the house so that Morag can work better (310–11). The tone of her relations with Maudie, A-Okay and Royland is more honest and less dependent than that of past contacts (she does not mind that Royland knows all about her and she knows nothing about him, even though his simple advice improves her mood). She no longer calls herself insane, as she used to in the year after leaving Brooke or while travelling to meet Dan in Crombruach. She accepts her limitations and her accomplishments. She takes her faith from a very realistic view of life's chances, and is able to make a joke of cynicism itself: "a

Presbyterian is someone who always looks cheerful, because whatever happens, they've expected something much worse" (312). At the end of her book, Morag has achieved self-definition and self-acceptance.

All three of Laurence's protagonists—Rachel, Stacey, and Morag—find their own voices, and in so doing, they assert their feminisms. Although upon first reading the endings may seem unfinished or ambivalent, Laurence does in fact provide many signs of progress in each novel. *A Jest of God* concludes with the prayer to God that is interpreted as Rachel's identification with her own internal voice of strength. She also stands up to her mother, finally telling her that she is a strain to live with. Stacey's book closes with several positive changes in her family's life: her daughter speaks her first words, finally finding *her* own voice; her other daughter shows maturity and a certain similarity to Stacey in refusing to pass moral judgment on her date; Mac makes love gently for the first time; Stacey gives up her "dancing," which may be read as a metaphor for her extramarital desires; and, finally, Mac's father comes to live with them, while Stacey's sister and mother come to live nearby, all of which enforce Stacey's role as caretaker, but reflect her nurturing capacities in a more positive light than that in which she had previously regarded them. Morag ends her book by returning from the river "to write the remaining private and fictional words, and to set down her title" (477). This final emphasis on her privacy reinforces our sense of her newly-acknowledged power in the gift of writing, but also poignantly reminds us of her aloneness, which she has finally come to accept as a part of her life. The final words of the novel, "her title," accentuate her claim to her own voice, her power of naming, and her assertion of control over the many mysteries and needs of her life.

The interior conversations of each of these characters are many-sided and playful. These protagonists refuse to shut up their rebellious, cynical and feminist voices, thus avoiding the common solution for many women, that is to squelch their plurivocality in the interest of relatively peaceful survival in a sexist society. By the act of writing and publishing these accounts of curious, conflicted, and struggling female consciousnesses, Margaret Laurence becomes, for me, an active feminist—one who not only strives to shape her existence primarily around her own needs rather than those of men, but who also disseminates her awareness to others, making public her commitment to struggle against the bonds of patriarchy.

Notes

1. Critics differ on whether Laurence's characters exhibit feminism or are "liberated."
   Two critics write about their frustration with the characters' sadness and passivity.
   John Moss writes that "one almost shouts at Morag to rage not against the dying of her
   special light but against passivity itself" (79) because he sees her "menopausal anxieties
   about her ability to create" at the end of the book overwhelming her, and Jules's death
   leaving a void. Having a similar wish to interact with the main character in *A Jest of God*,
   Robert Harlow writes that "the reader finds himself silently shouting at Rachel to get
   some eye-liner, save for a mink, strong-arm a man, kill her mother and stop bitching"
   (190). He finds her self-pitying, though, rather than anti-feminist.

   Nancy Bailey does not claim that Stacey is feminist, but rather that she performs
   "courageous mothering" and that we should recognize her role as nurturer as a positive aspect to life. Barbara Godard claims that Morag subverts the phallocentric
   literary canon when she rewrites the family legend in the feminine and undercuts the
   primacy of canonical Milton and Shakespeare by literally sneezing at them when she
   has a cold. Helen Buss describes a progressive movement toward hierogamy in
   Laurence's protagonists, finding positive aspects to the affairs with "dark lovers" Nick,
   Luke, Buckle, and Jules because they represent the un-integrated animus of the female
   characters who have not come to terms with the rebellious (and male) part of themselves.

   William New finds the Laurence characters feminist because they "discover the
   potentialities of their own natures." He believes, like myself, that their "freedom is
   articulated from within" (5).

2. I borrow the term "plurivocality" from an essay by Frances Restuccia, who reads Edith
   Wharton's *House of Mirth* as the clashing of two feminist discourses, one that requires
   women to lead independent lives in order to be considered "feminist," and the other,
   which she calls poststructuralist, that requires only that they refuse to define themselves according to societal labels. Restuccia finds Lily feminist because she refuses to
   be reduced to either a male's "objet d'art" or a female's gossip story; she struggles to
   define herself on her own terms. Lily questions the roles that women are expected to
   play in her rigid New York society, and ironizes her predicament. For Restuccia, it is
   enough that Lily, although victimized, is intelligent about it. Her plurivocality is itself
   a liberation (415).

3. Henry Phelps has recently interpreted this scene in a way that suggests that Nick is as
   shy as Rachel, that the photo he shows her is of his dead twin, that he perceives her
   response to it as one of rejection, and that he should not be judged as harshly as the
   majority of readers tend to do. If Nick's relationship with his dead brother is unresolved and constitutes Nick's greatest emotional block, then Rachel's seemingly
   dismissive reaction to the picture may have indicated "her impenetrable self-absorp-
   tion" to Nick and precipitated his callous-seeming departure from Manawaka (188).

8

"SISTERS UNDER

THEIR SKINS"

A Jest of God and *The Fire-Dwellers*

A Jest of God (1966) and *The Fire-Dwellers* (1969) are sister novels, both literally and figuratively. Laurence writes, "In *The Fire-Dwellers*, Stacey is Rachel's
sister (don't ask me why; I don't know; she just is)" ("Ten Years" 21).
Opposing personae of the author perhaps, Rachel Cameron, the heroine of
A Jest of God, and Stacey Cameron MacAindra, the protagonist of *The Fire-
Dwellers*, could not be more different in personality or situation, although
they share a common Cameron heritage. Rachel is a gawky, introverted
spinster schoolteacher who has returned home to Manawaka from university in Winnipeg, upon the death of her alcoholic undertaker father Niall
Cameron, to care for her hypochondriac mother May. Stacey is a broad-
beamed, hard-drinking, middle-aging extrovert who has escaped the
clutches of the Cameron clan in Manawaka to live in the big bad city of
Vancouver with her salesman husband Mac and their brood of four children.

Nevertheless, the family resemblance is obvious: their shared Scots
Presbyterian ancestry, which Laurence views as distinctively Canadian,

provides an armour of pride that imprisons both sisters (like all of Laurence's Manawaka heroines) within their internal worlds, while providing a defence against the external world.[1] To overcome that barrier between personalities, both sisters must learn to understand and accept their heritage in order to liberate their own identities and free themselves for the future. Both women must also learn to love themselves before they can love each other or anyone else. Rachel and Stacey each receive a sentimental education through a brief love affair: as a result of learning to empathize with their lovers, they learn to love themselves and the people they live with. The sisters have not seen each other for seven years, but by the end of each novel they will be en route to reunion. Laurence's emphasis is, as always, on the importance of love in the sense of compassion, as each of her solipsistic protagonists develops from claustrophobia to community.

A Jest of God and *The Fire-Dwellers* are sister novels in practical terms also. Published consecutively in 1966 and 1969, the two novels were composed simultaneously, since Laurence interrupted work on *The Fire-Dwellers* to write *A Jest of God*: "Stacey had been in my mind for a long time—longer than Rachel, as a matter of fact" ("Ivory Tower" 22), Laurence explains. Both novels are even set in the same summer, as Rachel and Stacey, aged thirty-four and thirty-nine respectively, endure parallel but opposing turning points in their lives. The letter Stacey writes to her mother in *The Fire-Dwellers* is the very letter that Mrs. Cameron reads to Rachel in *A Jest of God*. In fact, three letters form a framework for the novels, structuring the sisters' relationship.

With classic sibling rivalry, each sister envies the other, thinking that the grass is greener on the other side of the Rockies. Rachel reflects:

> It's all right for Stacey. She'd laugh, probably. Everything is all right for her, easy and open. She doesn't appreciate what she's got. She doesn't even know she's got it. She thinks she's hard done by, for the work caused by four kids and a man who admits her existence. She doesn't have the faintest notion. She left here young. She gave the last daughter my name. I suppose she thought she was doing me a favour. Jennifer Rachel. But they call her Jen. (*Jest* 105)

The two novels are an exercise in point of view, or the road not taken, as each woman must learn to empathize with her sister, to view her with compassion and charity. "Only connect" is a tall order, but one that Laurence believes in.[2]

The artistic parallels between the sister novels are just as striking as the literal ones. The two primary fictional techniques Laurence employs to delineate the sisters' character development are symbolism and structure. The titles, epigraphs, nursery rhymes, names and settings are all clues to the symbolism. The name *Rachel* inevitably connects Laurence's heroine with her Biblical namesake and her elder, more fertile sister Leah (Gen. 29:16). The titles of both novels, *A Jest of God* and *The Fire-Dwellers*, are very significant, generating central themes and motifs. Both sisters open their narratives with nursery rhymes—*"The wind blows low, the wind blows high"* and *"Ladybird, ladybird,/ Fly away home"*—containing keys to their characters, as well as to the patterns of imagery. The epigraphs for both novels are drawn from Carl Sandburg's poem "Losers": Rachel's archetype Jonah and Stacey's prototype Nero also provide crucial clues to their characters. But Laurence's losers win.[3]

Laurence interweaves structural with symbolic techniques to drama-tize the sisters' identity crises, manipulating narrative method to convey the divisions between the characters' inner and outer life, subjective and objective reality. This manipulation of narrative method also structures the time sequence in a flashback technique, relating memory and desire, as the protagonists try to come to terms with the past in order to free them-selves for the future. As Laurence explains, "Rachel and Stacey are threatened by the past," ("Sources" 15) for "the past and the future are both always present" ("Time" in New 157). Both sisters are haunted by their living death in the mausoleum of the Cameron Funeral Home, and they must both lay the ghosts of the past in order to survive for the future. While the polyphonic narrative structure dramatizes each protagonist's fractured psyche and the society's fragmented culture, the under-current of symbolism interweaves character and theme into an artistic unit.

Although *A Jest of God* and *The Fire-Dwellers* have been recognized as sister novels from the outset, the connections between them, curiously, have not yet been fully explored.[4] Let us consider first the structural and then the symbolic parallels between *A Jest of God* and *The Fire-Dwellers*.

Although *A Jest of God* won the Governor General's Award in 1966, early critical response to Laurence's first-person, present-tense narrative method was negative. In "Lack of Distance," Robert Harlow "applaud[s] with only one hand," judging, "this book is a failure": Rachel's character is "carpeted wail-to-wail with her failures…. The reader, instead of identify-ing, finds himself (herself, too, I should think) silently shouting at her to get some eye-liner, save for a mink, strong-arm a man, kill her mother and stop bitching"(189–90).[5] Clara Thomas judges that "artistically, as a novel, it slides out of balance. Because everything comes through Rachel's consciousness and because her mind is so completely, believably, neurotically obsessed, she cannot really see the world around her or the people in it" (*Margaret Laurence* 51). That, of course, is the point: Laurence shows us a schizophrenic character waking up to reality, as the narrative method recreates this development dramatically. Laurence defends her narrative method thus: "*A Jest of God*, as some critics have pointed out disapprovingly, is a very inturned novel. I recognize the limitations of a novel told in the first person and the present tense, from one viewpoint only, but it couldn't have been done any other way, for Rachel herself is a very inturned person" ("Ten Years" 21).[6]

Laurence's use of narrative method in *A Jest of God* mirrors Rachel's dilemma perfectly. The protagonist is her own narrator: "the thin giant She" (7) is our I/eye in both senses. As she relates her inner and outer experience, the narrative forms an exercise in psychoanalysis, for Rachel is in dire need of therapy. Hanging on to sanity by her fingernails, she is obsessed with fear of madness: "Am I doing it again, this waking nightmare? How weird am I already? Trying to stave off something that has already grown inside me and spread its roots through my blood?" (24). Consciousness for Rachel is "*Hell on wheels*," and she is bound to the clock's nocturnal circling as to a cosmic Catherine wheel (24). Oblivion is preferable, or at least the little death of sleep, for Rachel inhabits a nightmare world, which she describes in surrealistic pictures: "The darkening sky is hugely blue, gashed with rose, blood, flame pouring from the volcano or wound or flower of the lowering sun. The wavering green, the sea of grass, piercingly bright. Black tree trunks, contorted, arching over the river" (91–92). Laurence says "we must attempt to communicate however imperfectly, if we are not to succumb to despair or madness" (Killam, *Jest* as cited from *Long Drums* 124–25). *A Jest of God* records Rachel's struggle to save her sanity and survive in a sometimes insane world.

Nick Kazlik is not the only character with a phantom twin, for Rachel is a "divided self," in the terms of R.D. Laing. The 1969 film version of *A Jest of God*, directed by Paul Newman and starring Joanne Woodward, was appropriately titled *Rachel, Rachel*, for there are indeed two Rachels, and they live in two different worlds, seen through opposite ends of a telescope: "I have no middle view. Either I fix on a detail and see it as though it were magnified—a leaf with all its veins perceived, the fine hairs on the back of a man's hands—or else the world recedes and becomes blurred, artificial, indefinite, an abstract painting of a world" (91). Doubly divided, Rachel addresses herself as a separate person, saying, "We have discussed this a long time ago, you and I, Rachel" (77). Her ultimate humiliation occurs when two adolescent aliens overhear her address her image in a washroom mirror, saying, "Maybe it wasn't the sun" (159). She sees herself reflected in a glass window wearing her white hooded raincoat, like the negative of a photograph (35)—her own *döppelganger*. Scarcely a "material girl," she is not sure if she is even alive.

Rachel hardly inhabits the real world, so threatening does it appear. In her paranoid state, she interprets a former student's innocent greeting as hostility (62). Her former "children," grown into adolescents, appear to her as Venusians, with their jewelled eyes and candy-floss hair, invading her planet earth, dispossessing her (18). Instead, she lives in her own imagination, in the "deep theatre" (97) of the mind, where "I dramatize myself" (10). But this inner theatre is dangerous too, for the paranoid Rachel imagines "an unseen audience ready to hoot and caw with a shocking derision" (101). Not even the star of her own drama, the heroine of her own life, Rachel is an uneasy extra, fearing ridicule. Nor is she in control of her private theatre, for the willed masturbation fantasy of the "shadow prince" (25) gives way to the involuntary nightmare of the kingdom of death, where corpses powdered like clowns stare at her with glass eyes, their rouged lips twitching to mock her terror (25).

Laurence wants to help women find their own voice, to give her heroines "the gift of tongues" (32), but Rachel's voice is stifled in interior monologues. Her only real outcries are silent screams like Munch paintings, rendered in emphatic italics: "*My God. How can I stand—*" (23). When she does speak, it is in artificial or borrowed voices: the "Peter-Rabbitish voice" of a simpering schoolmarm (11) or the "robot's mechanical voice" (54) of the dummy she feels she is, or, most insidious of all, an echo of "Mother's voice, lilting and ladylike" (84)—and false: "Whoever said the truth shall make you free never knew this kind of house" (106). Not until the turning point of the novel will Rachel's inner and outer voices unite, when she enters the real world. Meanwhile, the only person she can talk to is a God she claims not to believe in.

Repressed, Rachel is like a volcano ready to explode. Her own voice, long stifled in the crypt on Japonica Street, finally surfaces in cryptic cries in the Tabernacle of the Risen and Reborn (35), where the "*gift of tongues*" has been given to the congregation. Rachel's friend Calla Mackie explains, "We hold ourselves too tightly these days, that's the trouble. Afraid to let the Spirit speak through us. Saint Paul...says *I thank my God I speak with tongues more than ye all*. And what about *the tongues of men and of angels*? What else does *the tongues of angels mean, if not glossalalia?*" (33). Rachel fears that Calla will "suddenly rise and keen like the Grecian women wild on the hills" (37), but it is Rachel who finds her tongue: "Not Calla's voice. Mine. Oh my God. Mine. The voice of Rachel" (43). But the outburst is abortive, for Rachel rejects it as hysteria, along with Calla's kiss, proffering love (44).[7]

The voice of Rachel is "mourning for her children" (187).[8] A childless spinster, Rachel calls her pupils "my children" (8), although she knows she must not. She mourns most for James Doherty, the creator of *splendid* spaceships, where astronauts ascend ropes "like angels climbing Jacob's ladder" (12). Since Rachel, unlike his mother Grace, has no right to touch him with tenderness, her repressed affections erupt in an act of violence, as she strikes him across the face with her wooden ruler, causing a river of blood, emblem of vitality, to stream down his face—prefiguring the Wachakwa River Valley where James likes to play hookey and where Rachel will come to life by learning to love (58–59).[9]

In both sister novels, a love affair with a man of different ethnic background provides the catalyst for the heroine's development.[10] Rachel has a summer romance with Nick Kazlik, a high-school teacher from Winnipeg visiting his parents in Manawaka for the summer. The Scots Presbyterian spinster from the right side of the tracks envies the indigent Ukrainians for having more fun—"Laying girls and doing gay Slavic dances," mocks Nick (94). Appropriately, "the milkman's son" awakens "the undertaker's daughter" (73), a modern sleeping beauty, on the banks of the Wachakwa River. "As private as the grave" (96), this tomb becomes a womb for Rachel, delivering her from the mausoleum of her Cameron Funeral Home. By making love to her, Nick gives Rachel "the gift of tongues," so that she can finally speak, touch, and love—even herself. Since Nick "inhabits whatever core of me there is" (153), Rachel learns to live in her own body at last, no longer wearing her hands "like empty gloves" (15).

Realizing that she can give houseroom to another creature, she says, "If I had a child, I would like it to be yours," echoing her Biblical namesake's cry, "*Give me my children*" (154). Nick's response, "I'm not God. I can't solve anything" (154), is a lesson to Rachel.[11] When Nick mysteriously disappears, after showing her a shadowy boyhood snapshot, Rachel realizes, "He had his own demons and webs" (197). Driven by parental pressure to replace his dead brother by inheriting the dairy farm from his father, "Nestor the Jester," Nick quotes Isaiah: "I have forsaken my house—I have left mine heritage—mine heritage is unto me as a lion in the forest—it crieth out against me—therefore have I hated it" (116). Rachel has a parallel problem: Laurence writes, "She tries to break the handcuffs of her own past, but she is self-perceptive enough to recognize that for her no freedom from the shackledom of the ancestors can be total" ("Ten Years" 21). Rachel has learned more than she realizes from Nick Kazlik.

Stacey's sense of identity is not as shadowy as Rachel's, but it has been badly bruised and battered in the marital wars. Somebody's wife, somebody's mother, somebody's daughter, and somebody's sister, Stacey has forgotten who she is: "I'm not myself" (156). She asks, "Who is this *you*?" and replies, "I don't know" (159). She begins to doubt that she even exists, "now that I'm not seen" (138). An invisible woman, she looks into the mirror "to make sure I'm really there" (132). She dreams that she is carrying her own severed head into the forest (115), suggesting the severing of her essence from her existence.[12]

Caught between her past name, "Stacey Cameron," and her present label, "Mrs. C. MacAindra," she addresses herself by various epithets, from "dream girl" (170) to "female saint" (231), from "clown" (122) to "doll" (189), from "idiot child" (177) to "rotten old bitch" (9). She also addresses herself in various voices, inquiring, "Who're you? One of your other selves" (106). Impatient with her Jiminy Cricket character, she exclaims, "Bugger off, voice" (189). Like Rachel, Stacey has no one but herself to talk to, except "God, Sir," although she is unsure of his existence. Bliss for Stacey means "no voices. Except yours, Stacey. Well, that's my shadow. It won't be switched off until I die. I'm stuck with it, and I get bloody sick of it, I can tell you" (158–59).

In *The Fire-Dwellers*, Laurence elaborates the fictional techniques that she developed in *A Jest of God*, manipulating narrative and structure skillfully to dramatize a crazily complex culture and the efforts of the individual to survive in a society that swamps her: "Narration, dreams, memories, inner running commentary—all had to be brief, even fragmented, to convey the jangled quality of Stacey's life" ("Gadgetry" 86). Communication is a central theme,[13] emphasized by the fact that Stacey's youngest child, Jennifer Rachel, her "flower," does not speak: the breakthrough of the novel occurs when Jen turns to her mother and inquires casually, "Want tea, Mum?" (273). Stacey cannot communicate with any of her children: "I can't get through the sound barrier" (203), she complains, as she contemplates "All your locked rooms" (198). Stacey's relationship with her eldest daughter Katie epitomizes the generation gap: a hangover from the jitterbugging generation of boogie-woogie, Stacey is "a stranger in the now world" (274)—the sixties counterculture of marijuana and flower power.

The major communication gap, however, occurs between Stacey and her husband Mac, who has escaped from frenetic family life into an underground cave inside his skull, where Stacey cannot follow (24): "whatever the game happens to be, its a form of solitaire for Mac" (44). The couple's communication gap is sexual as well as verbal: "in bed he makes hate with her, his hands clenched around her collarbones and on her throat until she is able to bring herself to speak the release. *It doesn't hurt*" (150).

Ostensibly *The Fire-Dwellers* is told in the third person, for Stacey is not the official narrator of her own experience that Rachel is in *A Jest of God*. But Laurence insists in "Time and the Narrative Voice" that *The Fire-Dwellers* "is really a first-person narrative which happens to be written in the third person, for the narrative voice even here is essentially that of the main character" ("Time" 155).[14] Stacey's salty vernacular, which Laurence calls "my own idiom" ("Ten Years" 22), does dominate the narrative, but her vivid undercurrent of imagery is just as poetic as Rachel's. *The Fire-Dwellers* is also as schizoid as *A Jest of God*, since Laurence creates a counterpoint of viewpoints, alternating first and third-person narrative techniques, as Stacey contradicts each actual utterance with a tacit comment introduced by a subtle dash: "These lies will be the death of me" (34), she fears; "God forgive me a poor spinner" (119), for "My kingdom extendeth it from lie to shining lie" (177). Stacey is split like Rachel in character and experience: she exclaims, "Help, I'm schizophrenic" (106), because "What goes on inside isn't ever the same as what goes on outside" (34), and it is always a shock to be transported "Out of the inner and into the outer" (161). Significantly, Stacey writes two letters home to her mother, the actual one and the imaginary one, as she wonders "what would happen if just for once I put down what was really happening?" (138).

Laurence symbolizes this schizoid existence by the mirror motif introduced on page eight of the novel, where "Stacey sees mirrored her own self in the present flesh," next to her wedding photograph (8). The real and unreal war in mirrors as on television, where newsreels of the war in Vietnam appear as unreal as western serial violence: "The full-length mirror is on the bedroom door. Stacey sees images reflected there, distanced by the glass like humans on TV, less real than real and yet more sharply focused because isolated and limited by a frame" (7). But Stacey is in control of her perspectives, whereas Rachel is the victim of psychic forces beyond her control. An escape artist, Stacey left the manacles of Manawaka far behind, emerging from the mausoleum of the Cameron Funeral Chapel. Stacey recalls her farewells: "Good-bye to Stacey's sister, always so clever. (When I think you're still there, I can't bear it.) Goodbye, prairies" (12). Stacey's children force her to keep a hold on reality, unlike Rachel, who realizes, "They think they are making a shelter for their children, but actually it is the children who are making a shelter for them" (56).

Counterpointing inner and outer realities is only the beginning in this novel, however. In *The Fire-Dwellers*, Laurence combines this technique used in *A Jest of God* with another method employed in *The Stone Angel*. The past is everpresent for Laurence's characters, and Stacey, whom Laurence calls "Hagar's spiritual grand-daughter" ("Ten Years" 22), counterpoints past and present in a series of memories indicated by indentation (11). Reminiscence becomes psychoanalysis, as Stacey lays the ghosts of her past, recognizing that her heritage from her parents' past will be her legacy for her children's future.

Laurence considers the form of *The Fire-Dwellers* wider than *A Jest of God*, including "third-person narration as well as Stacey's idiomatic inner running commentary and her somewhat less idiomatic fantasies, dreams, memories" ("Ivory Tower" 22). Parallelling Stacey's memories of the past are her fantasies of the future—daydreams and nightmares which Laurence presents in italicized paragraphs counterpointed with the actual occurrences (22). Many are science fiction fantasies, but none is more farfetched or poignant than this one: "*Out there in unknown houses are people who live without lies, and who touch each other. One day she will discover them, pierce through to them. Then everything will be all right, and she will live in the light of the morning*" (85).

The catalyst for overcoming Stacey's identity crisis and communication gap is the same as Rachel's—a summer romance. At the depths of her despair, upset by Mac's suspicion that she has gone to bed with his best friend Buckle Fennick, Stacey heads, as always when in need of spiritual sustenance, straight for the sea. Luke Venturi, an Italian dressed in an Indian sweater with Haida totems of eagle wings and bear masks (162), materializes beside her, fearing that she intends to drown herself. A cool counterculture type, sometime fisherman and science fiction writer, he invites her into his borrowed A-frame filled with fishnets where he dispenses, if not tea and sympathy, then "coffee and sex" (206). Every housewife's fantasy figure, he listens and loves—with no strings attached, assuring Stacey that "You're not alone" (165), that real mothers do cry, that *everything really is all right*. Fortified by fantasy come to life, Stacey can go home again to cope with her realities, for Laurence believes that "You have to go home again" (*Diviners* 324).

Both sister novels are very rich in symbolism, for Laurence employs titles, epigraphs, songs, names, and settings as clues to her themes. Both novels open with nursery rhymes. Rachel's rhyme reflects her duality:

The wind blows low, the wind blows high
The snow comes falling from the sky,
Rachel Cameron says she'll die
For the want of the golden city.
She is handsome, she is pretty,
She is the queen of the golden city. (7)

Poignant in its multiple implications, the song suggests the discrepancies between Rachel's repressive reality and her liberated ideal. The symbol of a golden city, echoed in the hymn "Jerusalem the Golden" (48), signifies Rachel's goal, but she fears the winds of fate that will waft her thither. Inserting her name *Rachel Cameron* into the song emphasizes her Cameron ancestry, as well as her Biblical namesake, mourning her lost children. But Rachel is not ready to be a mother, for she is still an infant, as Calla's continual epithet *child* (52) emphasizes. Hearing her "children" sing the same song that she sang in the same schoolyard twenty-seven years ago reinforces our impression that Rachel is entombed in a perpetual childhood in the mausoleum of the Cameron Funeral Home.

Settings are symbolic in Laurence's Manawaka novels, and Rachel's existence above the mortuary where her father reigned as king of the dead emphasizes her living death, even though she denies the facts of death: "No one in Manawaka ever dies, at least not on this side of the tracks. We are a gathering of immortals. We pass on, through Calla's divine gates of topaz and azure, perhaps, but we do not die. Death is rude, unmannerly, not to be spoken to in the street" (19–20). Rachel is a zombie, resembling a ghost in her white hooded raincoat. No wonder one suitor, a travelling salesman in embalming fluid, like an Egyptian Pharaoh's gravedigger, admired her for her "good bones" (23).

Both sister novels employ identical time settings, beginning with the approach of summer, and concluding with the onset of fall. Laurence makes rich use of seasonal and landscape symbolism, as well as imagery of flora and fauna. Calla, named for the lily, but brash as a sunflower (15–16), initiates the motifs of spring and rebirth by proffering Rachel "a hyacinth, bulbously in bud and just about to give birth to the blue-purple blossom" (15). "April is the cruelest month" for Rachel, recalling her humiliation at being ridiculed as a "peeping Thomasina" (85), outcast from life's feast by the young lovers when she crouched to smell the crocuses on the hill beyond the cemetery: "*I wandered lonely as a cloud*—like some anachronistic survival of Romantic pantheism, collecting wildflowers, probably, to press between the pages of the *Encyclopaedia Britannica*" (86).

Characters are also symbolized by birds and animals, emblems of the threat they represent to the paranoid Rachel. Willard Siddley, the sadistic school principal, appears to Rachel as a reptile (14); her mother May, named for spring, looks like "a butterfly released from winter" (46); and Nick slithers out of his flannels "like a snake shrugging off its last year's skin" (97)—like the slippery figure he turns out to be. Rachel's self-images are, of course, the most telling: she views herself as "a lean greyhound" (46), "a giraffe woman" (81), or as "gaunt bird[s]" (121)—an awkward "ostrich" (183), a "crane" (121), or "a tame goose trying to fly" (136), for she has yet to try her wings.

A Jest of God, almost as full of birds as *A Bird in the House*, is also inhabited by angels, birds of a different feather. Calla whistles, "*She's Only a Bird in a Gilded Cage*" (53), suggesting that Rachel's situation is symbolized by her canary's gilt cage. The canary is clearly a symbol for Rachel: Calla calls him Jacob, name of the Biblical Rachel's husband: "So-named because he climbs the ladder all the time. He won't sing. No ear for music. All he does is march up and down that blasted ladder.... Maybe the angel at the top can't be seen by me" (143). Like Jacob, Rachel has not yet found her voice; the question will be, can she see the angel at the top of her ladder? She does imagine angels, but they are the "Angel of Death" (100) or the "Angel-makers" of abortionists, until she eventually progresses to "a joke about an angel who traded his harp for an upright organ" (132).

The most important animal in *A Jest of God* is Jonah's whale, which provides the epigraph to the novel in this stanza from Carl Sandburg's "Losers":

> *If I should pass the tomb of Jonah*
> *I would stop there and sit for awhile;*
> *Because I was swallowed one time deep in the dark*
> *And came out alive after all.*

Resurrection from what Laurence calls "the tomb-like atmosphere of her extended childhood" ("Ten Years" 21) is essential for Rachel. The winds of tempest that God sent to engulf Jonah are also overwhelming Rachel. Stretched out in her bathtub, with its "claw feet taloned and grasping like a griffin's" (143), she considers her "flesh does have a drowned look" (145), as she recalls *The Tempest* and *Moby Dick*. Jonah cried, "The waters compassed me about, even to the soul" (Jonah 2:5), and Rachel also fears she has "drowned" (145). Like Jonah, Rachel will be rescued from the belly of the whale, but not until she has suffered a sea change.

Laurence echoes the Biblical Jonah in the name of Hector Jonas, the new proprietor of the mortuary downstairs. Rachel enters the whale's belly when she descends the forbidden steps of her early nightmare down to the land of the dead (25). The courage required to confront her fear of death, "the skull beneath the skin" (128), gives her the nerve to express herself: for the first time in her narrative, her inner and outer voices unite when she says to Hector, "Let me come in" (125). The Japonica Funeral Chapel is a comically grotesque Hades, resembling a cartoon version of "Ye Olde Dungeon" (124), presided over by a "comic prophet, dwarf seer" (131), who leads Rachel, a Persephone figure, "like a bride up the aisle" (132) of his Chapel of death in a parody ritual resurrection.

Rachel has always been haunted by the ghost of her dead father, and, to penetrate his mystery, she must quest him in his own kingdom. But she searches in vain among the green glass bottles for clues to his secret. Desperate, she turns to Hector Jonas to solve the mystery of her missing father. His reply, "he had the kind of life he wanted most" (131), prompts Rachel's recognition: "*The life he wanted most. If my father had wanted other-wise, it would have been otherwise. Not necessarily better, but at least different. Did he ever try to alter it? Did I, with mine?*" (131). Finally she realizes that she must be the author of her own life. Having accepted the fact of death, she now has the courage to face the facts of life.

But Rachel has another lesson to learn. Softened by Hector's sympathy, Rachel weeps—an outburst as significant as her first orgasm with Nick—when Hector serenades her with this saccharine song echoing her *"golden city"* (7):

> *There is a happy land*
> *Far far away—*
> *Where saints and angels stand*
> *Bright, bright as day—* (133)

Touched by her newfound vulnerability, Hector—named incongruously for the Trojan warrior prince—shares his own sore point (or Achilles heel) with Rachel: "At the crucial moment my wife laughs. She says...I look funny" (134). Hector's confession prompts Rachel to see another human being from inside for the first time: before, "Hector's eyes are lynx eyes, cat's eyes, the green slanted cat's eyes of glass marbles" (130), echoing her nightmare (25); but now, "I look into his face then, and for an instant see him living there behind his eyes" (134). Encouraged by this communion, Rachel aborts her compulsion to apologize and replaces it with appreciation (134). Having reached the turning point in her development, Rachel climbs the stairs out of Hades back to life.

But she has not yet emerged from the belly of the whale. A putative pregnancy provides the crucible in which Rachel is ground: "There are three worlds and I'm in the middle one, and this seems now to be a weak area between millstones" (100). Torn between her private desire for birth and the public need for abortion, Rachel agonizes: "*What will become of me*" and "It can't be borne" (166). Suicidal, she settles down with lethal legacies from both parents—a bottle of her father's whiskey and fourteen of her mother's sleeping pills—one for each of Rachel's years as a spinster schoolteacher in Manawaka and Jacob's years of labour for his Rachel. Realizing, "*They will all go on in some how, all of them, but I will be dead as stone and it will be too late then to change my mind*" (176–77), she tosses the pills onto the mortuary lawn, where they belong.

In the belly of the whale, she falls on her knees and prays to God, the "last resort": "*Help me*" (177)—like Jonah, who "prayed unto the Lord his God out of the fish's belly...out of the belly of hell cried I, and thou heardest my voice" (*Jonah* 2:1-2). But Rachel does not hear any reply: "If You have spoken, I am not aware of having heard. If You have a voice, it is not comprehensible to me. No omens. No burning bush, no pillar of sand by day or pillar of flame by night" (177). She finally realizes, "There isn't anyone, I'm on my own. I never knew before what that would be like. It means no one. Just that. Just—myself" (171). Rachel rejects death for the sake of the embryo she believes is "lodged" within her bonehouse (179). Realizing, "I could bear a living creature" (169), she elects life for herself and her offspring: "Look—it's my child, mine. And so I will have it. I will have it because I want it and because I cannot do anything else" (177). As a result of choosing to bear a child, with all the trials that must involve for a single woman, Rachel develops into an independent, responsible adult. She even liberates herself from her chains of guilt when her mother plays her trump card, a weak heart: "My mother's tricky heart will just have to take its own chances" (183).

Here comes the punch line, the jest of God of the title: Rachel is not gestating life but death. She imagines that Doctor Raven's waiting room is "death's immigration office and Doctor Raven some deputy angel allotted to the job of the initial sorting out of sheep and goats, the happy sheep permitted to colonize Heaven, the wayward goats sent to trample their cloven hoofprints all over Hell's acres. What visa and verdict will he give to me? I know the country I'm bound for, but I don't know its name unless it's limbo" (183). Doctor Raven, well named for a harbinger of death, sends her plummeting into purgatory when he discovers that she is incubating not an embryo but a tumour. "How can non-life be a growth?" (187), she questions. Overwhelmed like Jonah by the waters of grief, a new voice wells up from the depths of her spirit: "My speaking voice, and then only that other voice, wordless and terrible, the voice of some woman mourning for her children" (187)—the voice of Rachel. Surgery proves that "Doctor Raven was right, dead right" (189): the growth was a deadly, not a living one. Stretched on a metal table like the one in Hector's mortuary, with her feet strapped in the stirrups to ride birth, Rachel delivers death.

This is the ultimate jest of God, for the decision that cost Rachel so much seems all for nothing. However, the tumour is not *malignant* but *benign*—like God Himself, for Rachel does give birth—not to an infant but to an adult self. She has also gained a child, for she realizes "I am the mother now" (191, 203). God has the last laugh, but Rachel finally gets the joke. She has always been terrified of being foolish: "I'm not a fool" (52), she insisted, and "I can't bear watching people make fools of themselves" (34). She said, "If I believed, I would have to detest God for the brutal joker He would be if He existed" (48). St. Paul taught, "*If any man among you thinketh himself to be wise, let him become a fool, that he may be wise*" (141). Rachel has taken a long time to develop a spiritual sense of humour: embarrassed by her sexual awkwardness with Nick, she said, "All right, God—go ahead and laugh, and I'll laugh with you, but not quite yet for a while" (121). Finally, she gets the joke: "All that. And this at the end of it. I was always afraid that I might become a fool. Yet I could almost smile with some grotesque lightheadedness at that fool of a fear, that poor fear of fools, now that I really am one" (188). Having become a fool, she can now be wise—wise enough to pity the Joker: "God's mercy on reluctant jesters. God's grace on fools. God's pity on God" (209).[15]

Like Jonah and Job, Rachel has survived her suffering and learned joy, as she recalls the words of the Psalm: "Make me to hear joy and gladness, that the bones which Thou hast broken may rejoice" (208). The novel concludes with embarkation, as Rachel sets out on the road of life with her "elderly child" (208). Finally allowing the winds of fate to waft her, she sets off for her "golden city," en route to reunion with her sister Stacey in a new spirit of freedom, combining optimism with realism in an affirmative vision of the future: "Where I'm going, anything may happen.... The wind will bear me, and I will drift and settle, and drift and settle. Anything may happen, where I'm going" (208–9).

Stacey's journey parallels Rachel's artistically, for Laurence employs the title, epigraph, and opening nursery rhyme of the novel to symbolize Stacey's development. The title, *The Fire-Dwellers*, introduces the central symbol of the purgatorial flames that Stacey must endure before she can be saved.[16] Stacey's prototype, the Emperor Nero, who fiddled while Rome burned, underlines the main emblem of fire in this epigraph drawn from Carl Sandburg's "Losers":

> *If I pass the burial spot of Nero*
> *I shall say to the wind, "Well, well"—*
> *I who have fiddled in a world on fire,*
> *I who have done so many stunts not worth doing.*

The familiar nursery rhyme that opens Stacey's narrative emphasizes the fire motif further, while applying it to Stacey's situation as wife and mother:

> *Ladybird, ladybird,*
> *Fly away home;*
> *Your house is on fire,*
> *Your children are gone.*

This insidious little rhyme is repeated at three significant points in the novel: at the beginning (7), at the turning point (209), and at the end (280), structuring the entire narrative. The significance of the rhyme is double-edged for Stacey, the original Ladybird (13), suggesting both her desire to escape from the trap of her four walls and her fear that Providence will punish her for her sins through her most vulnerable point, her children, hostages to fortune.

The theme of Judgment (270) is underlined by the motif of thunder and lightning, echoed comically in the name of Thor Thorlakson, the phoney god of thunder, and Valentine Tonnerre, French for thunder, who will free Stacey from her false god. "I seem to believe in a day of judgment" (241), says Stacey, the original sinner. Recalling the fire that burned Piquette Tonnerre with her children, she fears the same fate for her own offspring: "Piquette and her kids, and the snow and fire. Ian and Duncan in a burning house" (241). Fear of fire fuels her paranoid fantasies: "The house is burning. Everything and everyone in it. Nothing can put out the flames. The house wasn't fire-resistant. One match was all it took" (141). Her first fantasy involves a forest fire, where she must traverse a tree bridge across a bottomless void, but she can rescue only one of her children from the fire, while she hears the voices of the other three calling to her from the flames—*Stacey's choice* (30–31).[17]

Stacey's world is on fire both literally and figuratively, internally and externally. Firey by nature, Stacey was always warned by her mother, "*you must learn to bank your fires*" (194). Surrounded by flaming red-haired MacAindras indoors and "the eternal flames of the neon forest fires" (154) outdoors, smothering her own flames proves difficult. Sexually and emotionally unsatisfied in her marriage, she recalls, "Better to marry than burn, St. Paul said, but he didn't say what to do if you married *and* burned" (193). Stacey is burned literally when she scorches her hand on the red-hot burner of her stove, branding her palm with two crescent lines—"My brand of stigmata. My western brand. The Double Crescent" (130)—recalling the crucified Christ.[18]

But it is not just Stacey's inner world that is burning; the whole outer world is in flames, as the news is constantly reminding us in capital letters:

EVER-OPEN EYE...MAN BURNING. HIS FACE CANNOT BE SEEN. HE LIES STILL, PERHAPS ALREADY DEAD. FLAMES LEAP AND QUIVER FROM HIS BLACKENED ROBE LIKE EXCITED CHILDREN OF HELL. VOICE: TODAY ANOTHER BUDDHIST MONK SET FIRE TO HIMSELF IN PROTEST AGAINST THE WAR IN (116)

"*Doom everywhere*" (58) is Stacey's impression, recalling "the fall of Rome" (117), when Nero fiddled. She watches transfixed as Napalm spreads its stain across an infant's face on a newscast (90), and listens appalled while a disembodied voice recounts another Vietnamese village burned or American city aflame.

The torch of war is carried back into the past and forward into the future: Stacey recalls her father's Great War, with his tears over the boy caught between the legs by an exploding shell, as well as her husband's Second World War, with the mine blast that left him forever responsible for the life of Buckle Fennick. Forecast of the holocaust triggers her fantasies, as she imagines escaping to the northern wilderness with her family. Her two lethal legacies from her undertaker father are, appropriately, "firewater" and firearms: she has saved his army revolver as a souvenir so that, in case of a cataclysm, she can dispatch the final thunderbolt that will free her offspring from suffering. Eventually, the purgatorial flames that persecute Stacey will become a refining fire from which she will emerge, if not purified, at least tempered.

The antidote to fire is water: after trying to drown her sorrows in spirits, Stacey awakens with a hangover, thinking, "Help. Water. Water. I'm dying of thirst" (104), but her need for healing water is spiritual as well as physical. If Stacey's nightmares involve fire, her daydreams concern water. Stacey lives in the "jewel of the Pacific Northwest" (10), and the first time she escapes from her "Home Sweet Home" (104), she heads straight for the waterfront, where she admires the freeflying gulls. Birds are a symbol of the spirit in all of Laurence's writing, and Stacey, living now on Bluejay Crescent, recalling her past persona whirling in the Flamingo Dance Hall, sees the seagulls as "prophets in bird form" (13), although vultures, the "tomb birds" (270), also threaten.

Fish, inhabitants of water, do not fare so well as waterbirds, if we think of Tess Fogler's goldfish, symbol of "Nature red in tooth and claw": "Dog eat dog and fish eat fish" (92), Stacey thinks, when Tess recounts watching the big fish eat the little fish, revealing the depths of her sickness (191). Fish symbolism is sinister for Stacey, always a strong swimmer (161), who envisions herself as a mermaid (15). Significantly, Luke calls her "merwoman" (166)—appropriately, for Stacey's thoughts are freefloating, like seaweed underwater:

> Everything drifts. Everything is slowly swirling, philosophies tangled with the grocery lists, unreal-real anxieties like rose thorns waiting to tear the uncertain flesh, nonentities of thoughts floating like plankton, green and orange particles, seaweed—lots of that, dark purple and waving, sharks with fins like cutlasses, herself held underwater by her hair, snared around auburn-rusted anchor chains (34)

Stacey's happiest memories are of lakes, as she recalls her first love-making with the airman from Montreal on the shores of Diamond Lake (71) and her Edenic honeymoon at Timber Lake, where she said to Mac, "I like everything about you," and he replied, "That's good, honey. I like everything about you too" (38). Regretting the loss of the loons from Diamond Lake, with their "voices of dead shamans, mourning the departed Indian gods" (159), she fantasizes about escaping with her family from the firey cataclysm to a cool lake up north in Cariboo country.

Timber Lake features in her "death wish" (14) also, for it is there that she drowns her father's infamous revolver. Like Rachel, Stacey sometimes longs for oblivion. She sings an escapist song that echoes the saccharine hymn with which Hector serenades Rachel in the underworld:

There's a gold mine in the sky
Faraway—
We will go there, you and I,
Some sweet day,
And we'll say hello to friends who said goodbye,
When we find that long lost gold mine in the sky.

Faraway, faraw-a-ay— (129)

In the depths of her despair, Stacey is blinded by tears of sympathy for her father-in-law Matthew, when he repeats the Psalm, "*Save me, O God, for the waters are come in unto my soul*" (164). But Stacey does not drown; like Rachel, she suffers her own significant sea change—a "change of heart" (221).

Stacey's lover Luke, a fisherman named for the Apostle, seems to Stacey "like the rain in a dry year" (187), bringing salvation. Surnamed Venturi, suggesting adventure, Luke offers to fulfill her escape fantasy by taking her north with him to Cariboo country. A fisher of souls, he invites her to blissful oblivion by crossing the Skeena River on a ferry driven by a "Charon" figure (208). Confronted by choice, Stacey knows she can never abandon her children. Mocking her sense of responsibility, Luke repeats the Ladybird rhyme for the second time (209), as Stacey decides, "I have to go home" (209). She returns home to a reprieve: sensing disaster, and fearing that Ian has died for her sins, she is forgiven when Mac explains, "Stacey—it's not Ian…. It's Buckle" (211). But Stacey does not escape disaster that lightly, and the motif of drowning is not yet finished, for her favourite, Duncan, is almost drowned at the seashore. Blinded by salt tears, she watches the seawater pump from his mouth until she hears him utter the infant wail of a newborn (267–68).

Finally, Mac confronts his ultimate fear, Stacey's suicide stunt, by asking her what she did with her father's revolver. Rejecting "pre-mourning" in favour of affirmation, she threw the gun into Timber Lake, drowning death, like Ethel Wilson's "Swamp Angel"—Excalibur in reverse. Ultimately, Stacey and Mac are reconciled and truly make love for the first time in the narrative, for Stacey has realized that Mac is not really an alien other or Agamemnon King of Men, but a person, like herself, who needs support and sympathy as much as she does.

At the conclusion of The Fire-Dwellers, Stacey repeats the Ladybird rhyme for the third and last time, thinking, "Will the fires go on, inside and out? Until the moment when they go out for me, the end of the world" (280). Speaking of her sister novels, Laurence writes, "Optimism in this world seems impossible to me. But in each novel there is some hope, and that is a different thing entirely" ("Sources" 15). So Laurence does not promise the reader perfect happiness, but Stacey has surfaced from her despair and survived: as she falls asleep on the eve of another decade, she prays, "Give me another forty years, Lord, and I may mutate into a matriarch" (281)— "Hagar's spiritual grand-daughter" indeed.

So both sister novels end with acceptance and affirmation, as Rachel and Stacey, having laid to rest the ghosts of the past and survived the present, are ready to embark on the future. Reconciled with the people they live with, but accepting their human limitations, they are ready for a change. At the end of *The Fire-Dwellers*, Stacey, who has recently given houseroom to Mac's aging father, receives a letter from Rachel announcing that she is moving to the coast with their elderly mother (276). Anticipating reunion, Stacey and Rachel realize that they can forgive each other for living. "Sisters under their skins," [19] they may even learn to feel for each other the compassion that their creator has taught us to feel for both of them.

Notes

1. G.D. Killam writes in his "Introduction" to *A Jest of God*, "The principal characters in the Canadian novels…live in almost total isolation from the world around them, unable to give expression to their most profound desires and concerns…."

2. "Only connect," the epigraph to E.M. Forster's novel *Howards End*, could serve as the epigraph to most of Laurence's novels also.

3. The final stanza of Sandburg's "Losers" suggests the kind of good losers or even tragic heroes that he had in mind:

    > I could ask people to throw ashes on their heads
    > In the name of that sergeant at Belleau Woods
    > Walking into the drumfires, calling his men,
    > "Come on, you…Do you want to live forever?"

4. When this paper was originally composed for the Margaret Laurence Memorial Conference in Brandon, Manitoba in 1988, there were few articles on either novel and none comparing them. Subsequently, numerous interesting essays have been published about each, but Coral Ann Howells is one of the first critics to explore their connections.

5. Patricia Morley responds to Robert Harlow thus:

    > Harlow misses the multiple voices of Rachel, who thinks and voices a very complex self…. The first-person point of view subsumes the many voices of Rachel, while the larger fictional form contains an ironic, implicit commentary through event, image, juxtaposition, and the reactions of the other characters. (90)

6. George Bowering writes, "The form of the novel, first person and present tense, works as Rachel's opening-out does, to get naked" (211). In "Gadgetry and Growing: Form and Voice in the Novel," Laurence says of *A Jest of God*:

> I tried again and again to begin the novel in the third person, and it simply would not write itself that way.... the character of Rachel would not reveal herself. So finally I gave up and stopped struggling. I began to write the novel as I really must have very intensely wanted to write it—in the first person, through Rachel's eyes. I knew that this meant the focus of the book was narrow—but so was Rachel's life. (84–85)

7. See van Herk's discussion of "The Eulalias of Spinsters and Undertakers."
8. These issues are developed further in *Rachel's Children*.
9. A nosebleed figures in *The Fire-Dwellers* also (232).
10. See Helen Buss's discussion of Laurence's dark lovers.
11. Stacey makes a similar remark to Mac about Buckle Fennick's death: "You're not God. You couldn't save him" (240). Laurence remarks to Donald Cameron that, as a novelist, you must "realize that you are *not* God" (104).
12. Christl Verduyn observes, "*The Fire-Dwellers* reflects a number of the predominant themes which have emerged in contemporary feminist writing" (134).
13. Laurence told Cameron, "I feel that human beings ought to be able, *ought* to be able to communicate and touch each other far more than they do, and this human loneliness and isolation, which obviously occurs everywhere, seems to me to be part of man's tragedy" (105). See C.M. McLay's "Every Man Is an Island: Isolation in *A Jest of God*."
14. F.M. Watt judges: "This book contains flaws enough to sink half a dozen books by lesser novelists.... *A Jest of God* stuck to the discipline of a single point of view; here the shifts to third-person narration are the technical aspects of the novel's lack of artistic rigour." Laurence explains:

> I did not want to write a novel entirely in the first person, but I did not want to write one entirely in the third person, either. The inner and outer aspects of Stacey's life were so much at variance that it was essential to have her inner commentary in order to point up the frequent contrast between what she was thinking and what she was saying. ("Gadgetry" 86)

15. Bowering concludes "That Fool of a Fear" eloquently: "God's jests are not just vocal—the word is made flesh, i.e., the eternal present. It is in understanding this that Margaret Laurence chose wisely to write in the present tense, to present the fool made wise by folly" (225).
16. A latter-day Hedda Gabler, Laurence says of her problems with *The Fire-Dwellers*, "I even once burned, dramatically, nearly a hundred pages of a second draft, and then sat down at my typewriter and wrote a deeply gloomy letter to a friend, which began 'I am a firebug'" ("Gadgetry" 87).
17. These issues are developed further in *Stacey's Choice*.
18. Alan Bevan discusses the "fire-hell symbol hunt" (xi).
19. Rudyard Kiping's 1896 poem "The Ladies" employs the refrain, "For the Colonel's Lady an' Judy O'Grady / Are sisters under their skins!"

9

ORPHAN AND AMPUTEE

The Search for Ancestors in *The Diviners* and

Wallace Stegner's *Angle of Repose*

In Margaret Laurence's *The Diviners* and Wallace Stegner's *Angle of Repose* the protagonists set out in search of ancestors. On one level they are engaging in traditional quests, seeking their forebears as confirmation of their own identities, but, more particularly, ancestors serve to focus their searches through the past for guidance in solving specific problems that confront them in the present. Morag Gunn and Lyman Ward are trying not simply to find their ancestors but to consult them.

These novels also invite comparison in other ways. Both Laurence and Stegner consistently sought to understand character in terms of heritage, family, and generational ties, Laurence throughout her Manawaka novels and Stegner in the novels and stories that extend from *The Big Rock Candy Mountain* (1938), which recreates his Saskatchewan childhood, to *Recapitulation* (1979), which closes his family saga. Both were novelists of the West, and each is increasingly recognized as the most accomplished prose writer in her or his region. *The Diviners* and *Angle of Repose* are their most critically acclaimed novels, and both have received national recognition, Laurence's novel winning the Governor General's award in 1974, Stegner's the Pulitzer Prize in 1971. These are arguably the best novels of the

Canadian and American Wests. They are also the novels in which Laurence and Stegner moved from more traditional forms toward contemporary metafictional narrative strategies. Morag and Lyman are both middle-aged writers secluded in rural cottages, composing the narratives that become the texts we read, and for each the creation of the narrative is itself the primary means of searching, of securing the past, interrogating it, and inducing it to yield up an understanding of the present.

Predictably, the differences that are thrown into relief by those broad similarities provide the most illuminating comparisons of these texts. Morag's and Lyman's stories differ in obvious ways. Lyman is an historian turned biographer, fictionalizing the documented evidence of his grandparents' lives as nineteenth-century pioneers in the American West. Morag is a novelist telling a story not primarily about a previous generation but about her own past, which begins in the Canadian West and includes her life-long search for what ancestors represent—an inheritance that can help her to define herself and address her present life. Their narrative searches differ less obviously than their stories but in equally systematic ways that reflect not only the personal, class, and gender differences of the narrators but characteristic differences in the cultures of the two Wests that have formed them.

These narrative differences are crystalized in two pairs of metaphors with which Laurence and Stegner represent their protagonists' relations to the past and the interaction of past and present. Lyman Ward is an amputee who regards his own condition as a metaphor for a modern world cut off from the past, particularly from the West his grandparents helped to build. He says at the outset, "As a modern man and a one-legged man, I can tell you that the conditions are similar. We have been cut off" (13). Morag is an orphan whose condition can also be metaphorically extended; her ancestral past is not simply cut off but dead, gone, leaving not even substantial documentary traces. Each protagonist is also given a kinetic metaphor for the passage of time and the observer's relation to the past. Morag is fascinated by an optical illusion on the river outside her window where a southward current is rippled by northbound winds to produce the appearance of a stream flowing both ways, and she interprets it as a metaphor for the interpenetration of past and present. Lyman is fascinated by the Doppler Effect, the phenomenon of sounds having a higher pitch when their source (such as a moving train) is approaching the listener than when it is going away. He later takes this as a metaphor for the differences in perspective, especially emotional perspective, given to events when they are approaching from the future or receding into the past.

These metaphors embody basic assumptions about time and the past that underlie Morag's and Lyman's searches and their ways of constructing narratives of discovery.

As the metaphors suggest, both protagonists are denied their pasts, blocked in distinct ways from possessing them. Lyman finds himself personally cut off, from his career by retirement and from marriage by his wife's sudden desertion at the time of his amputation. But he is also suffering what Stegner describes elsewhere as the common fate of western Americans, cut off from the past not only by their modernity but by their national mythology:

> Millions of westerners, old and new, have no sense of a personal and *possessed* past, no sense of any continuity between a real western past which has been mythicized out of all recognizability and a real western present that seems as cut-off and pointless as a ride on a merry-go-round that can't be stopped. ("History" 199)

The frontier myth of separation and beginnings, effective as a strategy for declaring America's independence from European history, has also obscured any local history with which western Americans might connect the prosaic present, and Lyman must reclaim his family past from the inscribed values of that myth before it can yield a meaning for his own life.

Morag has the opposite problem. She is both personally and culturally orphaned, with neither the generational continuity of family nor a public myth of origins that would place her in meaningful relation to her world. When Morag is a child, her foster-father, Christie Logan, feels obliged to invent a mythic past for her, and his tales of the clan Gunn are soon challenged by her reading of history. Morag's problem, like Lyman's, is nationally typical; as Robert Kroetsch has said, Canadians refuse to agree upon a "meta-narrative" that would assign meaning and value to their past ("Disunity" 21). Especially after their rejection of the British myth of empire, they are left, like Morag, with a plurality of contending narratives of meaning. Morag's lost parents, like the ubiquitous disappearing fathers in prairie fiction generally, are suggestive of this postcolonial condition in which history has abdicated or derelicted the ancestor function of defining the individual in a meaningful continuity. Morag, as she narratively reconstructs her past, can understand its meaning as a basis for her present actions only by discovering its generational and historical continuity.

Lyman Ward can be seen struggling with the frontier myth both consciously and unconsciously in his own life and writing. As he says, "When frontier historians theorize about the uprooted, the lawless, the purseless, or the socially cut-off who settled the West, they are not talking about people like my grandmother" (246). Susan Burling Ward is a sophisticated illustrator and writer, an intimate of nineteenth-century eastern literary society, whose work is sought by the most prestigious journals and publishers of her time. Her husband, Oliver Ward, is an engineer, also of good family, who pursues his dreams of achievement across the West from one idealistic failure to another. Their lives contradict the Turnerian narrative of a people descending to the primitive on the frontier and regenerating civilization in a form purified and authenticated by Nature. Lyman is at pains to dispell such "dubious assumptions" about the early West, about Adamic beginnings and "intractable self-reliance amounting to anarchy" (117). As he says, "Contrary to the myth, the West was not made entirely by pioneers who had thrown everything away but an ax and a gun" (35). His grandparents' lives depended on "continuities, contacts, connections, friendships, and blood relationships." With heavy irony he points out that "the West of my grandparents, I have to keep reminding others and myself, is the early West, the last home of the freeborn American. It is all owned in Boston and Philadelphia and New York and London" (133). Lyman's reading of western history is thus nearer to that of Earl Pomeroy, who emphasizes continuity, or to Patricia Limerick's *Legacy of Conquest* than to Frederick Jackson Turner's frontier thesis.

A second irony in Lyman's comment is that he must keep reminding *himself* of the gap between the myth and the actuality. The a-historical perspectives of his present environment reiterate the Adamic narrative—in the social science of his son Rodman, who "starts all fresh from his own premises" (13) and the utopian dreams of the Berkeley counter-culture of the 1960s. Lyman is eloquently scornful of those who imagine that they can reject history, tradition, and the "merely cultural": "How marvelously free they are! How utterly deprived!" (247). Yet he must still remind himself, because he has internalized many of the values of the frontier paradigm. The very act of establishing his research and writing in his grandparents' secluded cottage in Grass Valley is ambiguous. The ancient wisteria vine that embraces the cottage is a reassurance to Lyman that he is connecting himself tangibly with an organic past, but by isolating himself and resisting his son's help and his ex-wife's overtures, he is also clinging to frontier values of independence, freedom, and "intractable self-reliance." He is rejecting the "continuities, contacts, connections, friendships, and blood relationships" in the present that could restore his amputated life. Lyman faces a more difficult struggle with the effects of the frontier metanarrative internally than in his recuperation of western history.

Morag could equally be said to struggle with the consequences of her postcolonial history, with the absence of that one narrative that could define her. Her own narrative recapitulates that struggle as, in part, a search for literal and figurative ancestry. It begins with the repetition of a ritual, reviewing a handful of photographs of herself and her parents taken before the beginning of her connected memories. Morag recalls creating around these traces an evolving fiction of a conventionally happy and secure childhood. In her remembered Manawaka childhood, by contrast, Morag is excluded or marginalized as the foster-daughter of the town garbageman, and Christie's tales of Piper and Morag Gunn leading her ancestors from the Highland Clearances to the Selkirk Settlement give her something larger with which to identify. But Morag discovers that her past exists as a multiplicity of narratives: Christie's tales, her own inventions, Jules Tonnerre's Métis tales of the North West Rebellion that contradict Christie's, her school history that contradicts both. In her adolescent uncertainty, Morag even attempts briefly to identify with the ongoing social narrative of her puritanical Anglo-Scots prairie town. Once Morag conceives of herself as an aspiring writer, she finds she has a larger, more remote and ideal cultural heritage. Her escape to university and her marriage to her English professor, Brooke Skelton, represent attempts to identify with that literary heritage. Unfortunately, in her marriage she achieves only a colonial relation to that inherited culture; she is Brooke's newfound land, and must remain without a past and therefore without character or voice.

Morag's narrative thus recalls her earlier pursuit of a sequence of larger narratives of meaning in which she hoped to find herself expressed, but there is a turning point in her remembered quest. When she attempts to make a symbolic connection with her Celtic heritage by a pilgrimage to Sutherland, where her people came from, Morag stops just short of visiting the actual land, having learned something about her postcolonial identity:

> "It's a deep land here, all right," Morag says, "But it's not mine, except a long long way back. I always thought it was the land of my ancestors, but it is not." (415)

Morag does not claim to be able to explain this paradox, saying only that "The myths are my reality. Something like that" (415). She is discovering that what was real in her childhood was not the historical Sutherlanders but Christie's invented tales about them. Morag is developing a postcolonial awareness of the gap between actualities and the myths and cultural fictions that inscribe meanings on them. The land of her ancestors, she says, is "Christie's real country. Where I was born" (415). Morag is thus redefining "ancestors," not as literal progenitors of her blood but as those whose lives have made her what she is. The past that can explain her to herself lies in the Canadian West she has tried to escape, and with this realization Morag can at last turn homeward. She is emerging from a colonial condition in which she accepted her place in myths of colonization; those myths are now contained as parts of their own narrative of origins. At the intersection of all the contending narratives of her ancestral past she must formulate her own narrative of meaning, her own private mythology, to achieve a "personal and possessed past."

Morag's and Lyman's narratives of the past, while they tell very different stories, are both working out similar conflicts between separation and continuity, between independence and relationship, the divergent routes to self-realization or identity Carol Gilligan distinguishes in *In a Different Voice*. Orphan and amputee are both in obvious need of connection or reconnection, yet both are torn by contradictory impulses. Lyman is stubbornly resistive; in the eyes of his relatives, he is a "damned old independent mule-headed" fool; Morag's past is a record of severance from actual relationships in pursuit of identity with abstract or ideal ancestry and culture.

Lyman works through his conflict in the biography of his grandparents in ambivalent relation to the frontier myth. The contending impulses toward severance and relation therefore assume the form of familiar binaries of the frontier paradigm: man-woman, West-East, nature-culture, mobility-stasis, silence-words. In keeping with the hierarchies that these binaries inevitably become, Lyman cannot resist mythologizing Oliver Ward as western man, questing after transcendent achievement in the natural world, battling with the serpent earthbound destiny by opening new mines in the Rockies, devising new mining technologies, inventing a hydraulic cement to be exploited by eastern entrepreneurs, initiating a vast irrigation project in Idaho years before its time. Susan Burling Ward is eastern woman, exiled from gentility and intellectual stimulation, using her language and her art to appropriate each crude frontier to the styles of eastern culture, and struggling against their transience to preserve some semblance of continuity, of home and domesticity for their children. Lyman regards their conflict as inevitable. Oliver's identity is dependent on separation, beginnings, and transcendence; he has what Susan terms "the incurable Western disease. He had set his cross-hairs on the snowpeak of a vision, and there he would go, triangulating his way across a bone-dry future, dragging her and her children with him, until they all died of thirst" (328). Lyman sympathizes with Susan but sees her position as equally intractable: "So much that was cherished and loved, women like her had to give up; and the more they gave up, the more they carried it helplessly with them" (246). Susan is aware that just as Oliver's identity depends on transcendence hers as inevitably depends on continuity and relationship. In letters to her eastern friend she complains of "how we lose the sense of our individuality when there is nothing to reflect it back upon us" (89) and how "each move leaves me less myself" (409).

Canadian readers will recognize one of their own ancestors, Susanna Moodie, in Susan Burling, and will even find in her the same ambivalence toward the new land as potentially Eden or desert, but Moodie is situated differently in her own narrative than Susan is in Lyman's. Susan is not simply bound by loyalty; she is helpless before Oliver's heroic western silence and what she admires as his masculine strength: "It was his physical readiness, his unflusterable way of doing what was needed in a crisis, that she most respected in him: it made him different from the men she had known" (208). In the western context (historical or mythic) his are the higher virtues, and she feels the need to apologize for trying to make him over and to make him communicative: "I'm a foolish woman. I'm too much in love with talk and talkers. Talk isn't that important" (234). Yet the laconic Oliver also has innate good taste, and, like Owen Wister's Virginian, can offer sanative literary criticism that the cultivated eastern woman must recognize as sound (111). Lyman overtly honors his grandmother's civilized values, but the frontier metanarrative silently inscribes its heavily gendered values on the action of his story.

It might be expected that in western fiction, even removed from the American frontier, a similar pattern of questing male and domestic woman would assert itself. Robert Kroetsch, for example, has argued that the "basic grammatical pair in the story line (the energy-line) of prairie fiction," is horse:house, symbolizing motion:stasis, masculine:feminine ("Fear" 76). But the oppositions in Morag's narrative refuse to conform to any such binaries. Morag is herself a questing figure, while most of her men—Christie, Brooke, Dan McRaith—are static by comparison. Morag begins the search for her identity with a series of separations and beginnings, escaping from the constrictions of Manawaka to university, "Going to the whole world," as she imagines, then to Toronto with Brooke in a marriage that requires that she deny her own past. For Brooke, her appeal depends on her "'mysterious nonexistent past.'" In that relationship, Morag is West, virgin land; Brooke is East, culture, refinement, the Old World; Morag is silenced, and silence is not strength. Morag escapes constriction again, going west to Vancouver in search of independence and the freedom to develop her identity, her voice as a writer. In some respects Morag resembles a western hero "setting his cross-hairs on the snow-peak of a vision," but Laurence is not merely inverting the familiar binaries; she is breaking them down, denying their conventional logic. Morag rejects a subservient domestic role, but she wants a child, and at the breakup of her marriage she conceives that child with her first lover, Jules Tonnerre. As a Métis from Manawaka, Jules is more identified with the West and with Nature than Morag, and he too is mobile, an artist in song questing after his mixed-blood identity. Morag does not want marriage to Jules, but she does make their daughter, Pique, the centre of her life. In the story of Morag's past, the primary conflict between separation and continuity does not fit gender or other stereotypes and cannot be resolved into an either or choice; separation and relationship are equally essential to her identity. Morag cannot go back to the prairies but realizes that the voice within her that must find utterance is the product of Christie's language and her Manawaka past.

Morag's and Oliver Ward's quests are ironic in slightly different ways. Oliver exhibits the western phenomenon Howard Lamar has called "the mobility of defeat," as he is driven from one failed project to another. Oliver's coming to rest in Grass Valley as manager of the Zodiac Mine is not a fulfillment but merely his "angle of repose," that Lyman defines as the angle on a talus slope at which rocks and dirt stop rolling. Morag's journeying, like that of so many Canadian protagonists, is ironic in the sense that it is circular, a venturing out that unexpectedly enables her to find her way home. In the midst of her wandering, Morag has reflected on the necessity of this circular journeying:

> You Can't Go Home Again, said Thomas Wolfe. Morag wonders now if it may be the reverse which is true. You have to go home again, in some way or other. (324)

At the furthest extent of her journey, where she looks across the firth to Sutherland, she realizes where home is, and she can then secure her ancestors by returning to accept Christie as a father at the time of his death.

Morag achieves her balance of independence and relation, but not by returning, physically, to the prairies. Presumably, settling in Manawaka itself would pose a threat to that balance, but since she must go home "in some way or other," she chooses to return to what the prairies represent in her private mythology: the pioneer sources of a separate New World reality. Morag identifies the necessary mythic qualities in the cottage she buys at McConnell's Landing in southern Ontario:

> Land. A river. Log house nearly a century old, built by a great pioneering couple, Simon and Sarah Cooper. History. Ancestors. (439)

Here are the spiritual as distinct from biological ancestors Morag has sought, and as the narrator remarks on another occasion, "adoption, as who should know better than Morag, is possible" (458). Among the figurative ancestors the orphan Morag adopts is Catharine Parr Traill, the nineteenth-century pioneer settler and naturalist writer with whom she carries on a running, half-ironic dialogue. Traill was a more adaptable gentlewoman than her sister Susanna Moodie, and her approach to pioneering hardships is both a reassurance and a spur to Morag: "'In cases of emergency, it is folly to fold one's hands and sit down to bewail in abject terror. It is better to be up and doing'" (109). Traill is the ancestor Morag most directly consults.

In both *The Diviners* and *Angle of Repose*, narratives of past and present are interwoven, and their actions converge upon the present situation with a kind of inevitability beyond each narrator's conscious intent. Morag's entire exploration of her past is triggered by the departure of her eighteen-year-old daughter, Pique, who is hitch-hiking west. It is not a formed intention that sends Morag in search of those neglected snapshots from the past that had "never agreed to get lost." It is rather that "something about Pique's going, apart from the actual departure itself, was unresolved in Morag's mind" (13). In a sense her recalling is a search for that "something" that can be found only in her own past, and in the same sense the purpose of the entire narrative is to work out that mother-daughter relationship. The tension between independence and relation in her narrative of the past shadows a tension in the narrative present between holding Pique and letting her go. It is not until Morag recognizes in her own story of separations an indirect and paradoxical search for continuity, not until she finds in her journeying a pattern of return, that she can accept Pique's going. The "something" about Pique going west is resolved when Morag recognizes her own quest in her daughter's need to explore her mixed heritage—East-West, white-native—and reconcile the contending narratives that never quite define her. The present narrative ends with Pique's setting out again, this time for Galloping Mountain and her mixed-blood kin, but Morag, having completed the past narrative of her return to "ancestors," can at last say to herself, "Let her go. This time, it had to be possible and was" (464).

Lyman Ward is at first not merely uncertain but mistaken about his motives for researching the lives of his grandparents. He believes his interest in the past has taken over because he has no interest in the future, and he denies that his project has anything to do with what he calls "the Ellen business," his dismissive term for his wife's sudden betrayal at the time when bone cancer had crippled and disfigured him. But, like Morag, he is searching: "Many things are unclear to me, including myself" (12). Only gradually does he recognize the convergence of his past and present preoccupations. When he explains to his son that he is not writing about western history but about something else, "a marriage, I guess," (186), he surprises himself:

> I have never formulated precisely what it is I have been doing, but the minute I say it I know I have said it right. What interests me in all these papers is not Susan Burling Ward the novelist and illustrator, and not Oliver Ward the engineer, and not the West they spent their lives in. What really interests me is how two such unlike particles clung together, and under what strains, rolling downhill into their future until they reached the angle of repose where I knew them. That's where the interest is. That's where the meaning will be if I find any. (186–87)

Lyman, even then, does not consciously register the coincidence with his own marriage, though the main question his research may answer is whether and in what way Susan Burling Ward was unfaithful to her husband.

Later Lyman questions his motives more directly, asking "Is it love and sympathy that makes me think myself capable of reconstructing these lives, or am I, Nemesis in a wheelchair, bent on proving something—perhaps that not even gentility and integrity are proof against the corrosions of human weakness, human treachery, human disappointment, human inability to forget?" (391). At this point, four-fifths of the way through his research, Lyman begins to suspect the parallel not only between Susan's supposed act of betrayal and Ellen's but between Oliver's years of cold and silent reproach and his own bitterness and lack of charity toward Ellen, whose second husband has died and who appears to be seeking a reconciliation with Lyman. He still does not understand why, as he approaches the crisis of his grandparents' marriage, he finds he is getting "half stoned before lunch," though he questions himself about his drinking for more than a page of the text. Nor does he know why the inferences he draws from his fragmentary evidence favour Oliver and place the blame for his grandparents' marriage breakdown mainly on Susan. When he creates a scene of seduction between Susan and her husband's assistant, Frank Sargent, Lyman admits "I just made up the scene to fit other facts that I do know" (453). In a way reminiscent of Kroetsch's Demeter Proudfoot in *The Studhorse Man*, Lyman turns directly from that scene to imagining Ellen's seduction by the surgeon who amputated his leg. "Touch" he says, "It is touch that is the deadliest enemy of chastity, loyalty, monogamy.... By touch we are betrayed, and betray others.... those surgeon's hands laid on her shoulder in a gesture of comfort that lied like a thief...." (452). It is also after his recreation of Susan's efforts at reconciliation leading to his grandparents' achievement of their "angle of repose" that Lyman experiences his climactic dream of Ellen's visit and threatened return.

In their present circumstances, Morag and Lyman could be said to face the conflict between separation and continuity from opposite sides. Morag is threatened by separation, afraid to let her daughter go; Lyman is threatened by relationship, afraid to let his wife return. They have opposite lessons to learn from the past, and those lessons are reinforced by action in the narrative present. Morag, for example, makes one of her rare contacts with Jules, who is dying of cancer in Toronto, taking to the grave the ancient grief of his people which he has tried to express and to assuage in his songs. Morag sees in him their daughter's need to experience the other side of her heritage, and she heeds his urgent injunction: "You let her be, see? You just let her be" (470). Pique's separation, like those of Morag's own youth, is in pursuit of a larger continuity. Lyman is also provoked by events in the present to reformulate his view of the forces of separation and continuity he has been exploring in his grandparents' lives. He has an ambivalent and often contentious relationship with his editorial assistant, Shelly, a liberated young woman of the 1960s with a complete irreverence for tradition and the "merely cultural." Shelly is attracted to a utopian commune to be founded on a manifesto emanating from the Berkeley Ecology Center and devoted to "a serene and generous fulfillment of natural desires," where children would "grow up as part of the wild life" (458–59). Lyman's impatience with the naivete of the counter-culture provokes a review of his own beliefs that amounts to a personal manifesto:

"I don't think any of them is wise enough to play God and create human society" (462).

"I want to make a distinction between civilization and the wild life. I want a society that will protect the wild life without confusing itself with it" (463).

"Satisfying natural desires is fine, but natural desires have a way of being both competitive and consequential" (461).

"Civilizations grow by agreements and accommodations and accretions, not by repudiations" (463).

Lyman thus endorses his grandmother's position in the conflict he has been chronicling and rejects the frontier paradigm of separation, beginnings, and nature, along with its romantic primitivism and the radical elements of its individualism. His statement about the folly of trying to play God and create human society is, in fact, un-American, a challenge to the enlightenment philosophy on which the revolution was undertaken and justified.

Contact with Shelly also forces Lyman to recognize the unconscious sources of his fear of relationship in the present. He is ill-at-ease with what he calls her "ribald streak," and both titilated and threatened by her "body that flops and lounges." He senses aggression in her "bold-eye," "uninhibited tongue," and her fleshly ease and confidence, especially in the visible pressure of her erect nipples against the front of her pullover. Lyman's reactions betray his unwitting involvement in the gender stereotypes of the frontier myth. His stubborn desire for self-sufficiency, independence, and freedom, like that of the classic frontier hero, entails a fear of women. Women threaten the hero with relationship, domestication, a bond to his mortality, and with feeling. When Shelly attempts to draw out Lyman's feelings for his grandfather, he remarks that "if there is one thing above all others that I despise, it is fingers, especially female fingers, messing around in my guts" (390). Women, at the most basic level, represent the threat of sexuality, and having seen his wife run off with the surgeon who amputated him, Lyman understandably feels his manhood threatened sexually. In his climactic dream, while Ellen attempts to lure him back to relationship and dependence, Shelly intervenes to sexually assault him. Lyman does not interpret his dream, but he concedes it may represent some occult truth about himself (509). It suggests, among other things, an unconscious connection between his "juvenile fantasies of self-reliance" (29), his threatened manhood, and his responses to his grandparents' marriage and his own. Immediately after the dream, Lyman is ready to end his researches and face a reconciliation with Ellen. The amputee is prepared at least to consider a painful suturing together of his past and present in the future.

The second pair of controlling metaphors in *The Diviners* and *Angle of Repose*, the river that flows both ways and the Doppler Effect, embody different assumptions with which the protagonists approach their explorations of the past and their narrative recreations of them. Further, those assumptions confer in each case a different status on the narrative illusion, determining the way in which it can effect the resolution of the protagonists' internal conflicts. Both metaphors propose a dynamic relation to the past. Lyman is "teased" by the physical law that "the sound of anything coming at you—a train, say, or the future—has a higher pitch than the sound of the same thing going away," and he strives through his research to hear Susan Burling Ward's life as she heard it rather than in the receding sound of "expectations reduced, desires blunted, hopes deferred or abandoned, chances lost, defeats accepted, griefs borne" (20). The past can thus be differently perceived by placing the observer strategically in the flux of time, but it remains an immutable, one-way progression. As Lyman observes when he imagines himself intruding on a nineteenth-century drawing-room gathering, "the future is inexorable for all of them," and he is privy to its secrets (29). By contrast, Morag's fascination with the illusion of the river flowing both ways grows out of her awareness of a past created by her "invented memories," her "Memorybank Movies" that have been refilmed and edited in recollection, by the tales of Christie and Jules, and by the school histories. As Morag says,

> A popular misconception is that we can't change the past—everyone is constantly changing their own past, recalling it, revising it. What really happened? A meaningless question. But one I keep trying to answer, knowing there is no answer. (70)

The flux of time is thus not immutable or one-way or even linear, but reflexive, the past and the present ceaselessly recreating each other. The act of recapturing the past is not a matter of point of view and mimesis but of creation. Lyman proceeds from a firm belief that "what really happened" is determined and knowable; as "a historian under the crust" he believes his biography of Susan and Oliver Ward must "stick to the actual" (236). He is slow to recognize the fact that, in Stegner's own words, he "leak[s] his own story inadvertently between the lines" (*Conversations* 77).

These contrasting assumptions about the past generate narrative complexities in both texts. Lyman serves as third-person narrator of his grandparents' story and first-person narrator of his own, intruding into his third-person narration to comment upon it and to address his characters directly. Morag is narrated in the third-person past tense in the narrative present and third-person present tense in the recalled past, but she speaks out in italicized passages of first-person present tense reflection in both. Both texts sustain an ongoing narrative present; that is, scenes of present action in Lyman's and Morag's lives are presented as though the narrators had no knowledge of subsequent events. Both novels are metafictional in the sense that the protagonists draw attention to their own artifice in recreating the past. Almost all Morag's past takes the form of "Memorybank Movies," self-consciously presented as edited reconstructions, while Lyman Ward discusses his fictionalizing of his grandparents' lives, weighing the propriety, for example, of rendering their wedding night in graphically modern detail or with Victorian reticence. He admits his limitations, his inability to guess what the dialogue might be on important occasions, as at a meeting between Susan and the love-struck Frank Sargent: "Having brought them together, I find it difficult to put words in their mouths," and two pages later, "and now I can't avoid it any longer, I *have* to put words in their mouths" (400, 402). The "metafictionality" exists in a tension between Lyman as novelist and Lyman as historian and grandson.

Both texts make use of contained or interpolated forms of narrative. Lyman quotes letters, reminiscences, and published and unpublished essays, reports, and documents, and the entire text is presumed to consist of tape recordings, from Lyman's initial musings to the final twenty-four page dream, which ends with "I reached the microphone off the bed table and told my dream onto tape, for whatever it may be worth, and now I lie here on my back, wide awake, cold from my sweating, the plastic microphone lying against my upper lip and my thumb on the switch..." (510). *The Diviners* contains an astonishing array of interpolated forms, including pictures, memorybank movies, innerfilms (fantasies), self-contained tales by Christie, Jules, and Morag, songs, letters, conversations with Catharine Parr Traill, casualty lists, newspaper reports and ads, and passages from published books.

These myriad complexities, similar in many of their particulars, have opposite effects on the narrative illusions in the two novels. Lyman's documentary evidence reinforces the authority and authenticity of his narrative. To take the process back a step, Stegner was actually working from the papers of the nineteenth-century writer and illustrator, Mary Hallock Foote; hence his thanks on the acknowledgements page to "J.M. and her sister for the loan of their ancestors" (4 and Walsh). The device of the tape recorder also preserves verisimilitude in Lyman's self-revelations; as he says "If I were talking to anyone but myself I would have shut up long ago" (25). Even the attention he draws to his own artifice in recreating the moments of his grandparents' lives works to preserve the primary narrative illusion of Lyman in his cottage in time present speaking into his tape recorder. Lyman may be distanced from the reader emotionally by some of his attitudes, the reader may see Lyman's story "leaking" into the biography before he does, but the implied author, the creator of Lyman, does not show his hand. Lyman comes to the reader apparently unmediated.

Laurence's narrative complexities work to undermine and unsettle the primary illusion. The plethora of interpolated narrative forms and the polyphony of voices they create are sufficient to call into question the act of narration, including that of the primary, third-person narrator of the present action. In that on-going narrative present (narrated in the past tense), the intricacy and reflexivity of narrative point of view generates questions for the reader about who is narrating from what vantage point in time and where the "real" or unmediated actuality lies. The narration begins conventionally enough in the third-person, past tense: "The river flowed both ways," an "apparently impossible contradicton" that "still fascinated Morag." A few lines later we are told "Pique had gone away": past perfect tense, securely locating the action in some time prior to narration. Two paragraphs later, the first-person appears: "I've got too damn much work in hand to fret over Pique." This is not typographically signalled as internal monologue, but the use of first-person present tense is consistent with an intimate focalization within the mind of the narrated Morag in that past time. The next paragraph, however, calls these conventions into question:

Morag read Pique's letter again, made coffee and sat looking out at the river, which was moving quietly, its surface wrinkled by the breeze, each crease of water outlined by the sun. Naturally, the river wasn't wrinkled or creased at all—wrong words, implying something unfluid like skin, something unenduring, prey to age. (12)

Here, the first sentence focuses within Morag's perception of the river, but the second sentence is quizzical. It might be taken, like "I've got too damn much work in hand to fret over Pique," as the musings of the character, one who happens to be a novelist preoccupied with language, but if it is Morag questioning her first perception, it creates the "apparently impossible contradiction" of the narrated Morag in the past being aware of the specific words of the present narration that is creating her. If it is the narrator criticizing her or his own diction, then the narrative illusion is shattered, its artifice deliberately held up to scrutiny. The nameless, third-person narrator is emerging from behind his or her creation to establish separate contact with the reader, as visible first-person narrators sometimes do.

Narration of the ongoing action at McConnell's Landing is further complicated by italicized interventions. In the opening scene, for example, Morag is shown wondering why she has kept her clutch of miscellaneous snapshots:

> These photographs from the past never agreed to get lost. Odd, because she had tried hard enough, over the years, to lose them, or thought she had. She had treated them carelessly, shoved them away in seldom-opened suitcases or in dresser drawers filled with discarded underwear, scorning to put them into anything as neat as an album.... Not realizing that if she had chucked them out...her skull would prove an envelope quite sturdy enough to retain them. (13–14)

Some distance between narrator and focal character is implied by the phrases "or thought she had" and "not realizing." The narrator questions the character's understanding. An italicized passage is then interposed, in first-person, present tense:

> *I've kept them, of course, because something in me doesn't want to lose them, or perhaps doesn't dare. Perhaps they're my totems, or contain a portion of my spirit.* (14)

This is evidently the inner voice of Morag, but speaking when? At that time prior to the narration when, as the past-tense narration puts it, she "searched the house"? If so, how would she be aware of the questions the narrator has raised about her motives? Or does she speak at the time of narration? If so, we are once again presented with the "apparently impossible contradiction" of the past-tense-created Morag entering into dialogue in the present tense with her creator. At times the italicized "I" also refers more explicitly to the narration, as when the idealized childhood she created around the photographs has been described:

> *All this is crazy, of course, and quite untrue. Or maybe true and maybe not. I am remembering myself composing this interpretation in Christie and Prin's house.* (16)

Again, the signalling of time in "I am remembering" is ambiguous; it could be the time of Morag's review of the snapshots or the time of narration.

Readers can, and often do, escape this narratological dilemma by assuming some unusual conditions of narration. First, that the ongoing action at McConnell's Landing and the narration of that action are simultaneous, despite the use of the past tense. Second, that Morag is the narrator of this action, narrating herself in the third-person. The narrated Morag can thus enter into an ongoing dialogue with the narrating Morag, creating a special kind of reflexivity. From either vantage point, in Roman or italic type, Morag can question her written interpretations and her own language. Adopting these suppositions involves relinquishing traditional narrative authority and the realist's seamless illusion in favour of a "bivocal" text, but it preserves an orthodox, linear conception of time.

Unfortunately, this reading strategy does not finally resolve the dilemma, because it is not consistent with what happens in the rest of the text. The narration of the earlier past, the story of Morag's life, is conducted largely in the memorybank movies, set off and identified by headings and commented on in Roman and italic type by the narrating Morag:

> She could not even be sure of their veracity, nor guess how many times they had been refilmed, a scene deleted here, another added there. (36)

Morag's comments again unsettle the authority of these movies and all they contain, but render them consistent, like Lyman's tape-recordings, with the illusion of Morag in her cottage self-consciously calling up the past. The italicized "I," however, intervenes again in this recalled past, when action and narration could not be simultaneous. When Morag is shown, for example, dividing her time in London between Pique and her lover, Dan McRaith, while Dan divides his time between her and his wife, Bridie, she comments on the account of her situation in one such italicized passage:

> Dan is accustomed to that pattern, which presumably suits Bridie, but would not suit Morag.

Looked at that way, it's ideal. Why do I keep on feeling badly about it, then? I hate the fact that Dan's never even seen Pique.... And I'm jealous of his children and of Bridie, having so much of his life. Bridie, apparently cloaked in her disapproving silences. They're not happy together—for God's sake, why don't they part?

Morag's time of distress in London and her re-running of the memory-bank movie about it in McConnell's Landing cannot coincide. The italicized utterance is not apparently from the detached perspective of Morag narrating a decade later, but rather spoken with the passion of immediate involvement in the events. But neither can it pass for the musings of the narrated Morag at the earlier time, because the "I" speaking in the midst of that distress is aware of how her situation is being "looked at" in the present narration. Past and present are not discrete; narrative time is not linear; and there is no representational convention that can accommodate what Laurence is doing with it. Readers who approach the text with conventional expectations do, in fact, suffer confusion about time and sequence.

Laurence sustains this strange and equivocal narrative posture throughout the text, with Morag in the recalled past commenting on the present narrative and Morag in the present action jotting down recollections, such as the reference to the "Halls of Scion" in an old hymn, which become key elements in subsequent narration in memorybank movies (185). The final sentence of the novel confirms our growing conviction that what Morag has been struggling to write during the course of the action is the text we have been reading: "Morag returned to the house, to write the remaining private and fictional words, and to set down her title" (477). Morag is, in a quite postmodern sense, a self-creating protagonist, and her title, we suspect, is *The Diviners*.

Lyman's and Morag's searchers for ancestors proceed from different assumptions about language. As the Doppler Effect implies, Lyman adopts the realist assumptions that history is an immutable progression, though it may be variously perceived from different vantage points. He struggles to resist the frontier narrative of western history, but he believes there is one true past, rooted in "the actual," and that language is, at its best, a transparent medium for conveying the story and the self-evident meaning of that past. The fact that his own story "leaks" into his narration of Susan and Oliver Ward's life is Lyman's failure as historian. Morag is aware that the continual recreation of the past is inevitable, whether in the language of the academic historian, the novelist, the story-teller, the lyricist, or the private memory. As Michel Fabre, Theo Dombrowski, and others have convincingly demonstrated, Morag is intensely preoccupied with language, with its creative power, its limitations, its failures, and its dangers. She credits it with the occasional capacity to achieve "Magic. Sorcery. Even Miracle" (13), yet as novelist she feels ambivalent toward its power: "A daft profession. Wordsmith. Liar, more likely. Weaving fabrications. Yet, with typical ambiguity, convinced that fiction was more true than fact. Or that fact was in fact fiction" (33). Morag's and Lyman's assumptions about the relation between language and truth or reality may reflect the professional commitments of the novelist and the historian, but they are also consistent with differences in the two cultural traditions within which they search for the past. Morag's are the paradoxical assumptions of a decentred postcolonial culture, recognizing a gap between experience and the fictions that impose meaning on it while acknowledging that she lives within a linguistically, culturally constructed reality: "fact was in fact fiction." Lyman's, by contrast, are the product of a centred, ideologically defined culture with its underlying assumption that there must be one unifying narrative of actuality, meaning, and value, rooted in nature or "the actual." Under that assumption, language does not create, but only reflect or distort reality.

The presence or absence of an agreed-upon metanarrative of the West also affects the assumptions with which Morag and Lyman approach the act of narration. A metanarrative, what Robert Kroetsch calls "the shared story" or "assumed story," exists prior to the particular narrative ("Disunity" 21). No fiction of the American West, for example, can be written in the twentieth century without the assumption that both narrator and reader are familiar with the frontier myth. Lyman is able—even obliged —to play his narrative off against that myth. At the same time, the shared story constructs a position of narrative mastery for the teller; he is known to know the story of the West and its meaning, even if he chooses to question its validity or values. Lyman assumes that position of mastery emphatically in the guise of historical scholar. Morag is at an apparent disadvantage in this regard. To begin with, positions of narrative mastery are traditionally occupied by males. Also, her West has no single, authoritative metanarrative. Morag encounters and must contend with the various master narratives of white, European, Christian, capitalist, patriarchal western civilization, but none is specific to her West and none plausibly defines the identity of the orphan ward of the town garbage collector. All would tend to silence her; none would give her the voice she seeks. Morag must inevitably negotiate her narrative authority as well as her subject position among the multiplicity of stories that make up her past. She must therefore gain control of the creating power of language and liberate it from the assumptions that are implicit in the realist illusion of language as transparent medium. Her intricate, atemporal dialogues between narrated and narrating selves are all part of this negotiation. Morag's narration, beginning in skepticism and self-deprecation, can eventually create a self equal to the challenges she faces, complete with adopted ancestors and a private fiction or mythology that assigns meaning and value to the continuity in that she participates.

Ironically, Lyman Ward progressively loses rather than gains narrative authority. Beginning from a presumption of mastery, his narration slips toward a questioning of his objectivity and eventually into a loss of control. As Lyman gradually recognizes his unacknowledged motives for recreating his grandparents' lives, as he begins to suspect he is "bent on proving something," and as his story of Susan and Oliver's marriage converges with his tormented memories of his and Ellen's separation, he becomes suspicious of his own imaginative creation. At one point he says, "I not only don't want this history to happen, I have to make it up, or part of it" (467). In his state of growing agitation, Lyman's repressed fears break through his conscious control in the form of the nightmare that becomes the climactic scene of his narrative. In the face of this frightening, involuntary creation, the conscious, scholarly, authoritative narrator is silenced; Lyman is left with the microphone at his lips, wondering "if there is anything I want to say to myself" (510).

Both Morag's and Lyman's ancestor searches are successful in the sense that they yield the understanding the characters need to resolve their present conflicts between severance and relationship. Morag is able to see her daughter's separation as integral to a larger continuity of generations. Lyman can at least consider forgiveness and reunion with Ellen, not as a diminution but as an enlargement of his manhood. His last words are, "I lie wondering if I am man enough to be a bigger man than my grandfather" (511). But Morag's self-knowledge is more directly and deliberately achieved. Lyman sets out ostensibly to uncover the truth about his grandparents' lives, but his problem is not solved by discovering "what really happened"—for him as for Morag that turns out to be an unanswerable question. Lyman's problem is solved by his being overtaken in his labours by a recognition of the real motives for his search. He has unwittingly been seeking self-justification through finding in his sinning grandmother and his righteous grandfather a pattern for the wrongs he has suffered. As he once says, "Forgiving I have considered, though like my father and grandfather before me, I am a justice man, not a mercy man" (395). His motives have been moral; like the heroes of frontier myth, he is questing after justice. Morag also faces moral issues of injustice, betrayal, and guilt, but the driving impulse of her search is epistemological, a desire to know how she can know. Marital infidelity, for example, which focuses Lyman's sense of outrage, is significant in Morag's narrative primarily as a circumstance to be understood in relation to her and her child, not a question of conventional social morality or even as a private moral question between her and Brooke. Morag does not need moral justification; she needs to know what to do about her child. This difference in the emphasis on ethical and epistemological concerns in the two novels is again consistent with typical differences between the two canons of fiction within which Stegner and Laurence were writing.

Lyman's final dictum about wisdom could apply to both protagonists: "Wisdom…is knowing what you have to accept" (511), but Morag's state of acceptance is more active and more optimistic than Lyman's. The human relationships Lyman anticipates have the look of compromise, as his final interpretation of the novel's title metaphor, the angle of repose, suggests:

> the angle at which two lines prop each other up, the leaning-together from the vertical which produces the false arch. For lack of a keystone, the false arch may be as much as one can expect in this life. Only the very lucky discover the keystone. (510)

Looking forward to a "false" arch, a missing keystone, a static structure, Lyman seems more resigned than reconciled to the prospect of being reattached to his amputated world. Morag's acceptance of separations and endings is more organic and vital because it is generational, and she, too, envisions it in terms of the metaphoric title of her novel. All of the central characters in Morag's story are "diviners" or discoverers of hidden knowledge: her neighbour, Royland, who witches wells, herself as novelist, Christie, with his tales and his "gift" for the "garbage-telling," Jules in his tales and songs, and potentially Pique in her newfound gift for song-writing. From the aging Royland, whom she has adopted as a local "ancestor," Morag learns that the "gift" of divining is just that, something given that can be withdrawn, and that Royland can accept the loss of his divining powers as a sign that he must cultivate the gift in someone to take his place. Morag, as orphan, can recognize this passing along of gifts as the essence of the spiritual ancestry she has sought: "The gift, or portion of grace, or whatever it was, was finally withdrawn, to be given to someone else" (477). *The Diviners*, as it turned out, was Margaret Laurence's last novel, and as Dombrowski has argued, its conclusion with these references to the withdrawal of grace suggests that Morag's (if not Laurence's) divining is over, that she, like Lyman, has arrived at the point of silence. Morag, however, has achieved her place in a continuity of generations, so her voice is passed on, as Christie's voice lives on in her. The effect is not a silencing but a liberation of her voice.

The Diviners and *Angle of Repose* are exemplary without being typical of the fictions written about the two Wests. Unlike most classics of the western American novel, *Angle of Repose* is anti-frontierist, and in more fundamental and systematic ways than most of the parodic and postmodern texts of such writers as John Seelye, Thomas Berger, Tom Robbins, and E.L. Doctorow. Laurence's Morag Gunn is also a more mobile, independent, and anti-establishment hero than is usually found in western Canadian fiction. Readers might reasonably see a convergence of the two streams in these novels. At the same time, the amputee and the orphan are apt metaphors for the distinct kinds of cultural dispossession endemic to a culturally centred, ideologically committed, mythicized West on the one hand and a decentred, postcolonial West on the other. The metaphors of the Doppler Effect and the river flowing both ways also embody contrasting assumptions about time, language, and reality that follow logically from conditions of ideological commitment and from a postcolonial awareness of the gap between actuality and the plurality of fictions that impose meaning on it.

The two novels are perhaps more demonstrably typical of their canons in the nature of the action they generate around the shared central conflict between severance and continuity or independence and relationship. In *Angle of Repose*, as in novels of the frontier, the action, internal and external, is framed dramatically, as a conflict between irreconcilable binaries that can be resolved only by the triumph of one over the other. Lyman can defend the independence of his male ego or accept the need for others, and while acceptance promises to make him "a bigger man than his grandfather," the image of the false arch has the unmistakable air of defeat about it. In *The Diviners*, Morag's story includes external dramatic conflicts with others and with social and economic circumstances, but the essential conflict that must be resolved within Morag herself is framed as a dialectic opposition that cannot be resolved by the triumph of either independence or relationship. That apparent binary must be resolved by Morag's recognition that the two represent necessary, complementary, even mutually dependent impulses. Pique must separate not only for herself but to sustain the continuity of generations, just as Morag must find her place in the

succession of spiritual ancestors. In western Canadian fiction, as in the plu-
ralism of Morag's decentred, postcolonial imagination, dialectic resolutions
are more common than dramatic resolutions.

10

ANGELIKA MAESER LEMIEUX

THE SCOTS

PRESBYTERIAN LEGACY

J.D. Douglas writes in his essay, "Calvinism's Contribution to Scotland,"

> Calvinism has made a deep mark even on those who revolted from it. Some detest it, yet retain grudging admiration of it. The more famous have been in the literary field. One might think of Sir Walter Scott, Robert Louis Stevenson, Robert Burns, John Buchan, even David Hume. All of them, in one way or another, for better or for worse, were haunted by Calvinism, and in their writings returned to it again and again. (235)

To this list may be added Canadian novelist Margaret Laurence, whose writing throughout attests to the lasting imprint made by the Scots Calvinist tradition and her attempt to come to terms with its formative influence upon the lives of many of her characters and that of the larger society they inhabit.

Calvinism, or Puritanism as it came to be known in England and North America, had many nationalistic and ecclesiastical expressions; this must be remembered when considering the body of Reformed theology and ecclesiology known as Calvinism. Many diverse national religious developments and doctrinal positions proceeded from the Genevan reformer's original theory and practise. Thus, what is historically known as Calvinism has differed markedly from the thought of the man whose name has become identified with the various national formations in the Reformed tradition. It is the adaptations of Calvin's theology—subsequent products of a centuries-long process of debate and dissent—that have entered the stream of the Christian Reformed tradition and that have, to varying degrees, eclipsed Calvin. Beginning with Beza, his successors began to initiate changes in doctrine that would, in Basil Hall's words, alter "that careful balance in order to meet new needs or because they had never fully accepted or appreciated the whole range of Calvin's thought"; subsequently, Knox and seventeenth-century English Puritans, "omit[ted] or ignore[d] some of Calvin's essential emphasis to a degree which would have made Calvin deny that they were satisfactory expounders of his teaching" (20). This "going beyond Calvin," in Kendall's opinion, "became known as Calvinism in England" ("Puritan" 201), and Charles Bell contends "that Scottish theology did not remain true to the spirit and tenor of Calvin's teaching, and that the first traces of diversion and subsequent distortion can be found in Knox himself" (8).

The Scots Presbyterian elements of Margaret Laurence's longer fiction can be examined within three categories—moral order, church order, and social order—predominantly within the historic context of nineteenth and twentieth century Presbyterianism in Canada.[1] However, the theological disputes and positions on a variety of issues chequering Scottish church history cannot entirely be avoided in references to Canadian Presbyterianism, largely because of the intense ethnic loyalties and closely maintained links to the parent country and the virtual domination of Scots in colonial Presbyterianism (Moir 144).

I I I

In several interviews Laurence has elaborated upon the formative influence of her Scots Presbyterian background, particularly in relation to its strengths and weaknesses, its tribalism, and its connection with a chapter in Western Canadian history—namely, the role of the Scots in the fur trade and in the later settlement of the Red River.[2] These were themes Laurence would return to repeatedly as she strove to come to terms with the legacy of her ancestors, both those in her immediate memory—the generation of her grandparents and parents—and those of the more distant Old World past. "I think that I came to write about my own background out of a desire—a personal desire—to come to terms with what I call my ancestral past" (Thomas, "Conversation" 66). This has produced what she has called "spiritual" (but not literal) autobiography (Cameron 96–115).[3]

There is a sense in which the private journeys frequently extend into fictional ones and create a conflation of myth and reality, as, for example, Laurence's trip to Scotland that she called "making the obligatory pilgrimage to the town in Fifeshire where my people had come from" (Sullivan 47) and to the Highlands, to Ross and the Black Isle, which finds its parallel in Morag Gunn's eventual journey to the Highlands to discover the origins of Piper Gunn and the victims of the Clearances who came to settle in Manitoba in the early nineteenth century. However, both for author and protagonist of *The Diviners* the physical journey was ultimately less significant than what it confirmed—that the homecoming was spiritual (Sullivan 68; Kroetsch "Conversation" 47) and that home was the Canadian Prairie: "Christie's real country" (*Diviners* 415). Laurence realized, as she said, "that, if I came from anywhere, I came from a small prairie town of Scots Presbyterian stock" (Thomas, "Conversation" 66) and "I had to begin approaching my background and my past through my grandparents' generation, the generation of pioneers of Scots-Presbyterian origin, who had been among the first to people the town I called Manawaka" (Laurence, "Place" 16).

Scots Presbyterians came to Manitoba in substantial numbers only in the period between 1812–15 although some had come earlier in connection with the fur trade. These settlers, as opposed to nomadic traders and frontiersmen who were allied with the Native people through the nature of their work and unofficial marriages to Indian women, were the dispossessed victims of the Highland Clearances brought over to settle the Red River region by Lord Selkirk (Turner 76–91). For many years they unsuccessfully implored the Hudson's Bay Company and the Kirk in Scotland to send them a minister, but it would have to wait until after the Disruption in Scotland of 1843, from whose labour pains the evangelically-oriented Free Church was born, and then shortly thereafter the formation of the Canada Presbyterian Church (1844), for these long-standing pleas to be answered. It was thus the Free Church, both Scottish and Canadian, that took its missionary duty seriously enough to arrange for the eventual posting of the Scot, John Black, in 1851 as the first Presbyterian missionary to Manitoba at Kildonan. Between 1866–1902 James Robertson, another native of Scotland, supervised the work of Church extension on the Western frontier, creating local churches and working tirelessly for the

Presbyterian cause.[4] Thus from the start of the Presbyterian Church's presence in Manitoba, it was dominated by a Free Church spirit with a Calvinistic and evangelical theology (Vaudry 49, 53). By Calvinistic here is meant that body of belief formally expressed in the Westminster Confession that professes a moderated form of Federal or Covenantal Theology (Toon 26–28; Rolston III 11–22; Leith 91–95), and it is this latter influence going back to the early years of the Scottish Reformation in the sixteenth century and to the seventeenth century Covenanters that, I believe, makes itself felt in Laurence's novels. Although she has stated that the Scottish ancestors were not as immediately relevant and real to her as her nineteenth century forbears, that they only constituted something akin to a "Jungian racial memory" for her (Thomas, "Conversation" 66), I would argue that their faith has entered into the collective legacy of Presbyterianism along with later developments. The so-called "bloody-mindedness" of the Scots to which she sometimes refers has its origins, I suggest, in the "ages of darkness and blood," as James Barr describes a chapter in the history of *The Scottish Covenanters*. It was these "roots," "ancestors," and "gods" (Kroetsch, "Conversation" 47) she would confront through the medium of her art and thereby "in some way put to rest the threat that had been there" (Thomas, "Conversation" 66).

These pioneers, of whom she had some first-hand experience in the person of her grandfather, were a tough and rigid lot—"survivors" indeed (Fabre from *The Stone Angel* 193–209; Laurence, "Place" 18; *Diviners* 107)—who had brought their Old World religious traditions with them and the sense of moral, ecclesial, and social order they enshrined: firstly, a moral order that had bearing upon spirituality and conduct; secondly, an ecclesial order, the form of the confessing and worshipping community; and thirdly, a conception of social order that was predominantly conservative, hierarchical, and patriarchal.

In terms of moral order, three related categories should be borne in mind: (1) the universal, (2) the particular, and (3) the ethical. The conviction of faith that the universe in which one lives is supported by God's Providence and governed by law will logically extend to and affect one's spiritual life, relation to God, and ethical conduct. It follows that one's conception of God impinges intimately upon one's own self-understanding, as Calvin noted (35–39; bk.1, ch.1), and that one's spirituality, for better or worse, will reflect the degree to which one comprehends that relationship. One's image of God, conscience, and ability to interpret life meaningfully within a universal frame of reference (a myth of meaning, as Jung would suggest) are part of the interior aspect of moral order, as are the familiar, perennial issues that arise therefrom: faith and doubt, anxiety and assurance, guilt and justification, sin and sanctification.

The sense of a universal moral order, lovingly and providentially sustained by God at every moment, uninterrupted even by man's sinfulness (Bryden n.p.; Douglass 24–26), has been severely shaken and obscured for Laurence's protagonists. While some critics have correctly noted a "providential design" (Thomas, *Manawaka* 88, 170; Russell, "God and Church" 435–36; "Margaret Laurence" 245–48) operative in her novels, it must be pointed out that her characters are for the most part unaware of it and only come—if at all—with great difficulty to a belief in Providence. Even Morag, who, it may be argued, is in her middle-age the most spiritually intuitive and receptive of the heroines, must constantly be nudged by Royland to "have more faith" (*Diviners* 34, 115). Rather, the moral order in the world is depicted as too stultifying, too neat and tidy (*The Stone Angel, A Jest of God, A Bird in the House*) or else catastrophically destroyed (*The Fire-Dwellers* and *The Diviners*). Both possibilities obscure the Presence of God—that which will neither be boxed in by human conceptions nor vitiated by human evil.

We obtain the impression of the overly-civilized or cultivated order in *The Stone Angel*'s opening pages where the "tough-rooted…wild and gaudy flowers" are

> held back at the cemetery's edge, torn out by loving relatives determined to keep the plots clear and clearly civilized, for a second or two a person walking there could catch the faint, musky, dust-tinged smell of things that grew untended and had grown always, before the portly peonies and the angels with rigid wings, when the prairie bluffs were walked through only by Cree with enigmatic faces and greasy hair. (5)

This man-imposed moral order identified with the town is opposed to the order of nature where love, sexuality, and freedom become human experiential possibilities. The moral order of freedom of the spirit becomes possible for Rachel as she leaves for Vancouver at the end of *A Jest of God*.[5] Furthermore, the instinctive need of each individual to order life meaningfully, to discern a moral design, and to express it creatively may be hampered by the imposition of a static and repressive formalism that is at variance with a providential order of grace. This is seen in Vanessa McLeod's observation that, contrary to her grandmother's dictum "God loves order," she believes "whatever God might love in this world, it was certainly not order" (*Bird* 61). But the grandmother's conception of order, as Michael Darling has shown, is one of emotional repression and emotional self-denial, whereas Vanessa's own attempts to arrive at a moral ordering of her experiences "disproves [her] conclusion…. For as a narrator, the God-like recreator of life, she has ordered her memories and achieved some kind of unity out of the apparent disorder of her past" (Darling 202). This substitution of a dynamic, creative order for a static and repressive one appears to be what Laurence herself has accomplished in her fiction when she says, "Every serious writer is a moralist, and I am no exception" (*Margaret Laurence, First Lady of Manawaka*).

The other depictions, namely of moral order destroyed, figure in *The Fire-Dwellers* and *The Diviners*. Stacey's society—Vancouver in the 1960s—is portrayed in apocalyptic imagery; the entire social and moral fabric of the world is in tatters as the ravages of war, militarism, imperialism, the drug plague, and other evils threaten to destroy civilization in which all of us, by extension, are "fire-dwellers." This world conjures up a Yeatsian poetic association of "The Second Coming" in which "Things fall apart; the center cannot hold;/ Mere anarchy is loosed upon the world,/ The blood-dimmed tide is loosed, and everywhere/ The ceremony of innocence is drowned…" (210–11). Demonic forces of annihilation and vice are in apparent control of this hellish world. Stacey feels that the historical present is "like the fall of Rome" (117) and in her nightmare "she and Mac listen to the guards' boots. The legions are marching tonight through the streets and their boot leather strikes hard against the pavements and there is nowhere to go but here" (236).

Morag, in *The Diviners*, thinks, "The world seems full of more hazards now. Doom all around. In various shapes and forms" (35). One of these forms that reveals the breakdown of the moral order is the widespread destruction of the environment about which Morag frequently laments: "Soon there will be no more elms left" (12) and, in one of her imagined conversations with Catharine Parr Traill:

> I don't have your faith. In the Book of Job it says *One generation passeth and another generation cometh, but the earth endureth forever.* That does not any longer strike me as self-evident. I am deficient in faith, although let's face it, Catharine, if I didn't have *some* I would not write at all or even speak to any other person…The evidence of your eyes showed you Jerusalem the Golden with Milk and Honey Blest, at least if a person was willing to expend enough elbow grease. No plastic milk jugs bobbing in the river. No excessive algae, fish-strangling. The silver shiver of the carp

crescenting. My grandchildren will say *What means Fish?* Peering through the goggle eyes of their gasmasks. (186–87)

Small wonder that she thinks of the present generation as "children of the apocalypse" (*Diviners* 12).[6] What, we may ask, is the God-image that underlies these two disturbing versions of moral order in the world—one that is repressive, providing but a brittle veneer of stability, and the other that is inoperative, presaging a frightening collapse?

Kenneth Russell in his article, "God and Church in the Fiction of Margaret Laurence," concludes that "The God who rules here is a tall, threatening patriarch, the upholder of a strict law that clouds life and all its joys" and "the projection of [strong male figures] and their values (445–46).[7] Clara Thomas accounts for this same portrait by virtue of the difficult lives pioneers of all sects had in settling the frontier:

> [E]verything men and women found in pioneer experience would also confirm their belief that their God required hard service, not rejoicing, as the land demanded battle and did not repay love. The God who presided over their bleak lives must have seemed to the pioneers remarkably analogous to the Old Testament Jehovah, God of war and wrath and judgment. (Thomas, "Conversation" 66)

Thomas also attributes such a conception of deity to a Calvinism which

> shifted the balance of the Christian gospel from a message of hope, love, and redemption, to one of guilt, death, and damnation, backwards from the Christ of the New Testament to the Old Testament God of wrath and retribution. It was also particularly compatible with the entrepreneurial spirit of capitalism. (65)

While Thomas is correct in positioning the religious understanding of the pioneers within their immediate historical and environmental experiences of survival (for only the strongest could survive), the negative stereotypical representation of "the Old Testament God" (Yahweh) is misleading and unfairly one-sided.[8]

Rather than emphasizing an "Old" versus "New" Testament binary opposition, it might be more useful to examine how enculturated gender polarization enters into the representation of divinity in Laurence's novels. Clearly, the divine being is portrayed in terms of gender attributes that are reflective of a broken humanity: powerful, mean, tyrannical and rigid images of the masculine are associated with the Father (patriarchy) and weak, gentle, suffering and passive images of the feminine principle are connected to Jesus who, within a cultural context of patriarchal Protestantism, has to carry the repressed image of gentleness and victimization. The degree to which this culturally and historically perpetuated gender dualism has become pathological is revealed in the sadistic/masochistic character configuration presented in the God images.

In the years of her early religious education at Sunday school, Morag's God-image underwent a bifurcation as the harsh qualities were assigned to the Father and the gentle ones to the Son, thus making the Son the weaker person and victim of the all-powerful Father's wrath:

> Morag loves Jesus. And how. He is friendly and not stuck-up is why. She does not love God. God is the one who decides which people have got to die, and when Mrs. McKee in Sunday school says God is LOVE, but this is baloney. He is mean and gets mad at people for no reason at all, and Morag wouldn't trust him as far as she could spit. (87)

> Jesus is another matter. Whatever anybody says of it, it was really God who decided Jesus had to die like that. Who put it into the head of the soldier, then, to *pierce* his side? (*Pierce*? The blood all over the place, like shot gophers and) Who indeed? Three guesses. Jesus had a rough time. But when alive, He was okay to everybody, even sinners and hardup people and like that. (88)

Elsewhere, she describes the pictures of "Jesus with a Bleeding Heart, His chest open and displaying a valentine-shaped heart pierced with a spiky thorn and dripping blood in neat little drops" (154). She first sees this image at the Tonnerre shack and later again at Mrs. Crawley's house:

> Above Morag's bed, when she moved in, there hung The Bleeding Heart of Jesus. It looked familiar, and then she remembered—the Tonnerres' place. Even without this, the picture would have been hard enough to endure. Jesus with a soft, yielding, nothing-type face and a straggling wispy beard. His expression that of a dog who knows it is about to be shot. As usual in these pictures, the Heart Itself is shown in violent purplish red, His chest having apparently been sawn open to

reveal It, oozing with neatly symmetrical drops of lifeblood, *drip-drip-drip*. All tear-shaped. (191)

Lest we conclude that only Catholics have a monopoly of this image, it must be pointed out that the Heart makes one other important appearance as the crest of the Logans of Easter Ross:

> *"The Ridge of Tears,"* Christie roars. "That was the war cry. Oh Jesus. Think of it. The Ridge of Tears. And the crest, then. A passion nail piercing a human heart, proper. I always wondered what the hell *proper* meant, and now I'll never know, for who is there to tell me?" (178)

The salient feature that all the characters associated with the Heart have in common is that they are victimized and vulnerable.

Rachel also views her comfortable Presbyterian church's depiction on a stained-glass window as ineffectual and insipid; the power of love as a compelling and essential characteristic of God has been lost on the congregation and replaced by sentimentality at best and bourgeois security-mindedness at worst:

> The wood in this church is beautifully finished. Nothing ornate—heaven forbid. The congregation has good taste. Simple furnishings, but the grain of the wood shows deeply brown-gold, and at the front, where the high altar would be if this had been a church which paid court to high altars, a stained-glass window shows a pretty and clean-cut Jesus expiring gently and with absolutely no inconvenience, no gore, no pain, just this nice and slightly effeminate insurance salesman who, somewhat incongruously, happens to be clad in a toga, holding his arms languidly up to something which in other circumstances might have been a cross. (47)

Here the God-image that carries power is associated with cruelty and victimization; people are hapless victims of his jests: "If I believed, I would have to detest God for the brutal joker He would be if He existed" (48). Or else, He is aloof and indifferent to human cries, impassive in the face of suffering, yet morally correct: "I don't know why a person pleads with God. If I believed, the last kind of a Creator I could imagine would be a human-type Being who could be reached by tears or bribed with words" (101).

To Stacey God is both the "God Sir" (63) whom she addresses like a military commander and a possibly nonexistent, impotent, fiction of her imagination:

God knows why I chat with you, God—it's not that I believe in you. Or I do and I don't, like echoes in my head. It's somebody to talk to. Is that all? I don't know. How would I like to be only an echo in somebody's head? Sorry, God. But then you're not dependent on me, or let's hope not. (63)

God's Providence, affirmed in the biblical reference to the sparrow whose very mishap is noted by God, is cast in doubt as a childish Sunday school platitude that no one in adulthood really believes anymore. Matthew, the retired United Church minister addresses one of his grandsons, Duncan, as follows:

Well, Duncan, nice to see you. What did you learn at Sunday school?
Duncan, trapped, looks into the middle distance.
God loves birds.
Pardon?
Birds. Like sparrows and that.
You mean—"God sees the little sparrow fall?" Did you sing that hymn?
Yeh.
That's a fine hymn, especially when you really think about its meaning. It used to be your dad's favorite hymn, when he was your age. Did you know that? (67)

This ineffectual image of God corroborates the absence of moral order in the world of "the fire-dwellers."

Understandably, such images of deity do not inspire faith and trust let alone love. Proceeding from a flawed God-concept, it is inevitable that the interior spiritual life should be disturbed. When we examine the moral position of the self in relation to these internalized God-images several possibilities present themselves: firstly, the self may feel victimized, insecure, anxious, beset by doubts. Such is the predominant state of Rachel and Stacey. Interestingly, both sisters relate their own self-doubts to doubting God's existence, thereby confirming the association Calvin has made between knowledge of God and self. Rachel says, "My God, I know how suspect you are. I know how suspect I am" (177) and Stacey thinks,

At the Day of Judgment, God will say *Stacey MacAindra, what have you done with your life?* And I'll say, *Well, let's see, Sir, I think I loved my kids.* And He'll say, *Are you certain about that?* And I'll say, *God, I'm not certain about anything any more.* So He'll say, *To hell with you, then. We're all positive thinkers up here.* Then again, maybe He wouldn't. Maybe He'd say, *Don't worry, Stacey, I'm not all that certain, either. Sometimes I wonder if I even exist.* And I'd say, *I know what you mean, Lord. I have the same trouble with myself.* (14)

Secondly, the self may revolt against God and the power He represents, become rebellious and proudly self-sufficient to its own detriment, as does Hagar who compares herself to Lucifer and Napoleon. Yet a third possibility arises in the self whose experience is that of an outcast from the elect community without hope of finding favour and acceptance and thereupon takes a stance of defiance as does Morag. The conscience may become guilty (Stacey), cold (Hagar), cynical (Rachel), or outraged (Morag). It may seek assurance in good works, in marks of sanctification and election, as does Jason Currie, and as we may surmise, some other of the town's elders whose prosperity permits them to make generous contributions to the new Presbyterian church. Finally, in conduct (the outward expression of moral order) discipline has degenerated into rigid self-control and repression; work has ceased to be a joyful calling in service to neighbour and become instead a frustrating and mirthless duty or the means to amass wealth and court prestige.

How can these portrayals be accounted for in terms of Presbyterianism? We have a God who governs lawfully, if severely and coldly, who is the upholder of a moral order without a discernable basis in love, but we also see a God who is ineffectual and impotent and not at all actively engaged in maintaining the moral order, a God who has allowed the world to run out of control. I suggest that the influences of Federalism and the theological reactions it provoked can be discerned here. The doctrines expounded by Federal Theology, although classically formulated in the sixteenth and seventeenth centuries, had a lasting effect on Scots Presbyterianism, in particular their emphasis upon legalistic and contractual concepts of covenant, the introduction of a complex covenantal scheme of works, grace, and redemption, the separation of faith and assurance, the belief in supralapsarianism and limited atonement. Scottish Calvinism was in some respects not consistent with Calvin's original teachings, and, as Charles Bell has demonstrated, led to many unfortunate consequences for the spiritual life of its adherents—among them, doubt about one's faith and assurance of salvation led to greater moral scrupulosity ("self-examination and syllogistic deduction" (Bell 8)) and emphasis on the obligation to perform works to substantiate one's election, "a less helpful view of the nature of grace" (8), which made it conditional upon obedience and acting faith in Jesus Christ (9), and a diminution in the status of the sacraments to represent but "an empty title or seal of a legal covenant relationship" (9) limited for reception to the elect. The elaboration of the "twofold covenant scheme of works and grace resulted in an inversion of Calvin's *ordo salutis* by making the law prior to grace in the order of salvation, and led to a doctrine of preparation in which repentance precedes faith and forgiveness" (9). Finally, on the signal point of God's loving nature another conditionality was introduced:

> [T]he love of God, the person and work of Christ, the gift of saving faith, were of necessity limited to the elect. Such a theology made it difficult to proclaim to one and all that God is a loving Father in Jesus Christ. He is such, but, in this scheme, only to the elect. (10)

With hindsight it is possible to see the negative consequences of a line of thought that began as a reaction against scholastic Calvinism, particularly a hardening of the doctrine of predestination that emphasized God's immutable decrees at the expense of personal involvement. Among its positive features, Federal Theology attempted—in William Klempa's words—"to hold together the sovereignty of God and human responsibility, the rightful claims of God and human freedom" (142). Nevertheless, in the outworking of this theology an artificial contractualism entered into religious life, often expressed in most coldly mercantile metaphors (Bell 73, 85). Gone was the lively intuition of God's dynamic and gracious unconditional love for all people; it was shadowed by the image of a strong, uncompromising, and exacting deity who was the source of a repressive moral order.[9]

Orthodox Calvinism, therefore, retained this uncompromising quality although it was to produce its own dissenters over time, among them Unitarians. Interestingly, during her Vancouver residence Laurence taught Sunday school at the Unitarian Church but later left it and eventually returned to the church of her family, the United. Other voices of dissent from mainstream theological opinion would arise in the early nineteenth century, but among eighteenth century Moderates as well as Evangelicals, Cheyne maintains, "on the whole conformity…was the order of the day throughout that period" (11). It was only in the course of the nineteenth century and numerous heresy trials that "a formidable onslaught upon the Westminster fortress" (11) was made by men such as Campbell, Morrison, Balmer, and Brown who stood for a broader, kinder interpretation of Christ's saving work on behalf of all persons, yet this did not immediately occur but would proceed apace gradually as the later decades of the Victorian age brought with them other challenges from quarters outside of Scotland and generally polarized liberal and conservative groups (72–82). Eventually, in the 1870s the stringent application of the Westminster Confession was loosened as a consequence of The Great Confession Controversy (1860–1921) and a "conscience clause," permitting liberty of opinion, on "certain peculiarly controversial topics in the original Confession: 'the doctrine of redemption,' 'the doctrine of the divine decrees,' 'the doctrine of man's total depravity,' and the doctrines 'concerning the ultimate destiny of the heathen and of children who die in infancy'" (83–84) became part of the Declatory Act.

In nineteenth century Canada the Federalist tradition continued to find expression through the zealous, evangelically oriented and politically active Free Church which attempted to provide a well-organized, forceful moral leadership. Set apart from those who advocated a separation of the church from the state, Free Churchmen were institutionists who wanted to have the state acknowledge Christ's Headship over all matters, secular as well as spiritual. Those whose beliefs expressed an interventionist view of Providence, one might say, had very lofty, inflexible moral standards and believed in compelling adherence to them from all Canadians; in this may be detected the old Covenanter ideal of a nation sworn in loyalty to God, thereby ensuring continuous divine blessing.[10] Here was the basis for the first view of moral order and a concomitantly dynamic Providence but an authoritarian and orthodox God-image. However, as the century advanced, newer currents of thought and biblical scholarship from Continental Europe, scientific and technological advances, the aftershocks of the Enlightenment (rationalism, liberalism, moderatism, deism, skepticism) intruded upon the scene and had their unsettling effects upon religion in Canada no less than in Europe. Scottish Common Sense philosophy was seized upon by intellectuals and theologians as the *modus operandi* that would stop the deluge of skepticism and atheism from sweeping away the foundations of the older faith that had already been shaken (McKillop 23–58). For did not God seem to have retreated into the metaphysical clouds, leaving the world to its own moral confusion and men to the ungrateful task of locating Him and His purpose in creation ("Common Sense" would argue it was in "the moral sense" inherent in the mind which provided the important link between man's reason and God's being)? Had He, the Old Thunderer, not lost some of the electrical charge in His personality and now faded into the empyrean of abstract speculation about His own existence? (The poem *Dover Beach* by Matthew Arnold written in mid-century comes to mind as a troubled expression about the religious uncertainties of this age.) Here, I believe, is the second source of Laurence's unflattering depiction of the collapsed moral order and the lost God who has doubts about His own reality.

McKillop in the epilogue to *A Disciplining Intelligence* makes a summary but tantalizing reference to Laurence as being among those writers whose work bears "the direct marks of their nineteenth century cultural inheritance" (231) in terms of delineating the moral landscape of their country. I have indicated in some measure the terrain and the traditions to which she was heir by pointing out the two prevailing presentations of moral order and the God images and human responses that resulted.

I I I

The confessional aspect of church order has, to some extent, already been referred to in the context of the influence of the Westminster Confession upon Scots Presbyterianism in the seventeenth to nineteenth centuries and a gradual weakening of its centrality occurred. This led to more Arminian expressions of free will in matters of faith and salvation. The question is, in matters of faith how active a role did the individual play in exercising belief (Calvin had asserted true faith was passive and the gift of God) and was it something that could be produced voluntarily? Furthermore, in soteriological matters, how much latitude did the individual have in assuring his salvation; ultimately, how responsible was he for his eternal destiny? A cynical eighteenth century Catholic saying about Calvin's system was "You're damned if you do and damned if you don't" (qtd. in Stepanek 86). The hardening of Calvin's teaching and its codification in the five articles of the Synod of Dort in 1618 became the basis of confessional Calvinism and although Federal Theology was, in its more positive aspects, an attempt to circumvent the logical but horrible consequences of double predestination and the total depravity of man by stressing that man also had his part to do in keeping the covenant, it led to the inevitable shifting away of man's gaze from God to self and the door (which Calvin had wanted to keep closed) was thus opened to anxious introspection, doubt, and fear, as well as preoccupation with personal sin and the need to do good works to prove one's sanctification.[11]

The confessional element of the church's faith is not unrelated to the personal and social moral dimensions, for it produced in the former sphere the abiding sense of guilt (in some cases doom) and in the latter emphasis upon moral reform at large. Laurence's ironic quip about the definition of Presbyterian, put into the mouth of the Highlander, Dan McRaith, rings true here: "a Presbyterian is someone who always looks cheerful, because whatever happens, they've expected something much worse" (*Diviners* 312).

Laurence's protagonists have difficulty believing in God yet are haunted by negative images of Him. Nevertheless, the issue of faith remains unsettling and surfaces whenever Royland, a retired circuit rider and revivalist preacher, urges Morag to "have more faith." Because Wesleyans or Methodists did not believe in predestination and took an Arminian position, there was ample room to exercise personal choice, unlike orthodox Presbyterians for whom faith and salvation were not matters of free choice but consequences of God's efficacious grace and inscrutable will. Nowhere do any of Laurence's heroines produce faith and salvation by their own efforts. Jason Currie tries to, no doubt, but we are left wondering if his weekly confession of faith ultimately did secure him a place among God's elect. In each novel, faith, if it comes, and assurance of salvation, even if unusually interpreted, are always the free and gracious gifts of God's mercy. It is not "a decision for Christ" emotionally made but rather *God's decision for human beings in the unpredictable shapes of love* that is presented in the novels.

In the liturgical domain Laurence has vividly and frequently sarcastically presented some of the best of the worst forms of worship.[12] Emphasis on the psalms, which was the staple feature of Presbyterian worship, is replicated in her characters' spiritual experience; the powerful and stark qualities of the psalms resonate in the heroines' souls in times of trouble or grief. Hymns represent a later addition to Presbyterian worship and are not as favourably presented as the psalms. Whereas the words of the psalms present an unadorned emotionally-felt spiritual truth, the hymns often present an alienated form of spirituality that has the effect of putting the worshipper out of touch with his or her existential reality: "There is a happy land far, far away," and, "I know not what joys await us there" (*Jest* 138, 48). Hagar's belated conversation during Rev. Troy's unaccompanied singing of "All people that on earth do dwell," the "Old Hundredth" as it was called, links her with the Genevan Reformed worshippers of former centuries and provides that ancestral link to the living past. Laurence has reminded us that her own personal worship experiences made a lasting impression on her sense of ritual:

> But don't forget that I had come myself from a culture in which ritual was important, because although it wasn't the kind of ritual that you would find, say, in the High Anglican Church, I had grown up attending the United Church, which of course as you know is a union of the Presbyterian and Methodist—my people had been Presbyterians, so that I think that all my life, my young life, I had quite a strong sense of ritual. (Sullivan 67)

This combination of two very different theological and ecclesial traditions in the United Church seems somewhat incongruous and appears in all of Laurence's novels as a contrast between conservative middle and upper class staid, sombre, and decorous services for the Presbyterians and emotional, revivalistic, proletarian ones for the Methodists.

Lastly, the sacramental aspect of church order is significant because Laurence's heroines experience sacramental moments of healing love outside the church in so-called profane situations or contexts. These are always baptismal and eucharistic forms of experience. Evelyn Hinz has speculated that "what Hagar has missed most of all in her essentially Protestant upbringing...[are] rituals of atonement and exorcism" (87) which she could have had in a more pro-female Catholic Church (99). While this favorable assessment of the Catholic Church's beneficial psychological impact on women may be overstated and disputable, I would agree that the sacramental dimension is important in the heroines' spiritual journeys. The rejection of Calvin's teaching on the sacraments, especially the communion service, had unhappy consequences for Presbyterianism. Judging from the literature on worship in Scottish Canadian Presbyterian churches, there has been too much withholding of communion from members, too great an emphasis upon the sanctity and sinlessness of the communicant that reinforces a feeling of guilt or unworthiness in the layman. With sermons heavily concentrated upon moral purity, some people stopped attending services because they felt hopelessly unequal to meet the high standards the church set before them or else they went to the heavily-packed revivalists' camp and tent where the inviting call went forth to all sinners! [13] All of Laurence's protagonists are lapsed church-goers, except Rachel who attends merely as a concession to her mother. Stacey, the most guilt-ridden of them, entertains the idea of joining the Redeemer's Advocates—"Serenity, I thought" (*Fire-Dwellers* 38)—but drops it because she worries that her father-in-law, the elderly minister, would "have a fit."

I I I

With remarkable zeal for righteousness in private and public life, Scots Presbyterians in nineteenth century Canada directed their energies to transforming the social order. But this was not always the case. Indeed, Scottish Presbyterianism showed a scandalous neglect of the poor and presumably "unelect" of this world for most of its post-Reformation history. The tragic tale of that and the disregard of the prophetic element of biblical tradition has been thoroughly documented by Donald Smith. In Laurence's novels this disturbing aspect of the Scots Presbyterian legacy also appears. The well-to-do Manawakans, who are initially the first settlers of the town, self-made men of the commercial and professional classes like Currie, McVitie, and Pearl, and then their descendants who appear in *The Diviners*, are Presbyterians without social conscience in the prophetic sense—namely, "the care of the widow and the orphan" and "the least of my brethren." They are blind and deaf and cold toward the poor, the sinners, the social outcasts, the heathens. They do not mete out justice despite their concern for propriety, private morality, and righteousness. For example, Henry Pearl (so Christie tells Morag) "managed to winkle the piano and a few other things out and over to his place, and quietly sold them when he could, and no one who knew about it in South Wachakwa or Manawaka ever told on him" (*Diviners* 26). He apparently put the money from Morag's meagre estate into a bank account for her but after his death, five years later, no one ever saw the money again, so the orphan, Morag, was left doubly deprived—first of her family and then of her rightful inheritance. This thread of dispossession, of being denied one's justice, by those who are society's well-respected leaders and sanctimonious paragons of virtue in the eyes of the world, runs thematically through *The Diviners* and virtually pronounces a heavy judgment upon the elect—for, like the Pharisee of the Gospels, they have "washed the outside of the cup but left the interior unclean" and have "strained at a gnat but swallowed a camel." As Donald Smith has stated, the type of social concern that focused upon highly-visible moral issues such as "temperance reform, sexual morality, Sabbath observance, etc." frequently

> amounted to an evasion of genuine social criticism by implying that the sins and evils of society were due to the character weakness and moral faults of individuals rather than any shortcoming in the social and economic order. The cure was to change the individual, not society. (8)

This all produced a very hierarchical, class-defined, conservative and patriarchal social order wherein the dispossessed were left to fend for themselves and encouraged not to expect assistance from the well-to-do or from the state. An illustrative scene from *The Diviners* bears out this point: Christie and Morag are in town one evening, and as Christie is sauntering down the street looking at the goods in the stores ("gawking into the drugstore window at the boxes of chocolates and the hot-water bottles,") he runs into Simon Pearl and Archie McVitie, sons of Henry and Luke in *The Stone Angel*, and the following conversation ensues:

> "Well, well, hello there, Christie." Archie McVitie.
> Simon Pearl says nothing. A nod of the head, only. Brisk.
> "H'lo there, Mr. McVitie," Christie says. "Fine evening."
> *Christie.* But *Mr. McVitie.* Who decides?
> "Hear you're keeping off Relief so far, Christie," Mr. McVitie says.
> "Some are still on," Christie says sullenly, "despite this life-giving War."
> Then oh please NO
> Yep. Christie goes into his doormat act. Bone-grin, full of brown teeth.
> "Och aye, an honest job is all I ask in this very world, Mr. McVitie, and I tell you, sir, that's God's truth. An honest wage for an honest day's work, as you might phrase it."
> Mr. McVitie frowns, suspecting dirty work at the crossroads somewhere here but he can't put his finger on it.
>
> "That's more or less what I told the Town Council at the last meeting," Mr. McVitie says. "They want to get a truck, you know, for the um ah refuse collection. Younger man, and that. I said we'll only have one more on Relief if we do that. They claim the war's made a difference.

Not enough yet, I said. If it lasts another couple of years, yes, we'll be out of the doldrums."

Christie is looking hard at the two men. Deciding. Finally he speaks.

"God will no doubt hear you," Christie says.

And strolls on. (*Diviners* 131–32)

Christie's sarcasm does not penetrate the obtuse consciences of his social superiors who link war with economic recovery.

It might be argued that after the union of 1875 Canadian Presbyterianism became more sensitive to the distressing social problems that faced the country and the theological-philosophical ones as well. The Free Church spirit took the lead in working for widespread reform of the social order, as has been documented in Brian Fraser's study (*The Social Uplifters*; "Theology" 35–46). The "social gospel" was in vogue and Presbyterian progressives joined in the movement that swept through many North American Protestant churches in the Progressive Era in America and the post-Confederation period in Canada. As positive and well-intentioned as much of this no doubt was, it did have its shadow side that one must not fail to notice, and in some respects the old-fashioned Covenanter influence was still very much present. Although it spoke to broad social issues and aimed at the elevation and improvement of social, economic and political life for citizens of the new nation, the Free Church strategy was based upon moral regeneration of the individual and evangelicalism. It thus remained essentially conservative though presented in a newer progressive guise. What did late nineteenth to early twentieth century Canadian Presbyterianism wish to conserve? Four things, I propose:

1. political stability and British political institutions;
2. Anglo-Saxon ethnic ascendancy;
3. Christian cultural monopoly;
4. Anglo-American imperialism.

Presbyterians were not alone in holding these views but they were the most articulate, educated, and influential spokespersons for them. Goldwin French in his essay, "The Evangelical Creed in Canada," remarks, "In the end, possibly the most vital accomplishment of the evangelical denominations was to maintain the hold of the traditional conception of God's design for man in an increasingly antagonistic environment" (34). God's design was, however, identified with Anglo-Saxon ethnocentrism, racism, imperialism, and traditional power and class structures. The "antagonistic" forces in the environment that caused alarm were—to cite

but a few—waves of immigrants from non-Anglo-Saxon countries bringing with them different cultural, political and religious traditions, the
socialistic labour movement influenced by various European socialisms
(Marxist, Fabian, Christian), and the general mass of "unwashed,
unchurched, and unlettered" that were amassing in the cities.[14] In his
recent study of modern racism, *Infected Christianity*, Alan Davies has documented the ideology of Anglo-Saxon racial and political superiority that
tainted the churches from the latter half of the nineteenth into the twentieth centuries, particularly those dedicated to the social gospel mission
(81–85). As well, in his examination of the institution of the "school-homes
founded for the Ruthenian (Ukrainian) children sponsored by the
Presbyterian Women's Home Missionary Society to evangelize and
Canadianize the non-Anglo-Saxon 'new Canadians' of the Northwest"
(184) Michael Owen writes,

> When early-twentieth-century Canadian Presbyterians analyzed for-
> eign immigration, they perceived Canada as a leading Christian and
> British nation possessed of a special mission to evangelize the world.
> However, the missionaries, church members and concerned Canadians
> believed that the church must first transform Canada's own territory
> into "His Dominion." This Presbyterian vision of Canada as "God's
> country" apparently assumed a homogenous national value system
> committed to evangelical truth and British-Canadian customs and
> world views. (185)

Laurence's novels reflect the bias just described in connection with
Manawakans' attitudes toward Native peoples, Ukrainians, and other ethnic minorities. Some examples that stand out are the prejudices
experienced to varying degrees by immigrants, francophones, and aborigi-
nal peoples. The exclusion of others who are marked by difference
(physical, cultural, racial, ethnic) forms the basis of socio-political reality
in Manawaka. Whether it is the Métis who are ostracized as "the breeds,"
the Ukrainians who are ridiculed as backward, or the Chinese who are
prevented by Canadian immigration policy from reuniting with their
families, Laurence depicts the underlying ethnocentrism and racism of
the dominant Anglo-Saxon group. This is well symbolized by the
Canadian anthem eulogizing General Wolfe that used to be a staple of ele-
mentary school music classes and that Laurence parodies in *The Diviners*. In
the "Memorybank Movie: The Thistle Shamrock Rose Entwine the Maple
Leaf Forever" (70), Morag's grade six class "shuffles its feet" to sing O

Canada: "They are also learning it in French. The school board was a mite dubious at first, Miss McMurtie says, tee hee, but she won them over" (76). Not long after, she leads the class in singing "The Maple Leaf Forever," which Morag loves to sing because she can identify with her Scots emblem: "Thistle is Scots, like her and Christie (others, of course, too, including some stuck-up kids, but *her* definitely, and they better not forget it)" (80). Then: "Suddenly, she looks over to see if Skinner is singing. He has the best voice in the class…He is not singing now. He comes from nowhere. He isn't anybody. She stops singing, not knowing why. Then she feels silly about stopping, so she sings again" (80).

Commenting on the global pervasiveness of ethnocentrism, Laurence wrote in "Ten Years' Sentences":

> What one has come to see, in the last decade, is that tribalism is the inheritance of us all. Tribalism is not such a bad thing, if seen as the bond which an individual feels with his roots, his ancestors, his background. It may or may not be stultifying in a personal sense, but that is a problem each of us has to solve or not solve. Where tribalism becomes, to my mind, frighteningly dangerous is where the tribe— whatever it is, the Hausa, the Ibo, the Scots-Presbyterians, the Daughters of the American Revolution, the in-group—is seen as "the people," the human beings, and the others, an un-tribe, are seen as sub-human. This is not Africa's problem alone; it is everyone's. (31)

Throughout all her fiction and essays, Laurence has opposed imperialism, narrow tribalism, racism, and hypocrisy. She has been a forceful advocate of social justice and authentic spiritual values. All the more disconcerting that she was accused by fundamentalist Protestant groups of corrupting the morals of youth and writing morally dangerous books—yet, not too surprising from the vantage point of the evangelical creed which exhibited, according to French, "restrictive…attitudes toward many aspects of literature and the arts" (34). To be sure, there is swearing, drinking, fornicating, Sabbath-breaking and dancing (although only in Stacey's head!) in the novels. These targeted vices that the Free Church evangelicals also hoped to stamp out in the population by "creating a Christian collective conscience" (Fraser, *Social Uplifters*, 99) are presented not as the essentially evil acts that corrupt the soul but as the reactions against a repressive religious culture or the means by which, paradoxically, the psyche might express its spiritual totality.[15] For Laurence, finally, the real evils are related to violations of Jesus' Gospel and the Prophet's exhortations to "act justly, love tenderly and walk humbly with your God" (Micah 6:8). By drawing her readers' attention to the greater demands of the moral law, she has not pitted love against law, Old Testament against New, but rather shown that the two cannot be separated in an authentic religious expression. Likewise, I conclude, Laurence has not rejected the entire religious heritage of her Scots Presbyterian ancestors, for she has on occasion accorded them qualified admiration despite their shortcomings,[16] but indirectly, and without any trace of the didacticism she repudiated in art, she has also led us to explore and appreciate what it means to be a Reformed Protestant in our age.

Acknowledgements

This essay was prepared with the aid of a grant provided by SSHRCC.

Notes

1. A comprehensive evaluation of the religious sources of Margaret Laurence's art and an appreciation of the ways in which it could be considered to be sympathetic to Calvin's thought in certain respects and to the Reformation impulse goes beyond the scope of the present context. I am developing such an appraisal as part of a book-length study: *A Feminist Spirituality: Faith and Politics in the Fiction of Margaret Laurence*.

2. Interviews with Laurence and essays by the author on her work cited in this paper are the following:

    "Margaret Laurence," *Eleven Canadian Novelists*, Interview by Graeme Gibson (Toronto: Anansi, 1973), 185–208;

    "A Conversation about Literature: An Interview with Margaret Laurence and Irving Layton," Taped by Clara Thomas, *Journal of Canadian Fiction* 1.1 (Winter 1972): 65–68;

    George Woodcock, ed., *A Place to Stand On: Essays By and About Margaret Laurence* (Edmonton: NeWest Press, 1983);

    Donald Cameron, ed., "Margaret Laurence: The Black Celt Speaks of Freedom," *Conversations with Canadian Novelists* (Toronto: Macmillan, 1973): 96–115.

3. In this same conversation, Laurence says that "the thing that is autobiographical is not the events, not the characters, but some of the underlying response to life."

4. Robertson, like Black, was educated in Toronto, and yet further, at the staunchly conservative Princeton Theological Seminary in New Jersey, which had, in that ear, some informal, friend links to Knox College (Vaudry 50–55).

5. Jane Dempsey Douglass in *Women, Freedom, and Calvin* explores Calvin's "theology of freedom" and its significance for women.

6. See also Pesando 53–58.

7. Hinz argues that the decline of the Christian into "the effeminancy of the New Testament" and its "degeneracy" into softness is presented in Hagar's religious criticisms that privilege powerful God/masculine figures (82–100).

8. Rosemary Radford Ruether addresses the issue of Christian polemic against the Old Testament in chapter five, "Theological Criticism of the Christian Anti-Judaic Myth," especially page 258, in *Faith and Fratricide*. Thomas's allusion to the Weberian thesis linking the rise of capitalism with Calvinism, though not developed, is another debatable point; see Graham 365–66.

9. Michael Walzer, in his book *The Revelation of the Saints: A Study in the Origins of Radical Politics*, argues that in the "ideology" of Calvinism, the state becomes "an order of repression" that is based upon the moral self-discipline of the saints organized to perform God's will in the world. "Calvin's thought thus begins with alienation [man from God] and ends with a new religious discipline" (30); moreover, "Calvin describes and justifies a purely secular repression" (30–31).

10. Bell, in chapter 2 on Knox and the Scottish Reformation in *Calvin and Scottish Theology*, traces Knox's ideal of Scotland as a holy nation covenanted with God to his application of the Old Testament prophets to the contemporary historical and political situation (41–48). This covenant model was again used by the church adherents in Canada to justify their social reformation agenda, as Vaudry's thesis makes clear.

11. For a discussion of the differences between Calvin and the English Calvinists and Puritans see Toon, *The Emergence of Hyper-Calvinism in English Nonconformity, 1689–1765*; Kendall, "The Puritan Modification of Calvin's Theology," *John Calvin: His Influence in the Western World*; Kendall, *Calvin and English Calvinism to 1649*. As well, Bell's *Calvin and Scottish Theology: The Doctrine of Assurance* examines them in light of Federal Theology.

12. Russell in "God and Church in the Fiction of Margaret Laurence," *Studies in Religion*, notes that her "description of the local churches with which her characters come in contact is invariably negative. Neither the Presbyterian nor the evangelical churches fare very well in her fiction" (435). French in "The Evangelical Creed in Canada," *The Shield of Achilles: Aspects of Canada in the Victorian Age* (25–26) describes the contrast between Presbyterian and Methodist and Baptist worship in terms of "the conflict between reason and emotion."

13. In the nineteenth century, McLeod Campbell attempted to present a loving and inviting God-image to his parishioners in Scotland and thus incurred the ire of the conservative church leadership. As well, communion was usually reserved for a very small minority in the congregations, an indication of the spiritual alienation of the people and the sense of personal unworthiness inculcated by the clergy.

14. In 1909 James S. Woodsworth addressed this social problem in *Strangers Within Our Gates or Coming Canadians*, reissued in 1972 with an introduction by Marilyn Barber (VII–XXIII).

15. Carl G. Jung expounded the idea that the aim of the psyche is wholeness, not perfection, and that the integration of the "shadow" was an essential stage of the "individuation" process (a movement toward psychic totality). This idea is developed in many ways throughout Jung's enormous *oeuvre*; for example, see *Memories, Dreams, Reflections* (326, 33) and two relevant studies on this subject: *The Creation of Consciousness: Jung's Myth for Modern Man* by Edward F. Edinger, and *A Strategy for a Loss of Faith: Jung's Proposal* by John P. Dourley.

16. In "A Place to Stand On" (17), Laurence writes of Hagar and the people of her grandparents' generation, "I think I never realized until I wrote that novel just how mixed my own feelings were toward that whole generation of pioneers—how difficult they

were to live with, how authoritarian, how unbending, how afraid to show love, many of them, and how willing to show anger. And yet, they had inhabited a wilderness and made it fruitful. They were, in the end, great survivors, and for that I love and value them." See also Thomas, "A Conversation About Literature: An Interview with Margaret Laurence and Irving Layton" (67). For a comparison of Laurence to other well-known Presbyterian writers see, Joseph C. McClelland, "Ralph and Stephen and Hugh and Margaret: Canlit's View of Presbyterians" (109–22).

11

EARLY INFLUENCES

Laurence's Newspaper Career

Margaret Laurence's literary reputation rests on her fiction, but from 1947 to 1948 she had an important writing apprenticeship as a reporter for two different Winnipeg newspapers.[1] During that period more than 120 articles carrying her by-line appeared in these papers.[2] A close examination of her newspaper contributions, hitherto overlooked by scholars of Laurence's work, reveals that this period had a lasting impact on her.

In the spring of 1947, after graduating from United College, Winnipeg, Margaret Laurence (then known by her maiden name—Jean Margaret Wemyss or more commonly, Peggy) worked for several months as a staff correspondent for *The Westerner*, a weekly paper connected with the *The Canadian Tribune*. Both were Communist publications.[3] The staff was small and Peggy did much of the typical work of a young reporter, covering the Winnipeg scene and writing an occasional book review. The following year (1948), she was involved with an unusual newspaper enterprise, the *Winnipeg Citizen*. This fledgling morning paper was Canada's only, and perhaps the world's only, co-operatively owned daily newspaper.[4] Margaret Laurence recalled that she "loved working on the paper; the staff was small; everybody did three jobs."[5] The *Winnipeg Citizen*, was indeed an exciting and singular experiment in newspaper publishing. Before its first issue in March 1948 there had been hours of theoretical and practical discussions, months of fund-raising, and door to door soliciting of subscriptions. While working for this paper, Peggy Laurence "wrote a radio column, did book reviews, and covered the labour beat" (*Dance* 107).[6]

How significant was this experience in terms of Margaret Laurence's development as a writer? Her posthumously published memoirs *Dance on the Earth* (1989), contain brief comments that clearly refer to fond and long-cherished memories of her newspaper work. However, none of the many published interviews with Laurence contain comments about her newspaper experiences. Discussion of Laurence's journalism is absent, too, in critical essays on her work. And although Clara Thomas (*The Manawaka World of Margaret Laurence*) and Patricia Morley (*Margaret Laurence: The Long Journey Home*) in their studies of Laurence's life and work give a few sentences to her association with the *Winnipeg Citizen*, neither alludes to *The Westerner*.[7] In the face of such omissions, one might conclude that Margaret Laurence's experiences as a journalist were not significant. The very opposite is true. The variety of her assignments, the opportunities and experiences that journalism presented to this aspiring writer were very significant, particularly in terms of her subsequent literary career. The opportunities afforded Laurence through her early journalism were indeed formative and had a far-reaching and pervasive influence on her writing. These effects are reflected more in terms of content than in the development of her style.

While covering assignments for *The Westerner* and later for the *Winnipeg Citizen*, Peggy Wemyss/Laurence was in the midst of an exciting and controversial world. These papers featured news from post-war Europe, issues with Canadian wheat pools, local disasters, and routine social, political and fiscal problems of Winnipeg, one of Canada's most important post-war centres, bringing the young reporter in touch with a fast-paced and varied scene.

In addition, Laurence's radio columns include references to widely diverse programs such as: *The Farm Roundup, Sports Digest, Western Hour, Night Owl Club, Jr., Musical Club, Luncheon Club, Bonspiel Results, Supper Club, Movie News, 20 Questions, Music of Ukraine, Cuckoo Clock House* (a children's program), *Saturday Night Party, Hockey Broadcast,* and *Dancing Party.* Her articles contain specific references to many writers and lengthy reflections on specific broadcasts that she has heard. For example, Laurence discusses Bach's *St. Matthew Passion;* Shakespeare's *Richard II;* "The Dybbuk," a Jewish Folktale; Trotter's *Charter of Four Freedoms* and she comments on writers such as

Dorothy Sayers, Irwin Shaw, Jane Austen, John Donne, Alexander Dumas, and T.S. Eliot.

Her articles give some indication of the concerns and experiences that newspaper work afforded the young journalist. In the autumn of 1947, as a correspondent for *The Westerner*, Peggy Wemyss covers a disastrous train wreck and fire. While writing for the *Winnipeg Citizen* in March 1948, Laurence mentions on two occasions Louis Riel, the controversial Métis leader who figures so significantly twenty-five years later in *The Diviners* (1974). During May 1948, she writes about the terrible flood damage in Winnipeg and its environs and interviews the Lieutenant Governor when he visits the area.[8]

A good deal of insight about Margaret Laurence in her early twenties remains to be gleaned from further attention to her journalism. The topics covered in Peggy Wemyss's (or Laurence's) articles indicate the complexity and difficulty of trying to account for a novelist's later inspiration, and serve to remind us of a belief that is axiomatic among biographers, namely that their subjects never reveal all, and, that memory is selective—whether recalled in interviews or in memoirs.

After carefully reading through more than 120 of Peggy Wemyss's/ Laurence's contributions to *The Westerner* and the *Winnipeg Citizen*, at least four noteworthy aspects of her early journalism emerge: her articles for *The Westerner*; her book reviews; her analyses of radio dramas; and her coverage of the Canadian arts' scene for the *Winnipeg Citizen*. While Margaret Laurence's newspaper career was not lengthy, this essay will demonstrate that its influence and effects were significant and far-reaching in terms of her development as a writer.

The Westerner

On July 5, 1947, two months after her graduation from college, Peggy Wemyss's first signed article for *The Westerner* appeared.[9] From then until the end of December 1947, she contributed about 15 articles to this weekly paper whose banner proclaimed "Truth and Justice for the West."[10] During this period *The Westerner* published comments on the Saskatchewan Bill of Rights, the East Malarctic gold mines, old-age pensioners, the Marshall plan for Europe, and Mennonites departing Manitoba for Paraguay. With Mitch Sago as editor, John Marshall (who was later to be best man at her wedding) as associate editor, and Bill Tuomi as manager, the paper declared its intention of providing "honest news of the events and life around us—with the moral courage and the strength to tell it…. We will have none of the traditional press: cheap sensationalism and shoddy scandal" (*Westerner,* June 21, 1947). Peggy Wemyss's/Laurence's articles for *The Westerner* are good, sound reporting. Clearly, she did much of the work of a cub reporter, covering varied assignments, attending public hearings, writing about housing, health, welfare and labour issues. Having grown up during the Depression, she would have been aware of these issues, but as a young Winnipeg reporter with an urban beat, Peggy Wemyss must have discovered in these topics a dimension and an immediacy that had been lacking in her own adolescent and childhood experiences in the protected environs of Neepawa.

Her first article for *The Westerner* is a lengthy report that focuses on the postwar housing crisis in Winnipeg and the need for a municipal project, which would include "low-rent houses for workers and a permanent number of available houses for welfare cases." Peggy Wemyss details the situation in which 57 families might be evicted from Immigration Hall by order of the Minister of Mines and Resources (*Westerner*, July 5, 1947).

The following week she continues coverage of the housing shortage, reporting the clash among several of Winnipeg's committees over the needs of veteran's families and the needs of 1500 people who were currently in emergency shelters in the city.

Later that summer, Wemyss writes about the recent distribution of anti-Semitic leaflets in Winnipeg, quoting Winnipeg barrister Joseph Zukin who requested a police investigation of the incidents (*Westerner*, Aug. 30, 1947).[11] The next week, Wemyss contributes a lengthy article about the polio epidemic. In this she goes beyond the provincial situation to report that the opinions of doctors in Toronto differ from those of medical authorities in Winnipeg. She also refers to pamphlets issued by the Department of National Health and Welfare as well as U.S. experiments with polio serum and their newly established Infantile Paralysis Foundation (*Westerner*, Sept. 6, 1947). Perhaps her coverage was so thorough because she had witnessed first-hand the ravages of polio upon classmates and neighbors during her youth in Neepawa.

One of the most frightful and disturbing news events that Peggy Wemyss covered as a reporter for *The Westerner* took place on the night of September 1, 1947. A terrible train accident at Dugald, fourteen miles east of Winnipeg, caused at least 31 deaths and virtually wiped out six area families who were returning on the Minaki holiday train when it crashed into the No. 4 Transcontinental, standing at Dugald. Because Victorian-era gas lamps were used to light the thirteen flimsy wooden coaches, fire engulfed the train, compounding the tragedy.

Large headlines and photos accompany Wemyss's article. She opens with a quote from a CNR official, "'We have the charred bones of what we thought were two dogs, but it's not impossible that they were humans.'" Then Wemyss describes the scene:

> ...fire lashed through the 13 coaches, touching them with death and havoc. Oil tanks at the Imperial Oil depot went up in flames, and the Dugald grain elevator was demolished by fire.... The coaches were burned until nothing but their twisted skeletons of steel were left. Decapitated bodies and corpses, charred until unidentifiable, were part of the nightmare, as dazed survivors wandered around looking for friends and relatives and hysterical mothers screamed for their children lost in the blaze. (*Westerner*, Sept. 13, 1947)

Eight days after this terrible accident, thousands of Winnipeggers lined the route of the funeral cortege and 22 hearses and mourners passed long silent lines of citizens from the grounds of the legislative buildings to the graveside, while the flags of the city flew at half-mast.

During September 1947 no articles by Peggy Wemyss appeared in two issues of *The Westerner*. She was on her honeymoon, having married Jack Laurence on September 13, in the United Church in Neepawa.[12] The by-line "Peggy Laurence," her married name, appears for the first time in *The Westerner* on October 4, 1947. She contributes a lengthy account of the public hearings that she attended following the Dugald crash. Her account is a clearly written analysis in which she raises the questions one looks for in good journalism.

In the same issue, Laurence also interviews a fellow columnist at *The Westerner*, Margaret Chunn. One wonders what Peggy, who had recently married and who later struggled diligently to find a way to reconcile her talent and vocation as a writer with her need to be a "regular housewife and mother," thought of that interview. Mrs. Chunn, then mother of two small children, had managed to juggle many personal and professional demands. In addition to her domestic responsibilities, Chunn was president of the North Winnipeg Branch of the Manitoba Housewives Consumers' Association, a candidate for election to a local school board, and a regular contributor to *The Westerner* (*Westerner*, Oct. 4, 1947).

During autumn 1947, front page headlines in *The Westerner* carried the news that 3,000 workers were on strike in six packing plants. A few weeks later, after interviewing men at several plants: Swift's, Canada Packers, and Burns, Laurence wrote about the UPWA strikers who were picketing. The article is particularly interesting because here the young journalist slips into the fictional mode with descriptions of two strikers, Alf and Bill, followed by eight paragraphs of alternating dialogue between the two men:

> Alf was cleancut, fairhaired, probably in his early twenties. His alert eyes looked as if they knew how to laugh. Now he was in dead earnest, though.... "That's right." Bill said, shifting his massive frame on the bench beside the gateway. "And they say our demands aren't fair." (*Westerner*, Oct. 11, 1947)

This style, characteristic of fiction, contrasts markedly with Wemyss's/ Laurence's earlier journalism in *The Westerner* and leads one to wonder whether she was at that time working on her own fiction.

In mid-October, Laurence must have been excited when an article with her by-line appeared prominently on the front page of *The Westerner*. In it she excoriates the *Winnipeg Free Press*, which had juxtaposed a photo of Alderman Jacob Penner beside an article about bribe charges, giving readers the false impression that Penner somehow was implicated. Laurence calls this "one of the most brazen pieces of news distortion ever to hit the front pages of a Canadian newspaper" (*Westerner*, Oct. 18, 1947).

During October, Laurence also salutes a new publication *National Affairs Monthly*, singling out for praise Eugene Varga's essay on Europe's new democracies, and calling Nelson Clarke's "Wheat and Politics in Saskatchewan" one of the most honest and comprehensive analyses that she has seen. Laurence notes that this monthly presents both the achievements and the shortcomings of the Co-operative Commonwealth Federation (CCF) in Manitoba (*Westerner*, Oct. 25, 1947).[13]

While writing for *The Westerner*, Peggy Wemyss/Laurence contributed at least one radio column, a review of Joseph Schull's *The Shadow of the Tree* (a reference to the mushroom cloud from the atomic bomb). This drama, directed and produced by Andrew Allan, had premiered on CBC's new program, "Stage 48" (*Westerner*, Oct. 11, 1947). Laurence, quite moved by Schull's drama, referred to it several times in other columns during the months that followed. The drama's plot deals with a family as its members take up their lives after World War II. One son has been blinded, the other killed in combat. A daughter-in-law attempts suicide, but a physician persuades her that it is worthwhile to live, even if one is living in "the shadow of the tree." Laurence's review of Schull's work appears within Roland Penner's regular entertainment column "FanFare," which covered films, radio, music, and, on occasion, recent books. Penner, who later became a distinguished lawyer and Dean of the Faculty of Law at the University of Manitoba, was at that time an undergraduate there. The flavor of his youthful, idealist's views is captured in his Marxist comments about a recent film version of *Hamlet* starring Laurence Olivier, "[This is] the story of a humanist caught between the duties of a decadent feudalism and the cash-callousness of the rising bourgoise…" (*Westerner*, Dec. 6, 1947).

An important coincidence occurred in conjunction with Penner's column "FanFare." From late June to early September 1947, it was guest-edited by Adele Wiseman, who was to become an important Canadian writer and a life-long friend of Margaret Laurence. Wiseman, who was two years younger, was then an undergraduate at the University of Manitoba. When I interviewed her, Adele Wiseman related that she had first met Peggy at the Labour Temple where they both appeared seeking a job with *The Westerner*.[14]

Although Peggy Wemyss worked only six months for *The Westerner*, the atmosphere of that small paper and the people who wrote for it were to remain with her. The opportunities offered to learn more about newspapers, to write for deadlines, to cover incidents and to research information were skills that she would use later in her professional career. Although in the dozen or so signed articles which we know she wrote for the paper, a certain moral earnestness surfaces occasionally, this was not uncommon in the work of other writers at *The Westerner*.

Book Reviews

A second, very interesting area of Wemyss's/Laurence's writing in 1947–48 that invites attention are more than a dozen book reviews which she wrote for *The Westerner*, and later, the *Winnipeg Citizen*. Almost all of them deal with works by Canadian authors. These reviews offer a window into Margaret Laurence's literary concerns at the beginning of her writing career. The tone of these book reviews is confident and emphatic. While she applauds good Canadian writing, she does not hesitate to criticize the superficially Canadian or the stylistically ineffective, and even takes to task W.O.

Mitchell and Martha Ostenso (among others) for books that Peggy Wemyss/Laurence considers flawed. To those who only know her later book reviews, the tone of these early reviews will be a surprise.

William French, writing at the time of Laurence's death, recalled that when he had enlisted her to do some book reviews in 1969 for *The Globe and Mail*, he discovered that "her sympathies were always with the author, and she couldn't bring herself to say an unkind word about a novel, even when it was obviously necessary" (*Globe and Mail*, Jan. 6, 1987, A13). However, there is no indication whatsoever of such a tendency in her reviews during 1947–48. Wemyss's/Laurence's remarks step boldly from the page and she speaks authoritatively, delivering judgments about contemporary writers.

Peggy Wemyss's first book review appears in *The Westerner* on July 12, 1947. It comments on *Hurry Up Please, It's Time* by Elizabeth Hawes, a woman who had left a lucrative position in New York City, to work full-time as a union organizer. The review states that Hawes's sense of post-war America is that the country is headed for depression in a world of strife. Wemyss notes that Hawes "sees a country rife with red-baiting and capitalist propaganda, the last stand of an economic system which has outgrown its ability to work satisfactorily for the majority." While Wemyss remarks that Hawes's book is somewhat disjointed, she concludes the review by stating: "[This] is an urgent treatment of an urgent subject, a book which must be read" (*Westerner*, July 12, 1947).[15]

A few weeks after her twenty-first birthday, Wemyss's critique of *Who Has Seen the Wind?* appeared in *The Westerner*. "After the round of applause being given to *Who Has Seen the Wind?* has died down," she writes, "it may possibly be found that the book does not, after all, entirely capture the spirit of the west" (*Westerner*, Aug 2, 1947). Although Mitchell's novel was to become a Canadian classic, Wemyss finds much to criticize in it.[16] Her remarks are quoted at length because they address substantive issues with regard to dialogue, the relationship between the environment and the characters, and offer evidence of her early concern with fictional technique as well as content. She writes:

> Mr. Mitchell, himself a native of Western Canada, has a wealth of potentialities in his novel, but for the most part they remain on that level. Although the novel, which tells the early life and the gradual growing-up of the lad Brian O'Connal, is set in Saskatchewan during the drought period, little is said of the drought and depression....
> Practically the only person who mentions the environment and its effects on people is Brian's Uncle Sean, a farmer, who continually curses

the weather and the stupidity of the people in not attempting to use proper methods of irrigation and farming. However, Sean's effectiveness is limited by the exceedingly limited interpretation Mitchell puts on his character. The old man is not really taken seriously, for he is shown as the popular conception of the western farmer—bluff, uncouth, very rustic and something of a hill-billy. He swears incessantly (repeating "goddam" until this reader, at least, longed for a little colorful variety) and roars at everyone in his thick Irish brogue.

Many of the other characters—the hired man, the black-smith, et al., are treated similarly. Those of us who have lived all our lives on the prairies and among its people, may perhaps doubt the validity of presenting so many characters as merely "quaint." Western Canada has its oddities, but they are not specifically those of Dogpatch. (*Westerner,* Aug. 2, 1947)

Wemyss then praises the characters of Ben, the district ne'er-do-well, and his son, young Ben, saying that here Mitchell does his best work. In her concluding paragraphs, however, she states that "philosophically the novel is slim":

[*Who Has Seen the Wind?*] does not show people in the throes of life in a difficult time, as Steinbeck did in *The Grapes of Wrath*, and it does not make these people live. The total effect is one of vagueness of thought plus an attempt to portray the prairies and their people as charming and odd. The beauty of the prairie is here, but not its awe, its bleakness, its vast, terrifying presence. The amusing qualities of people, and some of their pettiness, is here [sic], but not the depths of their feeling. Gabrielle Roy, in *The Tin Flute*, and, in novels of the west, Sinclair Ross in *As For Me and My House*, have both done more to write Canadian novels that intensely portray people and their environment.

The prairie needs novelists. Mitchell has, despite the limitations of *Who Has Seen the Wind?* made a distinct contribution to this field of writing. Although the texture of the book seems rather too attenuated, he has achieved, at some points, a real poignancy and a rare descriptive quality. (*Westerner,* Aug. 2, 1947)

In this review, Peggy Wemyss's close attention to Mitchell's use of setting and portrayal of western characters is emphatically expressed. While she tries to be even-handed, Wemyss's strong negative feelings about the novel emerge very clearly. Her comments about *Who Has Seen the Wind?* are signifi-

cant, too, in the light of her own later choice of prairie setting and characters for her Manawaka novels. But, Wemyss's remarks about *Hurry Up
Please, It's Time* show that her affinity for subject matter may sometimes
result in greater tolerance for a writer's stylistic ineptitude.

After Peggy Wemyss left *The Westerner* (it seems the paper was strapped
financially, *Dance* 107), she was hired by the *Winnipeg Citizen* and her work
appears in their first issue on March 1, 1948. Although she states that she
covered the labour beat, her signed articles actually include her regular
radio columns as well as some interesting book reviews, but not labour
news.

In these book reviews, her attention to the nuances of her own prose
style is apparent in the use of periodic sentences and deliberate parallelism.
However, Peggy Laurence sometimes blends a hieratic and demotic style
in a way that produces a distracting effect. Generally, she writes with a
tone of confidence, though she can be carried away by her own sense of
humor. Reviewing a book about magic and the supernatural, she makes
the following pronouncement: "It has been said that *Great Mischief* may be
read as a psychological study. To this I say: a plague upon it: throw it to the
ravens. I prefer to see no subtle undertones of common sense or reality.
Seen with the cold analytical eyes of psychology, the story loses all point.
To be appreciated, it must be accepted for what it is: a cleverly woven,
totally unreal magic prescription, with more than a dash of the calculat-
edly theatrical" (*Winnipeg Citizen,* Apr. 10, 1948).

Laurence also can be succinctly ironic, for example, in reviewing
Everybody Slept Here, she notes, "Rarely can one get such a complete résumé
of the plot from the book's cover" (*Winnipeg Citizen*, Apr. 17, 1948). Another
time when critiquing a book about the Canadian Pacific Railway, she comments with tongue in cheek that the most dramatic thing about the book
is its title, *When the Steel Went Through: a C.P.R. Saga by an Engineer* (*Winnipeg
Citizen*, Mar. 20, 1948).

In longer reviews, such as that of Mitchell's *Who Has Seen the Wind?* and
Ostenso's *Milk Route*, Wemyss/Laurence addresses issues that will later
become central to her own novels, including the realistic evocation of
small prairie towns and the creation of authentic characters, not stereotypes. She asserts that "the tone of Miss Ostenso's latest production [*Milk
Route*] is just about as vigorous as the uninspired clip-clop of the milk-
wagon horse on the route which she describes." In Ostenso's vignettes
from life in the town of Wahwahnissa Creek, Laurence finds that "most of
the stock characters from the stock novel about a small town are here,

with little attempt at depth," and she concludes her review: "The tales of *Milk Route* are obviously calculated to inspire a little smile, a little tear. In this reviewer they inspired more than a little annoyance" (*Winnipeg Citizen*, May 24, 1948).[17]

Radio Drama

A third aspect of Peggy Laurence's newspaper work that reveals a good deal about the young writer is her handling of the radio column "In the Air," which she wrote for the *Winnipeg Citizen* six days a week from March to July 1948.[18] Although at least eight radio stations could be heard in Winnipeg, Laurence prefers to review programs from Canadian stations, including CKSB, St. Boniface (Manitoba), which sponsored French broadcasts, and the provincial station CKY, which also carried CBC (Canadian Broadcasting Corporation) programs but rarely adverts to CBS (the Columbia Broadcasting Station) or NBC (the National Broadcasting Corporation) which broadcast from the United States. Radio in Canada was then a tremendously significant medium of expression and communication, especially in the prairie provinces, and Laurence's daily column had many readers.[19] Her attention to radio drama and her admiration for its writers are worth examining because Laurence's discussions of radio drama often focus on literary features that later will become hallmarks of her fiction writing.

Peggy Laurence found live radio drama absorbing and exciting; she frequently comments on it and even suggesting a radio "trailer" (previews of upcoming programs) in order to gain a wider audience for radio drama and to lessen people's reluctance to tune in to "serious" programs such as those offered by "Stage 48" (*Winnipeg Citizen*, June 15, 1948).

Writing "In the Air," the *Winnipeg Citizen*'s daily radio column, required that Laurence concentrate on radio's varied offerings. Moreover, the routine of daily deadlines offered the young writer an important discipline as well as many opportunities to reflect on the elements that constitute effective writing, thus serving as a helpful preparation for her own later work as a novelist.

During the *Winnipeg Citizen*'s first week, Laurence's "In the Air" column commends radio drama which, she believes, has accomplished in the previous decade "things that are closed to stage plays." She particularly admires the way in which radio appeals to the listener's imagination.

Comparing stage drama with radio drama, Laurence remarks that the staging of *Peer Gynt* could not possibly satisfy us all as "radio drama can do by relying on the listener's own mind" (*Winnipeg Citizen*, Mar. 4, 1948).

A month later Laurence again focuses on the subject of radio drama with a rallying cry: "It's about time we aimed ourselves up and got rid of the national inferiority complex." Canada is "tops" in radio drama and CBC's "Stage 48" is "head and shoulders above most American productions" (*Winnipeg Citizen*, Apr. 6, 1948).[20] Laurence is convinced of the superiority of Canadian radio over American programs, particularly those of the "superficial Hollywood variety" and maintains that the presence of advertising sponsorship has had a deleterious effect on the style, type, and content of U.S. programs.[21]

She also touts the superiority of Canadian radio drama over most offerings of the British Broadcasting Corporation (BBC), including "London Playhouse" (*Winnipeg Citizen*, May 3, 1947). In fact, she writes a scathing review of BBC Theatre's new series: "moving with the sprightly pace of a lame elephant, *The Pile of Wood* was a mystery drama which concerned a young man who was killed and another young man who killed him." "All in all," she remarks, "*The Pile of Wood* sounded as if it had been written and produced by people whose mental equipment unhappily resembled its title" (*Winnipeg Citizen*, Sept. 15, 1948).

The young journalist's praise for Canadian radio programs and her encouragement of Canadian talent are linked to the fact that she envisions Canadian radio as a singularly important medium for "cultural advance" and national self-esteem among young people in particular. "We must…," she writes, "decide to integrate what is worthwhile in radio into our national culture and to give people a large chance to digest and appreciate what radio has produced" (*Winnipeg Citizen*, June 8, 1948).

Noting that good radio dramas are "such fleeting things," she declares, "It's not right that plays like Joseph Schull's *Shadow of the Tree* or Lister Sinclair's *Encounter by Moonlight* should simply vanish as soon as the broadcast is over." She suggests rebroadcasting, proposes that the ten best contemporary plays be published annually in an anthology, and recommends that several sets of records be made available to all CBC branches in Canada's chief cities so that anyone can go there and listen to programs from the record library (*Winnipeg Citizen*, June 8, 1948): "Surely some of CBC's radio programs deserve a permanent position as a feature both of art and of education. I think it is time we stopped thinking of radio as a passing phase. It is here to stay, and the sooner we integrate it fully into our national life, the better it will be able to fulfill its function not only as a source of entertainment but of education" (*Winnipeg Citizen,* June 7, 1948).

A natural corollary of this belief is Laurence's praise for writers of radio drama. Because she is especially concerned about recognizing and preserving the best work of Canadian radio dramatists, she urges: "Let us be honest with ourselves, Canadians have not turned out much that is worthwhile in the field of serious writing. Now when a few fine pieces of writing turn up, are we going to let them die simply because they appeared through the medium of radio?" (*Winnipeg Citizen*, June 7, 1948). In her column, Laurence certainly becomes an advocate for radio drama, recommending the preservation of drama, music and education programs.

Because Laurence believes that radio brings a drama to life in a way that no amount of text reading can do, she suggests making such radio programs available to school children. Her high praise for CKRC's free radio school and its drama lab under the direction of Mauri Desourdy and Kay Parking and her comments about their productions underscore this. Margaret Laurence's interest in and attention to young actors, writers, and musicians were to remain among her life-long concerns. In later years, after Laurence had won recognition in literary circles, she continued to encourage other writers through personal efforts, by letters in support of their work, and by becoming instrumental in founding The Writers' Union of Canada.

Laurence's enthusiasm for radio drama, however, does not cloud her critical judgment or blind her to some of radio's limitations. In her second column for the *Winnipeg Citizen*, she critiques a drama by the Canadian writer John Draine which, in her opinion, "fell far beneath the average" and was too much a "patchwork of events" (*Winnipeg Citizen*, Mar. 2, 1948). She later faults a CKY drama broadcast *Fear Comes First* for the following reasons: the plot and characters were stereotyped; every weary cliché of dialogue was used and the audience was told too often of the psychological implications of the plot. Pointing out that dramatic punch often rests in letting the audience gather its own conclusion without actually saying "This is the moral of the story," Laurence declares, "*Fear Comes First* may have had a moral, but it almost certainly had no story" (*Winnipeg Citizen,* June 25, 1948).

She also recognizes the difficulties of radio adaptations of the work of authors such as Henry James. Most of his novels, says Laurence, "are the sort in which it may take a man four pages or even a chapter to light a cig-

arette, but woven around that simple action, hundreds of minute psychological details are being revealed all the time. This sort of double pattern
would be hard to achieve in radio" (*Winnipeg Citizen*, May 31, 1948). In addition, Laurence notes that subtleties are communicated in a novel
"between mutually sensitive minds" by descriptions of a word, a look in
the eyes or sudden gesture of the hand are impossible to convey through
radio (*Winnipeg Citizen*, May 31, 1948).

Another indication of Laurence's thoughtful response to the medium
of radio may be found in her comments about adaptations of
Shakespeare's tragedies and histories. While mentioning that she had
hoped the CBC would produce more Shakespearean dramas, she admits
that she has modified her opinion after listening to an adaptation of
Richard II, and comments that listeners were confused because there was
such a "superabundance of characters." She says, "I thought I knew the
play reasonably well, but at times I found I had to refer to the written text
to be certain who was speaking" (*Winnipeg Citizen*, Apr. 29, 1948). She also
realizes that while the CBC presentation of *Romeo and Juliet* was effective,
Antony and Cleopatra was not, due to the tremendous range of time and space
and the rapid shift of rather brief scenes (*Winnipeg Citizen*, Apr. 8, 1948).

Although Laurence appreciated adaptations of Shakespeare, Greek
drama, and classics such as *Arabian Nights* and *Around the World in Eighty Days*,
she is quite emphatic about the need for radio dramas dealing with more
modern material. She notes that to address contemporary subjects and to
speak with the tongues, "not of biblical angels, but of truck drivers and
doctors and housewives is more difficult. It is also more desirable. More
difficult because less immediately dramatic and more controversial. More
desirable because so badly needed" (*Winnipeg Citizen*, Sept. 22, 1948).

In her columns for the *Winnipeg Citizen*, Laurence consistently cheers
contemporary radio writers who have dealt successfully with modern
issues. She praises Max Shoub for his series *My City*; and Len Peterson who
has done "the best job" of handling problems of the modern world
(*Winnipeg Citizen*, May 12, 1948). His play *Maybe in a Thousand Years*, dealing with
the marriage of an English girl and a Chinese sociologist, examines the
issue of racial prejudice. Laurence also comments at length on Joseph
Schull's work, finding "great sincerity" in his contemporary drama, *The
Little God*, but cautioning that it has a "certain vagueness of thought."
However, she has unqualified and frequent praise for Schull's *Shadow of the
Tree*, a play dealing with the atomic age. The twenty-one year old Laurence
predicts that Schull will probably become Canada's leading radio drama-
tist, for "his technical accomplishment has matured amazingly. His plays

are consistently well written and have about them a dramatic polish that comes from a thorough understanding of his medium" (*Winnipeg Citizen*, May 13, 1948).

While Laurence's comments about radio programs range rather broadly, there is one feature, voice, that consistently captures her attention and to which she frequently returns. Laurence's attention to nuances of speech pattern and to effective dialogue surely contribute to her own subsequent command of these same features in her novels and short fiction. In her very first "In the Air" column, Laurence applauds the wonderful narrative pace and suspense in an adaptation of Jules Verne's *A Courier of the Czar*, but remarks astutely that the mid-Victorian speech patterns make the play a bit of a burlesque (*Winnipeg Citizen*, Mar. 1, 1948). In comments about other programs, she notes that a daughter's voice is "too childish"; and that inconsistent speech patterns are given to an Indian woman, Leah (*Winnipeg Citizen*, May 28, 1948).

After writing her first month's columns for the *Winnipeg Citizen*, Laurence declares: "One of the things that always impresses me is the way in which voice can, through slight changes of tone, denote developing personality as well as moods" (*Winnipeg Citizen*, Apr. 6, 1948). She then recalls a broadcast of *Madame Bovary* during the winter months: "You could practically see Madame Bovary changing from a slightly ethereal girl to a self-centered, brittle woman, as the note of greed for excitement became more pronounced" (*Winnipeg Citizen*, April 6, 1948).

A month later, Laurence comments on *Winner Take All*, a play in which an elderly farmer marries a young waitress. Although the plot "showed imagination," Laurence is distracted by the use of voice: "the narrator (that strangely English voice that sounded so out of keeping with the environment) was totally unnecessary." Mike, the farmer, had a Swedish accent, but "rather than risk a poor dialect, it would have been better to leave it out entirely," she declares (*Winnipeg Citizen* , May 28, 1948).

These remarks about voice shed light on some of her own concerns as a writer. In comments about *Fire in the Snow*, a dramatization of Captain Robert Scott's ill-fated expedition to the South Pole, Laurence is intrigued by the fact that a woman was chosen to narrate the play: "This was the first time I had heard a woman narrator, and I thought the idea was a sound one. The contrast which she provided to the male voices was startling and served more than one purpose. On a more or less superficial level it made the distinction between the narrator and the characters in the play very clear indeed, a thing which is by no means always obvious to the audience. I know of only one type of play—Greek drama—in the radio adaptation of which the problem of the narrator does not appear." She adds that "in most plays the difficulty is to keep the narrator in direct communication with the audience by making him distinct from the other actors, and yet have him speak in a way suitable to the general tone of the drama." She also finds that the use of a woman narrator is effective because "[it] seemed to be so far removed from the setting of barren ice-wastes that she provided a fine contrast for the harsh suffering voices of the explorers, and gave an ominous tone to the whole, as though she were a sort of angel of death" (*Winnipeg Citizen*, May 27, 1948).[22] Laurence's comments on the impact of a female narrator are striking in the light of the fact that her own mature novels later made very effective use of female narrators.

Although some radio stations issued information bulletins for newspapers, Laurence's coverage of radio programs as well as her prose style are clearly original: reflective, humorous, sometimes acerbic, with an interplay of intelligence and energy: all of which are noteworthy in such a young writer. Laurence shows no hesitation in declaring that in a recent *Hamlet* she found Mavor Moore's interpretation "too loud and bombastic," but was impressed with Jane Mallett, who as Gertrude managed to convey to the audience "the touch of decadence that surrounded Hamlet's mother, her full-blown and fast-disappearing beauty, and her essential weakness" (*Winnipeg Citizen*, May 19, 1948). On another day, she concludes a critique with comments about the author's talent and expresses hope that in future his analysis of prairie people will go deeper (*Winnipeg Citizen*, May 28, 1948). Laurence is not timid about using "I," or "we" in her column. She frequently explains and illustrates her judgments, which are grounded in careful attention to numerous radio programs and in her own literary background. An energetic and confident tone pervades these radio columns.

Canadian Culture

After reading through Margaret Laurence's daily radio column for a seven-month period, I am struck by the way in which "In the Air" becomes in Laurence's hands an opportunity to celebrate many aspects of Canadian life. Her comments are perceptive and thoughtful. An overview of her daily radio column over this period reveals Laurence's concern for Canadian radio, drama, art, music and literature emerging as a consistent refrain. That Margaret Laurence, whose Manawaka novels are celebrated as being quintessentially Canadian, should have shown such a pronounced interest in the arts in Canada so early and so strongly in her career is quite significant.

Peggy Laurence's "In the Air" column often mentions Canadian radio dramas, books, writers and artists. But her concern with a distinctive Canadian cultural life extends as well to other areas: Canadian music, comedy, film, history and freedom of speech are recognized by Laurence. For example, she refers to a recent broadcast when she was "particularly impressed" with two movements from Alexander Brott's suite "From Sea to Sea," which portrayed in music British Columbia and the Prairie provinces (*Winnipeg Citizen*, Apr. 3, June 7, 1948). Believing that Canadian music has been "badly neglected" by the public, largely because it is not accessible to them, Laurence recommends that the CBC continue "the symphonic broadcasts which feature the work of young American and Canadian musicians" (*Winnipeg Citizen*, June 7, 1948). She believes that because most concerts are held in eastern Canada, such contemporary symphonic music should be made available to a wider audience through radio.

In other remarks about Canadian music broadcasts she recommends "Music of the Ukraine," to anyone who may still doubt the "large amount of richly varied culture that goes to make up the composite of Canadian culture" (*Winnipeg Citizen*, Apr. 9, 1948). She also includes laudatory references to Winnipeg's CKSB: "Orchids to our French language station for including on its musical menu more classical music, both light and otherwise than any other station. There are times when Count Basie becomes a little too exuberant for the weary mind, and one turns to CKSB with grateful relief" (*Winnipeg Citizen*, Mar. 8, 1948). She commends the station and its director Rene Dussault on several occasions and reports on April 1 that she enjoyed a recent tour of the St. Boniface station.[23] She also praises their "Let's Learn French Program," which then had 2,000 active English participants who received scripts for every broadcast (*Winnipeg Citizen*, Apr. 5, 1948).

Canadian folk music captured Laurence's attention, too, and she praises the work of Ed McCurdy, singer of Canadian ballads, but questions whether Canadians have been ignoring their own balladeers (*Winnipeg Citizen*, Apr. 1, 1948). She calls attention to the Manitoba Music festival, the largest of its kind in the British Commonwealth, which will be broadcast overseas by CBC's International Service; and mentions, as well, Canada's first festival of ballet which will be held in Winnipeg (*Winnipeg Citizen*, Apr. 26, 1948). Later, she endorses the "Ballet Club," pointing out that "since ballet in Canada is an art which is fast-maturing and gaining in importance in the national culture, it's a fine thing to see this trend recognized in such a novel [radio] program as the 'Ballet Club'" (*Winnipeg Citizen*, May 17, 1948).

In another vein, Laurence comments on Lister Sinclair's Friday night radio talks that had recently been discontinued. In this column we can learn a good deal about her own standards from what she appreciated in Sinclair's programs:

> We shall miss Sinclair's biting, pithy wit in "Mainly About Music." Perhaps we liked Sinclair because he agreed with our own ideas about Canadian art, (e.g., that a novel doesn't have to be crammed full of beavers and maple leaves to be Canadian). Although one might accuse Sinclair of a degree of intellectual snobbery, he never failed to criticize the cheap and tawdry and never used his wit to harm the genuine. For our money he is a good critic, and we'd like to see him back on the air, surveying Canadian books. (*Winnipeg Citizen*, Mar. 25, 1948)

A radio series, *The Happy Time*, based on the novel by the French-Canadian Robert Fontaine, receives praise from her on several occasions. Laurence calls it "the very best of Canadian humor," stating that she knows of no other Canadian book of its type (*Winnipeg Citizen*, Apr. 15, 1948). Another program with humor that appeals to her is Wayne and Schuster's comedy routine; this is a radio show that Laurence enjoys and recommends. She finds the pair less self-conscious than American comedians and feels that they are "our boys." The things they talk about are known to Canadians, not gags which centre around happenings in Ohio (*Winnipeg Citizen*, May 6, 1948). However, according to her, Canadian musical comedy is another matter—a rare species. She provides some telling commentary on the situation in Canada:

> It seems to be very difficult to capture the much more rugged atmosphere of Canada in a musical comedy.... They must deal in subtle wit, and the wit of this country is not generally found in the super-civilized repartee [sic]. They must be gay, and while this country has great potentialities for humorous writing, it is not basically gay.... I feel that the Canadian scene simply does not lend itself to good musical comedy. Just as great tragic drama flourished in Elizabethan England, the time and the tone of a country almost always set the pattern of its artistic creation. Until musical comedy actually fits in with the life of our peo-

ple, and until it can be written with more spontaneity than at present, I think we would be better to forget about it for awhile. (*Winnipeg Citizen*, July 14, 1948)

Films by Canadians or with Canadian content also receive attention from Laurence. She mentions, for example, "Un Homme et Son Péché," a radio program that has been aired for the past nine years and is soon to be made into a film. "Since this is one of the very few full-length films produced in Canada," she notes, "Canadians will look forward with a good deal of interest to its completion" (*Winnipeg Citizen*, May 25, 1948).

Laurence's enthusiasm for and appreciation of excellence in Canadian arts are obvious in two very revealing columns that appeared during her first month at the *Winnipeg Citizen*. Referring to the Jesuit priest Jean Brébeuf and "the passionate crusading ecclesiasticism of the Jesuits," she praises *Brébeuf and his Brethren*, a radio adaptation of E.J. Pratt's national epic. "Pratt's poem has about it the sweep of the Canadian wilds, in his sharp, realistic descriptions.... It is one of the most moving of all Canadian poems" (*Winnipeg Citizen*, Mar. 17, 1948).

Several days later she devotes most of her column to suggesting that Louis Riel's life would make an excellent radio drama. Because Laurence uses Riel and other Métis figures in her Manawaka novels, most significantly in her last novel *The Diviners* (1974), the context and extent of the young writer's remarks, as well as her deliberate prose style in this 1948 column are important to note.

She declares that if Joseph Schull were to walk into the office of the *Winnipeg Citizen* asking for ideas for a Canadian radio play, she would reply: "Why not write a play based on the life of Louis Riel?" And, noting that she has recently listened to "Lonesome Train," the saga of Abraham Lincoln, she points out that the main features of the Lincoln legend are present in the radio broadcast, with the funeral train as focus and flash-back as method. She then notes that:

There are few Canadian historical characters with enough color and significance to work into a similar drama. There are few Canadians who gather into themselves the salient features of their times and represent not only their individual story but part of the story of a growing country.

Louis Riel is one of these. Whether you think of him as a madman, a misguided reformer or a sincere man who was called by historical circumstances to be on the losing side, the drama of his life is indisputable. Into the person of a fiery French-Métis was gathered the whole inevitable struggle between red man and white, in a country where the railway to the west was beginning to have great possibilities, commercial and otherwise. There were two strong men in the west at the time. They knew each other well, and both were interested in the fate of the west, above all things. One was knighted by the queen and drove the last spike in the C.P.R. the same year as the other was hanged by the queen's men at Regina. The first was Donald Smith, Lord Strathcona. The other was Riel.

From the point of view of setting down our history, it would be a wonderful thing to see stories such as this done by "Stage 48." (*Winnipeg Citizen*, Mar. 22, 1948)

Here Laurence's understanding of the complexities of Canadian history and her interest in having stories that deal with that history set down and produced is clearly in evidence. This was to remain one of Laurence's continuing concerns, rather than a point of view that emerged only after her African sojourn, as some critics have claimed. Her interest in Canadian history is manifest as well in an early teenage story that she wrote ("Pillars of the Nation") that deals with pioneer life in Canada. And that interest appears later in her newspaper articles and reviews, and finally in her "bildingsroman," *The Diviners*. Moreover, national history and family history are not unconnected for Laurence as we learn from her abiding interest in her family histories and genealogies.

In her memoirs, Laurence relates that she left the *Winnipeg Citizen* in protest over allegations that she was a Communist (*Dance*, 107). I wonder whether the pain brought on in Laurence's later years by the harsh distortions of book-banners and their efforts to vilify Laurence's novels was augumented by memories of these unsupported allegations when she was a young reporter for the *Winnipeg Citizen*.

In what seems to be her last signed article for that paper, she focuses on freedom of speech and celebrates the unique freedom of radio programs such as "Points of View" which air opposing views on difficult questions.[24] In an earlier column, she had noted the freedom, diversity and initiative traditionally displayed by speakers in England's Hyde Park and in this, her last column for the *Winnipeg Citizen* on September 22, 1948, Peggy Laurence wholeheartedly endorses responsible freedom of expression:

Our radio writers must be allowed to keep every iota of writing freedom and even to extend and broaden it.

I believe that it is the business of all of us to insist upon this. For perhaps, after all, the most important job the CBC has to fulfill is that of holding up a mirror to our difficult times.

Public school history texts relate that Good Queen Bess destroyed all the mirrors in her house when she felt that she was losing her beauty. If the CBC ever reaches the point, as various information sources have been known to do, of allowing only one side of any picture to be shown, we shall have smashed our mirrors, and for reasons similar to those of the queen.

Although the mirror has flaws, the fact that it exists at all is a thing vigorously to be maintained through every apparent crisis. (*Winnipeg Citizen*, Sept. 22, 1948)

Here the young reporter elaborates on a theme which was to resound throughout her career—freedom and responsibility, for both individuals and nations. This also echoes in her newspaper articles and book reviews during her early career and appears thirty-six years later in one of her last essays, "The Greater Evil," in which Laurence quotes F.R. Scott's words, "'Freedom is a habit that must be kept alive by use.'" Then adding a characteristic note of her own, she states, "Freedom, however, means responsibility and concern toward others" (272).[25]

It is possible among Peggy Wemyss's/Laurence's contributions to *The Westerner* to find many themes, concerns, and situations which are similar to those in her later fiction. My point is that all of a novelist's life experiences may become threads for the cloth of fiction. Because the stitching may be changed, the threads dyed, elements from reading and conversation added, the result is magic, or, if you will, gift. Since the writer herself/himself is often unaware of each element that combines to form the threads, conclusions about a one-to-one correspondence between life and art seem to me fruitless and ultimately irrelevant. What is much more important are the workings of a young and vibrant literary imagination. There the raw material provided by Margaret Laurence's early journalism, however long it may have lain unbidden at the far reaches of her mind, becomes transmuted and transformed by the novelist's art.

These early newspaper columns remind us not of the older novelist with a secure place in Canadian literary history, but of the young Peggy

Wemyss who had moved from her family home in Neepawa to Winnipeg during the tumultuous closing years of World War II. Here is the young woman who had the drive to become a professional writer using the opportunities of journalism to hone her skills. The cultural diversity mirrored in the sights, sounds and pace of life in North Winnipeg combined with the competing agricultural and labour interests of the rest of Winnipeg to claim her attention.

In examining her articles for *The Westerner* and later for the *Winnipeg Citizen*, I find her analyses of radio drama reflecting more than a perceptive listener's comments; I hear the concerns of a reviewer who is herself a writer. In fact, the large body of Laurence's newspaper articles and columns provides a rich mine of material for critical analysis—with seams and layers waiting to be discovered and brought to light. This is an entirely new area of Laurence studies holding, no doubt, many rewards for readers and critics alike. I see this essay as the prolegomenon to this future study and one to which many scholars can contribute who want to see, as I do, the rich variety of Margaret Laurence's writings fully displayed.

Notes

1. These were *The Westerner*, and the *Winnipeg Citizen*.
2. Because Margaret Laurence in her early career signed her articles by her maiden name, Peggy Wemyss or Jean Margaret Wemyss (and after her marriage as Peggy Laurence), I have used those designations in the appropriate sections of this essay. Since her work with *The Westerner* lasted for several months after her marriage, I have used Wemyss\Laurence when referring to the period in which she was employed by that paper.
3. In her memoirs, Margaret Laurence states that she did not know about the paper's affiliation and was never a Communist (*Dance,* 106–7). Professor Roland Penner, Dean of the Faculty of Law at the University of Manitoba, told me that Peggy was never a member of the party or its youth organization.
4. The history of this unique newspaper has been chronicled in journalism theses by Kenneth Goldstein and by Noelle Boughton. One of the *Citizen*'s founders, Professor Harry S. Ferns, then a member of the faculty at United College, has also described its origins. During the early days of the paper one of Ferns's talented former history students, Jeannette Grosney '46, gave important direction to the running of the paper's first office (Fearns, 238–39).
5. Kenneth Goldstein, personal interview, October, 1991. He recalls that Laurence also mentioned working initially on the labour beat, which was "just wild."
6. By 1949 Peggy Laurence was no longer writing for this paper and there are no articles with her by-line in the *Winnipeg Citizen* during that year. However, she told Kenneth

Goldstein that she did return to the *Citizen*'s offices on the morning of April 13, 1949 when staff members gathered after the last issue of the *Citizen* had hit the streets of Winnipeg. During the previous months, the paper had been in financial difficulty. Ferns once noted that "falling in love with an idea is one thing, attempting to translate an idea into an instrument for social action is quite another matter." (251)

7. It may be that in interviews with the author their attention was focused on Laurence's novels.

8. Interview with Kenneth Goldstein.

9. In May of 1947 *The Western Tribune*, a weekly paper affiliated with *The Canadian Tribune*, came off the press in Winnipeg. This paper had gone through several changes of title over a period of time, but retained consecutive numbering. In fact, there was another change on June 21, 1947 when it became *The Westerner*, volume 1, no. 8 (383). On September 11, 1948 it merged with the *The Canadian Tribune* and carried the announcement that henceforth "The three prairie provinces will be served by a special Western edition bearing the new masthead *The Canadian Tribune* incorporating *The Westerner*."

10. There are two book reviews under her initials J.M.W. (which she had frequently used in writing for high school and college publications): five under her maiden name Peggy Wemyss, six under her married name Peggy Laurence, and a radio review under the initials P.L.

11. On the same page an article by a "staff correspondent" deals with the polio epidemic in Manitoba. I suspect this was written by Peggy Wemyss since the next week she contributes a very lengthy article about the epidemic (*Westerner*, Sept. 6, 1947). Possibly the editors felt it better not to have two signed articles by the same reporter featured on one page.

12. John Fergus Laurence, a World War II veteran and ten years older than Peggy, was then an engineering student at the University of Manitoba.

13. The non-Communist Left was the Co-operative Commonwealth Federation (CCF), a forerunner of the New Democratic Party (NDP).

14. Adele Wiseman, personal interview, October 1991.

15. This is vol. 1, no. 11 (386) which is incorrectly dated July 5, 1947 on page one, but then corrected to July 12 on all subsequent pages of the paper.

16. In 1962 she favorably reviewed Mitchell's novel *Jake and the Kid* in *Canadian Literature* 11 (1962): 68–70.

17. Some years later Margaret Laurence recounted that during this period she was phoned by an author in response to a negative review she had written. Peggy, consequently, felt bad about it and remarked to Kenneth Goldstein that thus she had learned that book reviewing is "a great responsibility." Interview with Kenneth. Goldstein.

18. "In the Air" was limited to two columns, but the length varied. This feature appeared six days a week from the paper's inception in March 1948 to mid-July 1948 when, as the result of an acute shortage of newsprint during the post-war period, the number of pages was reduced and Laurence's column then appeared only once a week rather than daily.

19. On several occasions she invites readers to send in a reply to her remarks.

20. Adele Wiseman, in a column she wrote in July 1947, noted that a brief which had been presented to the Commons Radio Committee alleged that Canada was nothing but a

"dumping ground for American talent;" and that the cost of "piping in" American programs was so little that advertisers preferred to bring in transcribed American programs rather than utilizing Canadian talent. The brief demanded, among other things, that some sort of tariff be established to protect Canadian talent. (*The Westerner*, July 12, 1947).

21. See her columns for *Winnipeg Citizen,* Apr. 7, Apr. 8, May 3, July 13, 1948.

22. Laurence concludes this column by noting that women have had no great part in radio until fairly recently. Men, she says, were always used as announcers, and still are, to a great extent. Pointing out that the actresses on "Stage 48" and some CBC produced talks have shown that women can speak effectively over the radio, she concludes the column, "I hope the idea of having a woman narrator will be explored further" (*Winnipeg Citizen,* May 27, 1948).

23. In 1948 CKSB reached every French community in the province of Manitoba. There were 52 communities within the station's primary coverage, which extended as far as Kenora.

24. In addition to her feature column "In the Air," Peggy Laurence probably wrote a number of unsigned articles while on staff at the *Winnipeg Citizen.*

25. "The Greater Evil," published in *Toronto Life*, September 1984, was included by Margaret Laurence in her memoirs *Dance on the Earth* (265–74).

Permission to quote from articles by Margaret Laurence in *The Westerner* and the *Winnipeg Citizen* granted by the estate of Margaret Laurence for the essay "Early Influences: Laurence's Newspaper Career" by Donez Xiques.

| THOMAS M.F. GERRY

12

"IN CASES OF EMERGENCY"

The Political Writing

> To revolt against an authority which you unconsciously believe to be in
> some way unassailable demands not only an act of will but also an act of
> the greatest faith, and it is never done without paying a terrible price in
> anxiety and pain.
>
> Margaret Laurence, "The Poem and the Spear" (1976)[1]

In Margaret Laurence's *The Diviners* Catharine Parr Traill's statement "In
cases of emergency it is folly to fold one's hands and sit down to bewail in
abject terror. It is better to be up and doing" (109) is quoted three times.
Laurence also perceived the times she was living in as times of grave crisis.
Being a writer, Laurence wrote what she could to try to be "up and doing"
something about the threatening predicaments she witnessed. Her writing—at times implicitly, and, as her career matured, more and more
explicitly—is deeply political.

Initially, I was drawn to examining the political dimensions of
Laurence's writings through learning more about Laurence's substantial
body of work on behalf of the anti-nuclear movement.[2] I quickly realized
that the topic needed to be more broadly defined, to include Laurence's
writing more generally, concentrating on its political implications. Being

opposed to nuclear weaponry was one facet of her approach, which also involved, as she observed in *Dance on the Earth*, "the wars, the pollution, the radioactive waste, the real possibility of nuclear reactors melting down, the slaughter of whales and dolphins" (99). This listing, however, does not include the aspect of Laurence's political thinking that I believe to be the major catalyst that empowered her to apply her pen directly, not through fiction alone, to her political work: the contemporary women's movement. The other catalyst was the book-banning controversy regarding *The Diviners*.[3] Laurence's deep commitment to social justice, especially in the spheres of women and peace is demonstrated not only by the evolution of Laurence's political views' informing her writings, but also by her struggle to write politically at all. From the concern to portray in fiction the "common humanity of men and women" (Thomas, "Introduction" xvii) of her early works, Laurence moves in her novels, essays, letters and speeches, to more practical concerns that she presents overtly, such as the denial of human rights experienced by the Métis people (as in "The Loons" and *The Diviners*), and the interconnections among women's disadvantaged status in our society, violence against women, nuclearism and war.

I I I

In her 1962 memoir, *The Prophet's Camel Bell*, her essays and throughout her fiction, Laurence did treat political issues. Consistently she restrained herself from didacticism, although at times political messages are just beneath the surface. During the 1980s Laurence became even more overtly concerned with the issues she had addressed obliquely in her earlier writings. Her nonfictional expression of these concerns marks a severe downturn in her career for many reviewers and critics. Robert Fulford's obituary in *Saturday Night* includes the remark that the fourteen years during which she published her novels comprised "her career as a serious writer" (6), as if her writing after *The Diviners* is not serious! The fact that she published no more adult fiction after *The Diviners* is often linked to her political commitments. In an article in *The Globe and Mail* marking the tenth anniversary of the publication of *The Diviners*, William French remarks about these commitments as a distraction, saying that since *The Diviners* "there has been only silence" (E1) . George Galt's review essay about *Dance on the Earth* in *Saturday Night*, takes the by-now-familiar line that it was Laurence's "moral sense and the acute distress it summoned that stalled and ultimately silenced her as a writer of fiction" (74–75). While Laurence did not write adult fiction after she returned to Canada from

England, nevertheless what she wrote was and is important to her and to us. To date, Laurence's political writing has not received the scholarly attention it deserves. Brief articles in the Fall 1987 issue of *Canadian Woman Studies/les cahiers de la femme* by anti-nuclear activists Metta Spencer (20–22) and George Ignatieff (19) are essentially personal testimonies to Laurence's contributions to their anti-nuclear work. Patricia Morley also discusses Laurence's political activities in her revised edition of *Margaret Laurence: The Long Journey Home* (30–33). These accounts are glowingly positive, but they do not focus on Laurence's writing.

Galt's and others' blindness to the value of writing that he considers nonliterary is part of the destructive pattern that feminist critics have pointed out, namely the canonizing of work with a so-called universal message regarding so-called universal human experience. The sexism of Galt's bias against Laurence's work of the 1980s, particularly *Dance on the Earth*, is evident in adjectives in the subtitle of his article, which questions, "had Margaret Laurence's fierce moral vision occluded her penetrating writer's eye?" (73). "Fierce" suggests an angry, irrational, bitch; "penetrating," what men are so good at. Even people who take a more positive approach to Laurence's work after the publication of *The Diviners* do so with the tone that something went wrong, that the gift of serious artistic writing had disappeared, and that Laurence was left with only a second-rate pastime.[4]

Surely, there is another way to look at this situation. Laurence's final published reading of her work appears in *Dance on the Earth*. (Once again, she makes her presence felt both through her work and through her commentary on it.) She points out one factor in the general dismissal of her late nonfictional work: "Writing by women in those [the 1940s] and the following years was generally regarded by critics and reviewers in this country with at best an amused tolerance, at worst a dismissive shrug" (5).[5] Not only was Laurence a female writer, but by the time of her memoir writing she had overcome her reticence regarding feminism, and repeatedly, right from the opening of *Dance on the Earth*, she proclaims that she is a feminist (4), leading to further marginalization.

Not only was Laurence a feminist female writer, but she chose to publish her writings in certain magazines and newspapers that critics and reviewers would generally disdain to consider as worthy sites of literature: *Toronto Life, Homemaker's Magazine, Maclean's, The Toronto Star*. She also wrote letters to the editors of newspapers as a feminist and as an anti-nuclear activist. She also wrote public letters on behalf of women's groups and anti-nuclear groups. Most often, as revealed by the collection of

Laurence's papers in the York University Archives, she wrote personal letters to friends and strangers advocating her political approach. How could such scurrilous material ever be permitted to join the exalted ranks of Literature? And the damning evidence does not stop here.

Not only was Laurence a feminist female writer who chose to publish her writings where they would be accessible to the masses, but she had the unmitigated gall to write didactically about political issues, about women's struggle for equality, about nuclear disarmament, about living in harmony with the environment. One put-down would be that these are all "apple pie and motherhood" issues, a particularly insidious anti-human phrase if there ever was one, because it dismisses the issues without even the thought that nurturance and motherhood are crucial to survival; and common sense tells us that threats to them ought to be addressed seriously and urgently.

Another way to perceive these issues that Laurence was writing so prolifically from 1975 to 1987 is to find opposition to the movement for equal status for women and opposition to nuclear weapons and generators deeply threatening to the established order—not at all as "trivial" as apple pie and motherhood. When an accomplished writer, an internationally respected woman of letters to whose writings many thousands of people turn for insight and wisdom about the human condition—when such a woman directs her attention and considerable energy to advocating equality for women, with all that such equality implies, and to advocating nuclear disarmament and the rejection of nuclear-powered generators, then the economic/military/political system that promotes traditional (patriarchal) values, including defence (nuclearism), might well swing into repressive action. The system is a way of thinking and acting that we have all learned and carry out to some degree.[6] Naturally women's writing is not as important as men's; who dismisses Stephen Leacock's or Mordecai Richler's nonfiction as unworthy? Naturally feminist writing does not express universal values; how could it? After all, it is arguing against our system (as if women are not part of it all.) Not only that, but it is biased, not objective; it is politics, polemics, propaganda—not literature. Without any overt show of force, the themes about which Laurence felt so intensely and wrote about directly for at least twelve years in her maturity, can be dismissed.[7]

I I I

Throughout her career, Margaret Laurence returned to her own work, at least in the sense that she was often called upon to comment on it in articles she wrote, in interviews and in her memoirs. Her insights concerning her work have markedly influenced, and continue to influence, responses to her writings. Laurence began as a New Critical reader in that she always insisted that her fiction had a life of its own, essentially independent of its author. In writing *The Stone Angel* Laurence claimed, she "did not consciously choose any particular time in history, or any particular characters. The reverse seemed to be true. The character Hagar in *The Stone Angel* seemed almost to choose me" ("Place" 16). She was also a thematic critic, however, in that she asserted a strong relationship between her fiction and life. Nevertheless, as Peter Easingwood has demonstrated in his essay, "The Realism of Laurence's Semi-Autobiographical Fiction," Laurence as a writer always contested any glib acceptance on the part of her characters of the knowledge that might come to them from other characters or their surroundings. Easingwood concludes, in fact, that Laurence can be seen as being a committed realist, "but as being deeply opposed to a form of realism which would appear to take for granted the conditions it described" (131).

This doubleness in Laurence's writing and in her own interpreting of her work helped her to create a wealth of extraordinary novels and stories. In a consideration of political aspects of her work, though, Laurence's and her other readers' New Critical, formalist isolation of the texts, combined with thematic claims of her fiction's relevance to daily life, lead to difficulties of interpretation that may partly explain why the most pressing political aspects of Laurence's opus have been avoided or overlooked.

Laurence often struggled to define the role of politics in her fictional writing. Her own struggle, interestingly, is parallel to the reception of her work by other readers. According to some readers her fictions include a political dimension, not as propaganda or polemics, but as a nicely balanced humanism emerging organically from her almost self-generating (in the New Critical sense) works. To others, the writings convey formidable political themes and even didactic messages, as shown by the work of many literary critics, by the letters of fans and political groups attracted to her work almost from the beginning, and later on by the attentions of would-be censors.

Another factor that significantly complicates the attempt to formulate a just assessment of Laurence's political writing is that in her last years, as part of the memoir composition process, in her responses to censors and fans, and in some essays, Laurence articulated readings of her own work that differ from her earlier statements about her writing, especially in its political dimensions. The evidence suggests that Laurence's perception of political aspects of her writings markedly developed, even though the principles informing her political positions did not change. Increasingly, for instance, she focused on particular issues—issues such as women's control over their bodies, and other aspects of men's violence, including nuclearism, colonialism and racism—and often drew upon her novels and essays to demonstrate how she had expressed her concerns in other words at earlier times in her career.

Laurence for much of her career accorded with the New Critics' claiming for literary work autonomy from its author and audience; but at the same time, Laurence often focused on thematic elements in a realist mode, namely that her fiction relates directly to life, reaching out beyond the ironic structures of words. This New Critical principle made it troublesome for her to admit to her artistry anything she regarded as specifically or personally—or politically—related to her.[8] A statement regarding "women's lib" that Laurence made during an interview with Donnalu Wigmore published in 1971 in *Chatelaine* magazine illustrates her stance at that time:

> There are a great many things those people are after which I have long felt and believed in, but the reason why I don't take part is not because I disagree with the aims, but because my way of dealing with it is not protest or propaganda. It's a case of reform tactics versus revolution and my way is at the individual psychological level using fictional characters. (54)[9]

An even greater acknowledgement of the role of politics entered Laurence's thinking about her writing a few years later. During an interview with Bernice Lever she states:

> I don't feel that you shouldn't make political statements but I personally feel disinclined to do it through my work. But what I'm dealing with in my work in fiction is that whole cultural background and characters

which start in my case with a small prairie town. This may be political in a different sense. (27)

Laurence's awareness of a directly political aspect to her art, the sharpening of which is evident in this passage from 1977, grew over the following years.

Another consideration when encountering Laurence's political writing is other readers' views of her work, which parallel Laurence's own two-fold reading. Generally, when dealing with political aspects of Laurence's writings, commentators either New Critically elaborate ways in which the works create political implications, or else they react directly—one could say "personally," in most cases—to the political themes and messages of the works. Commenting on *This Side Jordan*, David Richards exemplifies the formalist/New Critical approach. He notes that Laurence chose Africa as the subject of this novel because it is an apt setting, in her words in her article "Ivory Tower or Grassroots?: The Novelist as Socio-Political Being," for "the theme of an independence which was both political and inner" (22). Rather than dealing with the actual political/inner theme, however, Richards focuses on the "dualistic formal principle in the composition of *This Side Jordan* where the alternating voices of coloniser and colonised form the basic structure of the novel" (23).

Thematic commentary is exemplified by some critical articles and interviewers' questions, by the statements of various people who have tried to ban *The Diviners* from school curricula, and by the requests of members of political organizations who found in Laurence's work views harmonious with their own persuasions, and who tried to enlist her support for their causes. In an early critical article that focuses on theme from a Marxist perspective, Kenneth James Hughes's essay on "Politics and *A Jest of God*" characterizes Rachel as "a type of Canada in the post-colonial period" and "a national type seen from a particular class point of view" (121). Interviews that are also clear examples of thematic reading were conducted and recorded by Rosemary Sullivan and Michel Fabre, among many others.

The banning of *The Diviners* has been extensively reviewed; examples of requests to Laurence for support abound in the Laurence papers. In 1975–76 alone (and the following is not a complete list) Laurence joined and contributed money to Mel Hurtig's Committee for an Independent Canada; acted as honourary director of the Canadian Association for the Repeal of the Abortion Law (CARAL); helped to sponsor the Public Petroleum Association of Canada; supported the Civil Liberties Association's campaign against capital punishment; and helped to fund the anti-nuclear group Hiroshima-Nagasaki Relived.[10]

Whether they start from New Critical/formalist principles, or from a thematic position, then, readers do notice political dimensions to Laurence's work, as she herself did. But literary critics, no matter what their approach, for the most part become blind when Laurence treats real-life issues such as men's violence towards women and the nuclear crisis, particularly when such treatment is nonfictional. But even with her fiction this lack of critical attention applies. Walter Swayze comments, regarding her early story "A Queen in Thebes," with its anti-nuclear theme, that the story's "lack of recognition has really nothing to do with its quality. It is simply too horrible for most readers and critics" (18).

Before going on to suggest further reasons for this critical blindness to these political themes in Laurence's work, and to argue that this political writing ought to be included as an integral part of her literary achievement, I need to offer a definition of "political" writing, and to suggest the range of types of Laurence's political writing, in order to more fully contextualize this writing.

The dictionary provides a starting-point for defining "politics," one to which Laurence also turns in her contribution to *A Political Art: Essays and Images in Honour of George Woodcock*, "Ivory Tower or Grassroots?" Laurence cites and concurs with the *Concise Oxford Dictionary's* definition of "politics": "Science and art of government, political affairs or life; political principles." Particularly appealing to Laurence is the generality of the definition, its connotation that politics is not primarily the activity of political parties. Her own definition of politics is "a social commentary at a grassroots level" (16). The openness and flexibility of politics in Laurence's conception are underscored by her term "social commentary," implying as it does, an ongoing conversation. At this point in her essay, Laurence claims for all fiction a political role, in the sense of its being social commentary (16); nevertheless, for Laurence, there are emphatically two kinds of politics. Near the end of "Ivory Tower or Grassroots?" she reiterates her sense of the imperative to keep separate fiction and politics in its narrower meaning:

I have not taken an active or direct part in the women's movement, just as I have not taken an active or direct part in any party politics, simply because my work resides in my fiction, which must always feel easy with paradox and accommodate contradictions, and which must, if anything, proclaim the human individual, unique and irreplaceable, amazingly strong and yet in need of strength and grace. (23)

Keith Louise Fulton has used this statement of Laurence's to demonstrate the novelist's being unconscious of the role that the language of humanism has played in suppressing women; according to Fulton, "this historical movement has enshrined hierarchy, privilege, and the corresponding oppressions in every aspect of our lives, our society and our knowledge" (102). Fulton also observes that "amazingly, humanism is widely regarded as egalitarian, while feminism is frequently held to be ideological with all the implications of narrow polemics" (103). Amazing as this mindset may be, in valorizing a humanism oppressive to more than half of the people, while underrating feminism's goal of universal equality, it is still far from uncommon, and Laurence shared it at that point—1978—in her career. "Ivory Tower or Grassroots?" also indicates, though, that Laurence was prepared to acknowledge the presence in her work of specific political themes such as the patriarchal oppression of women, as opposed to the general "universal" humanistic "truths" that she had previously regarded as the only appropriate political themes for fiction. She describes how

The growth of some of the themes in my writing—those themes which in the broadest sense I may define as political—took place in my mind in an intertwined and simultaneous way. My sense of social awareness, my feelings of anti-imperialism, anti-colonialism, anti-authoritarianism, had begun, probably, in embryo form in my own childhood; they had been nurtured during my college years and immediately afterwards in the Winnipeg of the old Left; they had developed considerably through my African experience. It was not very difficult to relate this experience to my own land, which had been under the sway of Britain once and was now under the colonial sway of America. But these developing feelings also related very importantly to my growing awareness of the dilemma and powerlessness of women, the tendency to accept male definition of ourselves, to be self-deprecating and uncertain, and to rage inwardly. (24)

Clearly these themes are much more specifically focused and less the vague humanistic project of proclaiming "the human individual, unique and irreplaceable" that Laurence had earlier in the essay avowed to be the province of fiction. She immediately goes on, however, to interpret these themes of social awareness, anti-imperialism, anti-colonialism, anti-authoritarianism and the dilemma and powerlessness of women, which do appear in her work, in the universalistic terms of traditional humanism:

> The quest for physical and spiritual freedom, the quest for relationships of equality and communication—these themes run through my fiction and are connected with the theme of survival, not mere physical survival, but a survival of the spirit, with human dignity and the ability to give and receive love. (24)

I I I

Even in Margaret Laurence's early writings, her political views emerge. In *The Prophet's Camel Bell*, Laurence reflects on her experiences in the early 1950s in Somaliland. She makes direct comments on the manners and mores of the native people, as well as on the British and other imperialists living there. Her awareness of the destructiveness of imperialism, which she expresses in the second chapter of the book (25), is tempered by the fact that her and her husband's presence also constituted imperialism, certainly in the eyes of the Somali people they met (70), even if the reservoir construction on which Jack Laurence worked, and the translations of Somali poems and stories on which Laurence worked, were worthy projects. In her chapter on "The Imperialists," after a humorous introduction to the British as they appear at a ceremony to mark the queen's birthday, she presents the imperialists in individual character sketches, not as part of a larger political force. Laurence insists on this distinction, in fact, emphasizing the psychological dimension to the point of completely excluding political motives:

> The English enclosure in particular was a scene of well-intentioned but uncoordinated action. People sat down hopefully, then bobbed up again when they noticed that no one else was sitting down....
> The Somalis, watching from a slight distance, did not appear surprised. They had always known the *Ingrese* were demented.
> And of course, a good many of them really were demented, and not in the harmless and rather touching musical-comedy manner of the Birthday Parade, either. I found the sahib-type English so detestable

that I always imagined that if I ever wrote a book about Somaliland, it would give me tremendous joy to deliver a withering blast of invective in their direction. Strangely, I now find that I cannot do so.... They bear no relation to most parts of Africa today, and however much Africans may have suffered at their hands, it is to be hoped that one day Africans may be able to see them for what they really were—not people who were motivated by a brutally strong belief in their own superiority, but people who were so desperately uncertain of their own worth and their ability to cope within their own societies that they were forced to seek some kind of mastery in a place where all the cards were stacked in their favour and where they could live in a self-generated glory by transferring all evils, all weaknesses, on to another people. (226–27) [11]

In *The Prophet's Camel Bell* Laurence also devotes much attention to women's role in the imperialist and native societies. On this topic she primarily describes women as individuals, the absurdities and injustices of systemic oppression being mentioned but left unremarked. Laurence's attention characteristically moves from the women's dilemmas to self-reflection. For instance, as an illustration of the limit to which her inadequate medical supplies and abilities were pushed by needy Somalis, Laurence describes some women who had to walk for miles over the desert in the driest time of year with burden camels, and who requested a remedy for their severe menstrual pain, which was intensified by their having been subjected as children to "either a removal of the clitoris, or a partial sewing together of the labia, or perhaps both" (75). Laurence notes that this practice was perpetuated not only by the men, but also by the older women. Her response, though, turns back on herself, on her position in relation to these women:

> What should I do? Give them a couple of five-grain aspirin? Even if they had money to buy future pills, which they had not, the lunatic audacity of shoving a mild pill at their total situation was more than I could stomach.
> "I have nothing to give you. Nothing." (76)

These two examples from *The Prophet's Camel Bell* suggest Laurence's approach to political issues in her 1962 memoir. Even in this form, when the literary standard of refraining from polemics is less of a concern than with fiction writing, Laurence is more obliquely than directly concerned with political issues she encounters, such as imperialism and men's oppression of women.

Paradoxically, considering Laurence's disinclination towards the use of protest or propaganda in her fiction, her stories and novels actually present more directly political views than does *The Prophet's Camel Bell*, although these opinions and arguments are always within fictional contexts. Perhaps it is the fictional contexts that enabled Laurence to incorporate these views, since she was also able to remain true to her New Critical principle of authorial absence.

The Fire-Dwellers takes place against the background of what Laurence calls "The Ever-Open Eye"—the television, with its mix of reality and fantasy, mainly violent. The following excerpt from Stacey's interior monologue demonstrates Laurence's epitomizing women's social position and men's violence as the television constantly displays them:

—The Ever-Open Eye. Western serial. Sing yippee for the days of the mad frontier. Boys were sure men in those days all right and men were sure giants. How could they miss? Not with them dandy six shooters. *Tak! Tak! Splat!* Instant power. Who needs women?

The program ends, and then the News. This time the bodies that fall stay fallen. *Flicker-flicker-flicker.* From one dimension to another. (57)

Often the news concerns the war in Vietnam. At one point Stacey attends a peace rally. Clearly, political issues are present in the novel, and, the political message is not far beneath the surface.

This technique, providing background or context with political implications is a constant feature of Laurence's fiction. Another example is the damage caused by the First and Second World Wars—damage to a generation of young men who were killed or injured, but also to their families in Manawaka. While *A Bird in the House*, *A Jest of God*, and *The Diviners* are not propagandistic in their treatment of war, nevertheless, the anti-war message is plain.

Similarly, as Laurence herself pointed out in "Ivory Tower or Grassroots?" her female heroines/narrators, who struggle for freedom and survival, enact aspects of women's coping with "the dilemma and powerlessness of women, the tendency to accept male definition of ourselves, to be self-deprecating and uncertain, and to rage inwardly" (24). Also, as she indicates, her political theme of dispossession, like other themes of social justice, "must sometimes be defined in fiction by the lack of it." Laurence instances the plight of the Métis, the lower class citizens in her work, the depressions of the 1930s, and the wars (25). The conclusion to this 1978 essay reasserts Laurence's concept of fiction: fiction, she writes, "speaks first and foremost of individual characters, and through them it speaks of our dilemmas and our aspirations, which are always in some way or other those both of politics and of faith" (25).[12]

I I I

Looking at Laurence's writings that explicitly handle women's issues and nuclearism, I notice first that Laurence ties these two areas of concern closely together. Diana Brydon's observation about Laurence's fictional mothers provides insight into the novelist's conception of this relation: "In Laurence's fiction, taking on motherhood means taking on responsibility, not just for one other life, but for the continuity and development of humanity" (197). Again, we find Laurence's pattern of moving from the individual to the social level, and it is not difficult to see how the threat of nuclear annihilation would be a major element in any mother's acting on the responsibility for the continuity of humanity (not that such a responsibility should be solely that of mothers). Laurence writes in her Foreword to a collection of essays on *Canada and the Nuclear Arms Race* that

> Our lives and the lives of all generations as yet unborn are being threatened, as never before, by the increasing possibility of nuclear war. I believe that the question of disarmament is the most pressing, practical and spiritual issue of our times. If we value our own lives and the lives of our children and all children everywhere, if we honour both the past and the future, then we must do everything in our power to work nonviolently for peace. (xi)

The connection between women's issues, particularly men's violence towards women, and nuclearism is evident in Laurence's writing in more specific ways. In her lead article, "Prospects for Peace," in a 1986 issue of *Homemaker's Magazine* devoted to "Peace: A Passionate Plea," Laurence repeats the last sentence in the previous quotation, and then, showing her awareness of the magazine's audience, goes on:

> I hope that every reader of this magazine—literally millions of Canadians—will ponder these words. Each of us must find the means, make the time, to rise up out of our demoralized self-in-isolation and

join together so that our concerns about nuclear weapons will be heard and heeded. Put aside other issues—many of which are divisive of society—and concentrate on this one goal that truly matters: making the planet earth a peaceable kingdom, or at least ensuring that if men are misguided and perverse enough to persist in their war games that they do not wipe out the lot of us as a consequence. (18)

Her term "demoralized self-in-isolation" is reminiscent of her statement about "the dilemma and powerlessness of women" in "Ivory Tower or Grassroots?": "the tendency to accept male definition of ourselves, to be self-deprecating and uncertain, and to rage inwardly" (24). That Laurence read about connections between feminism and nuclearism is indicated by the presence in the Laurence papers at York University of Ann Morrissett Davidon's piece "On Feminism and Militarism"; the opening of *Dance on the Earth* is a meditation on these connections (3–7).

Laurence's article, "Prospects for Peace," is also a further instance of her strategy, common to her fiction and nonfiction alike, of presenting themes on an individual scale, then interpreting their implications for society at large. She opens the article with words about herself, how she found her way out of this dilemma:

The first time I spoke out publicly on the subject of nuclear arms—in a speech entitled My Final Hour,...I felt that at last I had overcome the helplessness and depressed passivity that all citizens are encouraged to feel in today's society when they think about this particular problem. (18)

Laurence then cites Traill's words from *The Diviners* on what to do "In cases of emergency (109)," and goes on to interpret this advice in the light of her present context: "We are faced with an emergency that concerns not only our own personal lives, but the lives of all people and all creatures on earth" (18). Near the end of the article she returns to the implications for her personally of being "up and doing":

I don't like calling myself "an artist." But I guess I am, and as a writer— an artist, if you will—I have a responsibility, a moral responsibility to work against the nuclear arms race, to work for a recognition on the part of governments and military leaders that nuclear weapons must never be used and must be systematically reduced....

I do not claim to pass on any secret of life, for there is none, or any wisdom except the passionate plea of caring. (22)

Caring, for Laurence, is related to imagination, as she makes clear also in this article: "I fear greatly that many of the world's leaders have so little imagination and so little real caring that they cannot visualize at all what a nuclear holocaust would mean" (18). She proceeds to sketch (with her writer's care) a possible scene after the explosion of a nuclear bomb, in contrast to the fatuous language of the military:

> Such words as "overkill" and "megadeath" do not convey in any sense at all what would really happen—the dead, mutilated and dying people clogging the ruined cities and towns like so much unvalued discarded rubbish, the suffering humans screaming for help with no medical help available, no water, no relief at all for the unbearable pain of millions of humans except finally the dark relief of death for all. (18)

"A Constant Hope," an article Laurence contributed to *Canadian Woman Studies/Cahiers de la femme* in 1985, shows another link she made between women and peace:

> Any speculation about women in the future must be preceded by a question. Will there be a future, not only for women but for everyone, for the planet itself? Unless the nuclear arms race can be halted, unless the nations that possess nuclear weapons, and especially the two superpowers, can be persuaded to make genuine efforts to end this lunacy, the prospects do not look promising. Women have taken a large part in the growing peace and disarmament movement, and I believe we must take an even greater part in the future and on behalf of the future. (12)

Laurence also focused on the individual woman and her experiences of male violence through her writing on abortion, rape and shelters for women battered by men. The following excerpt from a letter to Brenda Fleet of CARAL, dated 28 May 1982, shows Laurence's caring imagination at work, this time moving from the general problem to an individual, perhaps fictional, instance.

> I do not think any of us would favour abortion if any other viable and workable alternative exists. But it just seems to me—and believe me, I

have given great thought to the matter—that there are times when to remove the fertilized egg at a very early stage is a better alternative than forcing a mother to have an unwanted child. What I worry about are the many many child-mothers, teenage girls of 13, 14, 15, victims of incest or rape or simply their own terrible ignorance, who become pregnant and have no notion of what parenthood will mean. Often these girls are unable even to cope with the thought that they are pregnant, and more often than one would like to believe, their own parents are not supportive but rather feel punitively. The babies born to these girls often become abused children…the lonely child-mother doesn't know how to deal with a demanding baby who is not a cute and cuddly little doll but a real live needful person, and in her despair and hysteria, the young mother hurts the baby, sometimes dreadfully.

From her overall view of political methods one appreciates Laurence's wisdom, however often she denied having any. Her wisdom is based on all of her life experiences, her being a writer, a mother and citizen of Canada in particular. Another excerpt from a letter selected from her correspondence with CARAL, to Kathleen Martindale, the Association's president, dated 6 August 1982, reveals Laurence's alertness to language in the political arena. She is discussing hate mail she had received after writing a public letter to appeal for funding for CARAL:

I agree that the anti-abortionists do tend to control the language of the debate [in terming themselves "pro-life"], and of course that is just one more reason why it is so important…. This was, of course, why I pointed out in my replies to these guys that I am indeed pro-life, pro-family, pro-baby, etc. etc.! But precisely that belief determines my stance. However, we will never convince them, just as writers like myself will never convince some of the fundamentalists etc. who say we write "blasphemous" "pornographic" books! (Which mainly they haven't read, of course.) It's a long struggle, and we carry on, not to convince the opposition, but simply to ensure that their views will not be forced on the rest of the people.

Laurence's integration of her experiences so that she is able to convey wise judgments is also evident in a letter she wrote a couple of weeks later, to the President of Operation Dismantle, James Stark, who had asked her to discuss disarmament issues in a public forum. Laurence writes,

I cannot bring myself to go on a panel with Barbara Amiel. In my last letter to you, I said that my heart sank at the thought, but I see now that it is more than that.... This is in no way a personal thing—I have never met her....

I question—forgive me for saying so—the value of confrontation with such a person. To me, it would be somewhat like discussing reasonably the question of blacks in America with a member of the Ku Klux Klan. No true discussion is possible. Another paralell [sic] in my mind would be trying to discuss my novel *The Diviners* with the fundamentalists who have tried to have it banned in this country. I have avoided this kind of confrontation because I believe it to be fruitless. I certainly do not believe in speaking only to the converted, as it were, but there are persons with whom one cannot speak at all and indeed should not even try to do so. I am more interested, in terms of the peace movement and disarmament, in such practical work as the referendums at community levels, and pressuring our government not to allow testing of the cruise missile.

Laurence's practical approach resulted in a host of letters, essays, speeches and written statements that share important characteristics with her fiction: the imaginative creation of and focus on the individual, accompanied by a movement towards society-wide concerns; a powerful awareness of the powers of language; and a vision, informed by tolerance and wisdom, of an egalitarian, peaceful world for all. In the early 1980s she admitted that she was "trying to write a novel which will not be didactic but which will bring in some of these [anti-nuclear] themes," because, as she put it, "I have to try to put some of my life-views down in fiction, again, and to proclaim a belief in life and human individuals and all creatures, in that way" (letter to James Thurlow). As we know, she did not do so. My belief is that Laurence perceived the threats to life on earth, in the various forms of male violence, including that directed toward women, and nuclearism, as so urgently in need of action, that she decided to devote her writing energies to more direct, didactic appeals to politicians and the public. At the same time, she also interpreted her fictional works in the light of her most pressing concern. In 1984 Ellie Kirzner reported, for example, that Laurence's anti-nuclear position was not a recent development for her:

"I've had these feelings for many, many years," she says. And so it is no accident that Laurence has infused her novels with a strong strain of social justice. "It comes into my writing. My feeling about war comes into all my Manawaka books. I'm not going to write a novel which is didactic, but as writers we have to tell the truth as we see it and as much as we can." (6)

Even though Laurence clearly placed such a high value on her fiction in contrast to her political essays, speeches and memoirs, as do many reviewers and critics, I think it is time for us to heed Laurence's words, and to understand that what she did in all her work—fictional or otherwise— was to tell the truth as she saw it and as much as she could. The political writing she created is often eloquent, moving, and glowing with wisdom. Instead of the emphasis on symbolism, characterization and other formal considerations involved in fiction writing, she focused in her political writing on persuasive techniques, logic and theme. These techniques are not inferior, but different.[13] Laurence shared, however, in reducing our estimation of this work because she thought of it as being didactic. But propaganda and didacticism are usually noticed and condemned only when the writer is promoting a challenge to established authority; otherwise, promoting established values—such as the values of traditional humanism—is regarded as proper and laudable.

That Laurence chose to enter directly the women's movement and the anti-nuclear movement, and by doing so, largely through her writing, to make a great contribution to enhancing the prospects for life, is a cause not for disappointment about the literary forms she chose, but for celebration, and for renewed attempts to realize what she was advocating.

Notes

1. To balance the self-reflective sombreness of that statement, here is an anecdote Laurence tells in a letter to her New York agent, John Cushman, written shortly after the event she describes, a fundraising dinner for the Writers' Development Trust, called "Night of a Hundred Authors," organized by Jack McClelland on September 29, 1982. The one hundred authors are lined up in a basement tunnel of the Sheraton Centre hotel in Toronto, waiting to be introduced.

   The corridor was airless, hot, without windows and without a place to sit down. We lined up, alphabetically, being guided by bewildered and worried young helpers who obviously thought we were all strange creatures from outer space. We were to be taken into the dining room and introduced individually. Never has

L seemed so far from the beginning of the alphabet. Thank God my name does not end with a Y.

We stood and we stood and we stood.

My feet hurt. I got more and more irritated....

After 45 minutes on my feet in this steamy dungeon, my Scots anger took sway, or, I guess, I got a little bit insane.

"If this line does not move soon," I proclaimed, "I AM GOING HOME."

Of course, one never gets to protest to the people in command. Instant panic among the young marshalling people, who did not know me well enough to know that OF COURSE I would not march out and let J.G. McC. down. One should never pull rank for this reason. "I think," said partly insane M.L., "that I am going to faint."

I have never fainted in my entire life and probably never will. But flutterings went on, and a young man who was one of the marshalling kids who would ultimately escort me to the SCENE, came up to me and said, "Oh, Mrs. Laurence, if you're really so troubled, we'll take you in right now, before anyone else."

Oh, John.

"Are you out of your head?" I yelled at him, with, as I now see, almost perfect absurdity, "I'm a socialist!"

2. I had written an article on nuclearism and literature, and was curious about Laurence's involvement in this crisis.

3. John Ayre gives a detailed account of this often-treated subject. Other articles which deal with the attempts to suppress *The Diviners* include Patricia Morley (158–59), Per Seyersted, and Timothy Findley. Laurence's own views on censorship were fully expounded in a speech she presented to a group of judges and their wives on June 2, 1983; the documentation, background notes and drafts of the speech are in the Margaret Laurence Papers, York University Archives, Scott Library (MLP): Accession 3 & 4, Series 1, Box 6, File 147. This crisis forced Laurence into a political arena, of course, but it was a small part of her overall analysis of the "emergency" that she believed we were facing.

   Thank you to Jocelyn Laurence for granting me permission to study and to quote from her mother's papers.

4. Hilda Kirkwood suggests disease as the cause of weaknesses in *Dance on the Earth* (30). Morley's empathetic treatment of the post-*Diviners* phase of Laurence's career indicates in some detail the ways she and other sympathizers account for the loss of the gift, whether through stress associated with the censorship issue, or physical health problems. Walter Swayze adds to the health problems Laurence's "frightening knowledge" about the threats of nuclearism as an explanation for its becoming "impossible for her to write fiction" (19). Laurence's friend Lois Wilson suggested, noting the immense differences between Ontario and the prairies, that Laurence stopped writing fiction because she wasn't "grounded enough in Ontario to carry on."

5. Galt's review is an outstanding example of the "dismissive shrug"; "the following years" include the present.

6. Barbara Godard's article and Betty Reardon's monograph *Sexism and the War System* provide an introduction to the analysis of these interrelated topics, as well as useful bibliography.

7. Although I am not directly relying on them here, Joanna Russ's arguments on *The Suppression of Women's Writing* could be applied to Laurence's writing too.

8. Coral Ann Howells illuminates the relation between the political and the personal in her comment on one of Laurence's authorial strategies:

> She uses the conventions of autobiographical fiction which privilege subjectivity in order to create spaces for her characters' dreams and fantasies, and such breathing spaces in their turn expose the limits of realist fiction as a construct of private or social reality. These novels problematise distinctions between personal and political as they insist on possible connections across the boundaries between fantasy and realism as modes of discourse. (96)

Wayne Fraser also studies the connections in literature between the personal and the political.

9. In a letter to Laurence, dated January 18, 1971, which Laurence must have received around the time of this interview, Margaret Atwood expresses similar reservations about joining a "women's lib" group, concluding with the words "just writing the truth is in a way a better contribution anyway." In her article "Face to Face" Atwood quotes Laurence, indicating the latter's wariness regarding women's lib (23).

10. The relevant documents are in MLP: Accession 1: box 9, file 12, item 801; box 10, file 15, item 1016; box 10, file 15, item 1025; box 10, file 15, item 1055; and box 10, file 15, item 1125.

11. Considering the disasters wrought at least in part by further waves of imperialists, including the most recent U.N. interventions, I doubt that Laurence's hope for the Somalis' vision has been fulfilled.

12. Parenthetically, I should add that often her early essays and memoirs, also approach political issues through individuals. The epigraph to this essay, from "The Poem and the Spear," is a general statement arising from Laurence's study of the career of Mahammed'Abdille Hasan, for example.

13. A critic such as Wayne Booth argues that all literature is a species of rhetorical argument.

BIBLIOGRAPHY

Works by Margaret Laurence

Books

Laurence, Margaret. *A Bird in the House*. New Canadian Library. Toronto: McClelland and Stewart, 1989.

————. *The Christmas Birthday Story*. Toronto: McClelland and Stewart, 1980.

————. *Dance on the Earth: A Memoir*. Toronto: McClelland and Stewart, 1989.

————. *The Diviners* [1974]. New Canadian Library. Toronto: McClelland and Stewart, 1992.

————. *The Fire-Dwellers* [1969]. New Canadian Library. Toronto: McClelland and Stewart, 1992.

————. *Heart of a Stranger* [1976]. Seal Books. Toronto: McClelland-Bantam, 1988.

————. *Jason's Quest*. Toronto: McClelland and Stewart, 1970.

————. *A Jest of God* [1966]. New Canadian Library. Toronto: McClelland and Stewart, 1989.

————. *Long Drums and Cannons: Nigerian Dramatists and Novelists 1952–1966*. London: Macmillan, 1968.

————. *The Olden Days Coat*. Toronto: McClelland and Stewart, 1979.

————. *The Prophet's Camel Bell* [1963]. New Canadian Library. Toronto: McClelland and Stewart, 1991.

————. *This Side Jordan*. 1960. New Canadian Library. Toronto: McClelland and Stewart, 1992.

————. *Six Darn Cows*. Toronto: James Lorimer, 1979.

————. *The Stone Angel* [1964]. New Canadian Library. Toronto: McClelland and Stewart, 1989.

————. *The Tomorrow-Tamer* [1963]. New Canadian Library. Toronto: McClelland and Stewart, 1990.

————. *A Tree for Poverty: Somali Poetry and Prose*. Nairobi: Eagle Press, 1954. Rpt., Hamilton: McMaster University Library Press and Shannon: Irish University Press, 1970. Rpt., Hamilton: McMaster University Library Press and Toronto: ECW Press, 1993.

Essays

————. "A Place to Stand On." *Heart of a Stranger*. Seal Books. Toronto: McClelland-Bantam, 1976. 1–7. Rpt., *A Place to Stand On: Essays By and About Margaret Laurence*. Ed. George Woodcock. Edmonton: NeWest Press, 1983, 15–19.

————. "A Constant Hope: Women in the Now and Future High Tech Age." *Canadian Woman Studies/les cahiers de la femme* 6.2 (1985): 12–15.

————. Foreword. *Canada and the Nuclear Arms Race*. Ed. Ernie Regehr and Simon Rosenblum. Toronto: Lorimer, 1983, xi–xiii. Rpt., *Dance on the Earth*, 287–90.

————. "Gadgetry or Growing: Form and Voice in the Novel." *Journal of Canadian Fiction* 27 (Summer 1980): 54–62. Rpt., *A Place to Stand On: Essays By and About Margaret Laurence*. Ed. George Woodcock. Edmonton: NeWest Press, 1983, 80–92.

————. "Ivory Tower or Grassroots? The Novelist as Socio-Political Being." *A Political Art: Essays and Images in Honour of George Woodcock*. Ed. W.H. New. Vancouver: University of British Columbia Press, 1978, 15–25.

————. "My Final Hour" [1983]. *Canadian Literature* 100 (1984): 187–97. Rpt., *Margaret Laurence: An Appreciation*. Ed. Christl Verduyn. Peterborough: Broadview, 1988, 250–62.

————. "The Poem and the Spear" [1976]. *Heart of a Stranger*. Seal Books. Toronto: McClelland-Bantam, 1988, 37–76.

————. "Prospects for Peace." *Homemaker's Magazine* (January/February 1986): 18–23.

————. "A Queen in Thebes." *Tamarack Review* 32 (1964): 25–37.

————. "Sources." *Mosaic* 3.3 (1970): 80–84. Rpt., *Margaret Laurence*. Ed. W.H. New. Toronto: McGraw-Hill Ryerson, 1977, 12–16.

————. "Ten Years' Sentences." *Canadian Literature* 41 (1969): 10–16. Rpt., *Margaret Laurence*. Ed. W.H. New. Toronto: McGraw-Hill Ryerson, 1977, 17–23. Rpt., *A Place to Stand On: Essays By and About Margaret Laurence*. Ed. George Woodcock. Edmonton: NeWest Press, 1983, 28–34.

————. "Time and the Narrative Voice." *Margaret Laurence*. Ed. W.H. New. Toronto: McGraw-Hill Ryerson, 1977, 156–60. Rpt., *A Place to Stand On: Essays By and About Margaret Laurence*. Ed. George Woodcock. Edmonton: NeWest Press, 1983, 155–59.

Letters

————. Letter to Brenda Fleet. 28 May 1982. The Margaret Laurence Papers, York University Archives, Scott Library: Accession 3 & 4, Series 1, Box 4, File 125.

————. Letter to James Stark. 23 August 1982. The Margaret Laurence Papers, York University Archives, Scott Library: Accession 3 & 4, Series 1, Box 5, File 136.

————. Letter to James Thurlow. 21 June 1981. The Margaret Laurence Papers, York University Archives, Scott Library: Accession 2, Box 1, File H/9.

————. Letter to John Cushman. 2 October 1982. The Margaret Laurence Papers, York University Archives, Scott Library: Accession 3 & 4, Series 1, Box 6, File 155.

————. Letter to Kathleen Martindale. 6 August 1982. The Margaret Laurence Papers, York University Archives, Scott Library: Accession 3 & 4, Series 1, Box 4, File 125.

————. Interview with Rosemary Sullivan. In *A Place to Stand On: Essays By and About Margaret Laurence*. Ed. George Woodcock. Edmonton: NeWest Press, 1983, 61—79.

Newspapers
The Westerner. 21 June 1947—11 September 1948.
Winnipeg Citizen. 1 March 1948—13 April 1949.

Secondary Sources Cited

Achebe, Chinua. "English and the African Writer." *Transition* 4.18 (1965): 27—30. Rpt. as "The African Writer and the English Language." *Morning Yet on Creation Day: Essays*. Studies in African Literature. London: Heinemann, 1975.

————. *Hopes and Impediments: Selected Essays 1965—1987*. London: Heinemann, 1988.

Agheyisi, Rebecca N. "The Standardization of Nigeroan Pidgin English." *English World-Wide* 9.2 (1988): 227—41.

Alcoff, Linda. "The Problem of Speaking for Others." *Cultural Critique* 20 (Winter 1991—1992): 5—32.

Arnold, Matthew. "Dover Beach." *The Norton Anthology of English Literature*. Ed. M.H. Abrams et al. New York: W.W. Norton & Co. Inc., 1962, 1632—33.

Ashcroft, Bill, Gareth Griffiths and Helen Tiffin. *The Empire Writes Back: Theory and Practice in Post-Colonial Literatures*. London: Routledge, 1989.

Ashcroft, W.D. "Is That The Congo? Language as Metonymy in the Post-Colonial Text." *World Literature Written in English* 29.2 (1989): 3—10.

Atwood, Margaret. "Face to Face" (1974). In *A Place to Stand On: Essays By and About Margaret Laurence*. Ed. George Woodcock. Edmonton: NeWest Press, 1983, 20—27.

————. Letter to Margaret Laurence. 18 January 1971. The Margaret Laurence Papers, York University Archives, Scott Library: Accession 1, box 1, Atwood file folder.

————. *Survival: A Thematic Guide to Canadian Literature*. Toronto: House of Anansi Press, 1972.

Axthelm, Peter M. *The Modern Confessional Novel*. New Haven: Yale University Press, 1967.

Ayre, John. "Bell, Book and Scandal." *Weekend Magazine* (28 August 1976): 9—10.

Bailey, Nancy. "Identity in *The Fire-Dwellers*." In *Critical Approaches to the Fiction of Margaret Laurence*. Ed. Colin Nicholson. London: Macmillan, 1990, 107—18.

Barker, Francis, Peter Hulme and Margaret Iversen. Introduction. *Colonial Discourse/ Postcolonial Theory*. Manchester and New York: Manchester University Press, 1994, 1—23.

Barr, James. *The Scottish Covenanters*. 2nd ed. Glasgow: J. Smith, 1947.

Bell, Charles. *Calvin and Scottish Theology: The Doctrine of Assurance*. Edinburgh: The Handsell Press, 1985.

Bevan, Alan. "Introduction." *The Fire-Dwellers*. Toronto: McClelland and Stewart, 1969, viii—xiv.

Birbalsingh, Frank. *Novels and the Nation: Essays in Canadian Literature*. Toronto: Tsar Publications, 1995.

Blodgett, E.D. "Is a History of the Literatures of Canada Possible?" *Essays on Canadian Literature* 50 (1993): 1—18.

Bök, Christian. "*Sybile*: Echoes of French Feminism in *The Diviners*." *Canadian Literature* 135 (1992): 80–93.

Booth, Wayne C. *The Rhetoric of Fiction*. 2nd ed. Chicago: University of Chicago Press, 1983.

Boughton, Noelle. "The Fall of the Winnipeg Citizen." Carleton University, Journalism Thesis, 1978.

Bowering, George. "That Fool of a Fear: Notes on *A Jest of God*." In *A Place to Stand On: Essays By and About Margaret Laurence*. Ed. George Woodcock. Edmonton: NeWest Press, 1983, 210–26.

Bryden, Walter. "John Calvin, Apostle of God's Sovereign Power." *Presbyterian History* 15.2 (1971): n.p.

Brydon, Diana. "Silence, Voice and the Mirror: Margaret Laurence and Women." In *Crossing the River: Essays in Honour of Margaret Laurence*. Ed. Kristjana Gunnars. Winnipeg: Turnstone, 1988, 183–205.

Busia, Abena. "Silencing Sycorax: On African Colonial Discourse and the Unvoiced Female." *Cultural Critique* 14 (Winter 1989–90): 81–104.

————. "Miscegenation as Metonymy: Sexuality and Power in the Colonial Novel." *Ethnic and Racial Studies* 9.3 (1986): 360–72.

Buss, Helen. "Margaret Laurence's Dark Lovers: Sexual Metaphor, and the Movement Toward Individualization, Hierogamy and Mythic Narrative in Four Manawaka Books." *Atlantis* 2.2 (1986): 97–107.

Butler, Judith. *Gender Trouble: Feminism and the Subversion of Identity*. New York: Routledge, 1990.

Calvin, John. *Institutes of the Christian Religion*. Ed. John T. McNeill. Ind. Ford Lewis Battles. *The Library of Christian Classics*. Vol. 20. Philadelphia: The Westminster Press, 1960.

Cameron, Donald. "Margaret Laurence: The Black Celt Speaks of Freedom." *Conversations with Canadian Novelists*. Toronto: Macmillan, 1973, 96–115.

Cheyne, A.C. *The Transforming of the Kirk: Victorian Scotland's Religious Revolution*. Edinburgh: St. Andrews Press, 1983.

Clark, David, ed. *The Sociology of Death*. Oxford and Cambridge: Blackwell, 1993.

Coetzee, J.M. *White Writing: On the Culture of Letters In South Africa*. New Haven: Yale University Press, 1988.

Cohan, Steven and Linda M. Shires. *Telling Stories*. New York: Routledge, 1988.

Darling, Michael. "'Undecipherable Signs': Margaret Laurence's 'To Set Our House in Order.'" *Essays on Canadian Writing* 29 (1984): 192–203.

Davidon, Ann Morrissett. "On Feminism and Militarism." *Peace and Freedom* (October 1980): 6–7. The Margaret Laurence Papers, York University Archives, Scott Library: Accession 3 & 4, Series 1, Box 4, File 121.

Davidson, Arnold E. "Cages and Escapes in Margaret Laurence's *A Bird in the House*." *University of Windsor Review* 16 (1981): 92–101.

Davies, Alan. *Infected Christianity: A Study of Modern Racism*. Montreal: McGill–Queen's University Press, 1988.

Davies, Richard. "'Half War/Half Peace': Margaret Laurence and the Publishing of *A Bird in the House*." *English Studies in Canada* 17.3 (1991): 337–46.

Dombrowski, Theo Quayle. "Word and Fact: Laurence and Language." *Canadian Literature* 80 (1979): 50–62.

Douglas, James Dixon. "Calvinism's Contribution to Scotland." In *John Calvin: His Influence in the Western World*. Ed. Stanford W. Reid. Grand Rapids, Michigan: Zondervan Publishing House, 1982, 217–37.

Douglass, Jane Dempsey. *Women, Freedom, and Calvin*. Philadelphia: The Westminster Press, 1985.

Dourley, John P. *A Strategy for a Loss of Faith: Jung's Proposal*. Toronto: Inner City Books, 1992.

Easingwood, Peter. "The Realism of Laurence's Semi-Autobiographical Fiction." In *Critical Approaches to the Fiction of Margaret Laurence*. Ed. Colin Nicholson. Vancouver: UBC Press, 1990, 119–32.

Edinger, Edward F. *The Creation of Consciousness: Jung's Myth for Modern Man*. Toronto: Inner City Books, 1984.

Egejuru, Phanuel Akubueze. *Black Writers: White Audience. A Critical Approach to African Literature*. Hicksville, NY: Exposition, 1978.

Fabre, Michel. "From *The Stone Angel* to *The Diviners*: An Interview with Margaret Laurence." In *A Place to Stand On: Essays By and About Margaret Laurence*. Ed. George Woodcock. Edmonton: NeWest Press, 1983, 193–209.

———. "Words and the World: *The Diviners* as an Exploration of the Book of Life." *A Place to Stand On: Essays By and About Margaret Laurence*. Ed. George Woodcock. Edmonton: NeWest Press, 1983, 245–69.

Ferns, H.S. *Reading from Left to Right: One Man's Political History*. Toronto: University of Toronto Press, 1983.

Findley, Timothy. "A Life of Eloquence and Radicalism." *Maclean's* (19 January 1987): 52–53.

Forster, E.M. *Howards End*. Harmondsworth: Penguin, 1910.

———. *A Passage to India*. 1924. London: Penguin, 1979.

Foucault, Michel. "What is an Author." In *Contemporary Literary Criticism*. Eds. Robert Con Davis and Ronald Schleifer. London: Longmans Press, 1989.

Fraser, Brian J. *The Social Uplifters: Presbyterian Progressives and the Social Gospel in Canada, 1875–1915*. Waterloo, Ontario: Wilfrid Laurier University Press, 1988.

——. "Theology and the Social Gospel Among Canadian Presbyterians: A Case Study." *Studies in Religion/Sciences Religieuses* 8.1 (1979): 35–46.

Fraser, Wayne. *The Dominion of Women: The Personal and the Political in Canadian Women's Literature*. Westport, CT: Greenwood, 1991.

French, Goldwin. "The Evangelical Creed in Canada." In *The Shield of Achilles: Aspects of Canada in the Victorian Age*. Ed. W.L. Morton. Toronto: McClelland and Stewart, 1968, 15–34.

French, William. "Margaret Laurence: These Days Peace Is One of Her Top Priorities." *The Globe and Mail* (4 February 1984): E.1.

———. *The Globe and Mail* (January 6, 1987): A.13.

Freud, Sigmund. "Mourning and Melancholia." *The Freud Reader*. Ed. Peter Gay. New York: Norton, 1989, 584–89.

Frye, Northrop. *The Bush Garden: Essays on the Canadian Imagination.* Toronto: Anansi, 1971.

Fulford, Robert. "Orphan from Neepawa." *Saturday Night* (May 1987): 5–6.

Fulton, Keith Louise. "Feminism and Humanism: Margaret Laurence and the 'Crisis of the Imagination.'" In *Crossing the River: Essays in Honour of Margaret Laurence.* Ed. Kristjana Gunnars. Winnipeg: Turnstone, 1988, 99–120.

Galt, George. "Morally Bound." *Saturday Night* (October 1989): 73–75.

Genette, Gerard. *Narrative Discourse: An Essay in Method.* New York: Cornell University Press, 1980.

Gerry, Thomas M.F. "The Literary Crisis: The Nuclear Crisis." *Dalhousie Review* 67.2–3 (1987): 297–305. Rpt. in *Twentieth-Century Literary Criticism.* Ed. Laurie DiMauro. Detroit: Gale, 1993, 384–90.

Gibson, Graeme, ed. "Margaret Laurence." *Eleven Canadian Novelists: Interviewed by Graeme Gibson.* Toronto: Anansi, 1973, 185–208.

Giddens, Anthony. *The Consequences of Modernity.* Cambridge: Polity, 1990.

———. *Modernity and Self-Identity.* Cambridge: Polity, 1991.

Gilligan, Carol. *In a Different Voice: Psychological Theory and Women's Development.* Cambridge: Harvard University Press, 1982.

Godard, Barbara. "Caliban's Revolt: The Discourses of the (M)Other." In *Critical Approaches to the Fiction of Margaret Laurence.* Ed. Colin Nicholson. Vancouver: UBC Press, 1990, 208–27.

Goldstein, Kenneth J. Interview with Donez Xiques, October 1991.

———. "*The Winnipeg Citizen.*" Ryerson Polytechnical Institute. Thesis for Diploma in Journalism, 1966.

Graham, W. Fred. "Recent Studies in Calvin's Political, Economic and Social Thought and Impact." *In Honour of John Calvin: Papers from the 1986 International Calvin Symposium, McGill University.* Ed. E.J. Furcha. Montreal: ARC Supplement #3, Faculty of Religious Studies, 1987, 365–66.

Groß, Konrad. "Margaret Laurence's African Experience." In *Encounters and Explorations: Canadian Writers and European Critics.* Edited by Franz K. Stanzel and Waldemar Zacharasiewicz. Würzburg: Königshausen und Neumann, 1986, 73–81.

Gunnars, Kristjana, ed. *Crossing the River: Essays in Honour of Margaret Laurence.* Winnipeg: Turnstone, 1988.

———. Preface. *Crossing the River: Essays in Honour of Margaret Laurence.* Ed. Kristjana Gunnars. Winnipeg: Turnstone Press, 1988.

———. "Margaret Laurence." *Encyclopedia of Post-Colonial Literatures in English.* Vol. I. Eds. Eugene Benson and L.W. Conolly. London and New York: Routledge, 1994, 822–24.

Hall, Basil. "Calvin Against the Calvinists." *John Calvin: A Collection of Essays.* Ed. G.E. Duffield. Grand Rapids: Eerdmans Press, 1986, 19–37.

Harlow, Robert. "Lack of Distance." *Canadian Literature* 31 (1967): 71. Rpt., *Margaret Laurence.* Ed. W.H. New. Toronto: McGraw-Hill Ryerson, 1977, 189–91.

Hart, Jonathan. "Comparative Poetics, Postmodernism, and the Canon: An Introduction." *Canadian Review of Comparative Literature/Revue Canadienne de Litterature Comparée* XX 1.2 (1993): 1–8.

Hinz, Evelyn J. "The Religious Roots of the Feminine Identity Issue: Margaret Laurence's *The Stone Angel* and Margaret Atwood's *Surfacing*." In *Margaret Laurence: An Appreciation*. Ed. Christl Verduyn. Peterborough: Broadview Press, 1988, 82–100.

Hjartarson, Paul. "Storytelling, Loss, and Subjectivity in *The Diviners*." In *Crossing the River: Essays on Margaret Laurence*. Ed. Kristjana Gunnars. Winnipeg: Turnstone Press, 1988, 43–64.

Holm, John. *Pidgins and Creoles*. Vol. 1. Cambridge Language Surveys. Cambridge: Cambridge University Press, 1988.

Howells, Coral Ann. "Weaving Fabrications: Women's Narratives in *A Jest of God* and *The Fire-Dwellers*." In *Critical Approaches to the Fiction of Margaret Laurence*. Ed. Colin Nicholson. Vancouver: UBC Press, 1990, 93–106.

Hughes, Kenneth James. "Politics and *A Jest of God*" [1978]. In *Margaret Laurence: An Appreciation*. Ed. Christl Verduyn. Peterborough: Broadview Press, 1988, 101–27.

Hunter, Lynette. "Consolation and Articulation in Margaret Laurence's *The Diviners*." In *Critical Approaches to the Fiction of Margaret Laurence*. Ed. Colin Nicholson. Vancouver: UBC Press, 1990, 131–51.

Hutcheon, Linda. *The Canadian Postmodern: A Study of Contemporary English-Canadian Fiction*. Oxford: Oxford University Press, 1988.

Ignatieff, George. "Margaret Laurence, Peace Worker." *Canadian Woman Studies/les cahiers de la femme* 8.3 (1987): 19.

Jacobus, Mary. *Reading Woman: Essays in Feminist Criticism*. New York: Columbia University Press, 1986.

JanMohamed, Abdul. "The Economy of Manichean Allegory: The Function of Racial Difference in Colonialist Literature." *Critical Inquiry* 12 (Autumn 1985): 59–87.

Jones, Eldred Durosimi, Eustace Palmer and Marjorie Jones, eds. *The Question of Language in African Literature Today: Borrowing and Carrying*. Trenton, NJ: Curry, 1991.

Jung, Carl G. *Memories, Dreams, Reflections*. Rec. and Ed. Aniela Jaffé. Trans. Richard and Clara Winston. 1961. New York: Vintage Books, 1963.

Kearns, Judy. "Rachel and Social Determinism: A Feminist Reading of *A Jest of God*." *Journal of Canadian Fiction* 27 (1980): 101–23.

Keith, W.J. *A Sense of Style: Studies in the Art of Fiction in English-Speaking Canada*. Toronto: ECW, 1989.

Kendall, R.T. "The Puritan Modification of Calvin's Theology." *John Calvin: His Influence in the Western World*. Ed. S.W. Reid. Grand Rapids: Zondervan, 1982, 199–214.

———. *Calvin and English Calvinism to 1649*. Oxford: Oxford University Press, 1979.

Kertzer, J.M. *"That House in Manawaka": Margaret Laurence's A Bird in the House*. Toronto: ECW Press, 1992.

———. *"The Stone Angel*: Time and Responsibility." *The Dalhousie Review* 54 (Autumn 1974): 499–509.

Killam, G.D. "Introduction." *A Jest of God*. Toronto: McClelland and Stewart, 1974, n.p.

———. Introduction. *This Side Jordan*. New Canadian Library. Toronto: McClelland and Stewart, 1976, ix–xvii.

Kirkwood, Hilda. "Last Words." Rev. of *Dance on the Earth*. *Canadian Forum* 69.790 (1990): 29–30.

Kirzner, Ellie. "Margaret Laurence Making Peace." *Now* 22–28 (March 1982): 6.

Klempa, William. "The Concept of the Covenant in Sixteenth and Seventeenth Century Continental and British Reformed Theology." *A Covenant Challenge to Our Broken World*. Ed. Allen O. Miller. Atlanta: Darby Printing Co., 1982, 130–43.

Kolodny, Annette. *The Lay of the Land: Metaphor as Experience and History in American Life and Letters*. Chapel Hill: University of North Carolina Press, 1975.

Kristeva, Julia. *Powers of Horror: An Essay on Abjection*. Trans. Leon Roudiez. New York: Columbia University Press, 1982.

———. "Stabat Mater." *Tales of Love*. Trans. Leon Roudiez. New York: Columbia University Press, 1987.

Kroetsch, Robert. "A Conversation with Margaret Laurence," *Creation*. Toronto: New Press, 1970, 53–63.

———. "Disunity as Unity: A Canadian Strategy." In *The Lovely Treachery of Words: Essays Selected and New*. Ed. Robert Kroetsch. Toronto: Oxford University Press, 1989, 21–33.

———. "The Fear of Women in Prairie Fiction: An Erotics of Space." In *The Lovely Treachery of Words: Essays Selected and New*. Ed. Robert Kroetsch. Toronto: Oxford University Press, 1989, 73–83.

Lacan, Jacques. *Ecrits: A Selection*. Trans. Alan Sheridan. New York: Norton Press, 1987.

Lamar, Howard R. "The Unsettling of the American West: *The Mobility of Defeat*." In *Crossing Frontiers: Papers in American and Canadian Western Literature*. Ed. Dick Harrison. Edmonton: University of Alberta Press, 1979, 35–54.

Leith, John H. *Assembly at Westminster: Reformed Theology in the Making*. Richmond, Virginia: John Knox Press, 1973.

Leney, Jane. "Prospero and Caliban in Laurence's African Fiction." *Journal of Canadian Fiction* 27 (1980): 63–80.

Lennox, John. Introduction. *Margaret Laurence-Al Purdy: A Friendship in Letters*. Ed. John Lennox. Toronto: McClelland and Stewart, 1993, xi–xxxvii.

———, ed. *Margaret Laurence-Al Purdy: A Friendship in Letters*. Toronto: McClelland and Stewart, 1993.

Lessing, Doris. *This Was the Old Chief's Country: Collected African Stories* [1951]. London: Paladin, 1992.

Lever, Bernice. "Literature and Canadian Culture: An Interview with Margaret Laurence." In *Margaret Laurence*. Ed. W.H. New. Toronto: McGraw-Hill Ryerson, 1977, 24–32.

Limerick, Patricia Nelson. *The Legacy of Conquest: The Unbroken Past of the American West*. New York: Norton, 1987.

Margaret Laurence, First Lady of Manawaka. Dir. Robert Duncan. National Film Board of Canada, 1978.

Mannoni, Octave. *Prospero and Caliban: The Psychology of Colonialization*. New York and Washington: Praeger, 1964.

Martens, Debra. "Laurence in Africa." *Paragraph* 16.1 (Summer 1994): 9–13.

McCance, Dawne. "Julia Kristeva and the Ethics of Exile." *Tessera* 8 (1990): 23–29.

McClelland, Joseph C. "Ralph and Stephen and Hugh and Margaret: Canlit's View of Presbyterians," In The *Burning Bush and a Few Acres of Snow: The Presbyterian Contribution to Canadian Life and Culture*. Ed. William Klempa. Ottawa: Carleton University Press, 1994.

McCormick, K.M. "Code-Switching and Mixing." *The Encyclopedia of Language and Linguistics*. Eds. R.E. Asher and J.M.Y. Simpson. 10 vols. Oxford: Pergamon, 1994.

McGann, Jerome. *Theoretical Issues in Literary History*. Ed. David Perkins. Cambridge: Harvard University Press, 1991.

McKillop, A.B. *A Disciplined Intelligence: Critical Inquiry and Canadian Thought in the Victorian Era*. Montreal: McGill-Queen's University Press, 1979.

McLay, C.M. "Every Man Is an Island: Isolation in *A Jest of God*." *Canadian Literature* 50 (1971): 57–68.

Mellor, Philip. "Death in High Modernity: The Contemporary Presence and Absence of Death." *The Sociology of Death*. Ed. David Clark. Oxford and Cambridge: Blackwell, 1993, 11–30.

Memmi, Albert. *Portrait du colonisé* [1957]. Montréal: l'étincelle, 1972.

Miller, Nancy K., ed. *The Poetics of Gender*. New York: Columbia, 1986.

Moi, Toril, ed. *French Feminist Thought*. Oxford: Blackwell, 1987.

Moir, John. *Enduring Witness: A History of the Presbyterian Church in Canada*. 2nd ed. Toronto: Eagle Press Printers, 1987.

Morley, Patricia. *Margaret Laurence: The Long Journey Home*. Rev. ed. Montreal and Kingston: McGill-Queen's University Press, 1991.

Moss, John. *Sex and Violence in the Canadian Novel*. Toronto: McClelland and Stewart, 1977.

New, W.H., ed. *Margaret Laurence*. Critical Views on Canadian Writers. Toronto: McGraw-Hill Ryerson, 1977.

———. Introduction. *Margaret Laurence*. Ed. W.H. New. Toronto: McGraw-Hill Ryerson, 1977, 1–11.

———. "The Other and I: Laurence's African Stories." In *A Place To Stand On: Essays By and About Margaret Laurence*. Ed. George Woodcock. Edmonton: NeWest, 1983, 113–34.

Nicholson, Colin, ed. *Critical Approaches to the Fiction of Margaret Laurence*. Vancouver: UBC Press, 1990.

———. "'There and not there': Aspects of Scotland in Laurence's Writing." In *Critical Approaches to the Fiction of Margaret Laurence*. Ed. Colin Nicholson. Vancouver: UBC Press, 1990, 162–76.

Nixon, Rob. *London Calling: V.S. Naipaul, Postcolonial Mandarin*. New York and Oxford: Oxford University Press, 1992.

Okara, Gabriel. "African Speech…English Words." *Transition* 4.10 (1963): 15–16.

Ondaatje, Michael, ed. *From Ink Lake*. Toronto: Lester & Orpen Dennys, 1990.

Osachoff, Margaret. "Colonialism in the Fiction of Margaret Laurence." *Southern Review* 13.3 (1980): 222–38.

Owen, Michael. "'Keeping Canada God's Country': Presbyterian School-Homes for Ruthenian Children." *Prairie Spirit: Perspectives on the Heritage of the United Church of Canada in the West*. Ed. Dennis L. Butcher et al. Manitoba: University of Manitoba Press, 1985, 184–201.

Palmer, Jerry. "Genre." *Potboilers*. New York: Routledge, 1991, 112–27.

Pascal, Roy. *Design and Truth in Autobiography*. Cambridge: Harvard University Press, 1960.

Penner, Roland. Interview with Donez Xiques, 5 October 1992.

Perkins, David. "Introduction: The State of the Discussion." In *Theoretical Issues in Literary History*. Ed. David Perkins. Cambridge: Harvard University Press, 1991, 1–8.

Pesando, Frank. "In a Nameless Land: The Use of Apocalyptic Mythology in the Writing of Margaret Laurence." *Journal of Canadian Fiction* 2.1 (1973): 53–58.

Phelps, Henry C. "Nick's Picture in *A Jest of God*." *Canadian Literature* 138/139 (1993): 186–88.

Rabinowitz, Peter J. *Before Reading: Narrative Conventions and the Politics of Interpretation*. Ithaca: Cornell University Press, 1987.

Reardon, Betty A. *Sexism and the War System*. New York: Teachers College (Columbia University Press), 1985.

Renault, Mary. "On Understanding Africa." Review of *This Side Jordan*, *Saturday Review* (10 December 1960): 23–24. Rpt. In *Margaret Laurence*. Ed. W.H. New. Toronto: McGraw-Hill Ryerson, 1977, 103–04.

Restuccia, France L. "The Name of the Lily: Edith Wharton's Feminism(s)," *Contemporary Literature* 28.2 (1987): 222–38.

Richards, David. "'Leave the Dead Some Room to Dance!' Margaret Laurence and Africa." In *Critical Approaches to the Fiction of Margaret Laurence*. Ed. Colin Nicholson. Vancouver: UBC Press, 1990, 16–34.

Rimmon-Kenan, Shlomith. *Narrative Fiction: Contemporary Poetics*. London: Methuen, 1983.

Rolston, Holmes, III. *John Calvin Versus the Westminster Confession*. Richmond, Virginia: John Knox Press, 1972.

Rosengarten, Herbert. "Inescapable Bonds." In *Margaret Laurence*. Ed. W.H. New. Toronto: McGraw-Hill Ryerson, 1977.

Ruether, Rosemary. *Faith and Fratricide: The Theological Roots of Anti-Semitism*. New York: Seabury Press, 1974.

Russ, Joanna. *How to Suppress Women's Writing*. London: Women's Press, 1984.

Russell, Kenneth C. "God and Church in the Fiction of Margaret Laurence." *Studies in Religion/Sciences Religieuses* 7.4 (1978): 435–46.

———. "Margaret Laurence's Seekers After Grace." *The Chelsea Journal* 3.5 (1977): 245–48.

Sacks, Peter. *The English Elegy*. Baltimore: Johns Hopkins University Press, 1985.

Scholes, Robert and Robert Kellogg. *The Nature of Narrative*. London: Oxford University Press, 1966.

Seyersted, Per. "The Final Days: Margaret Laurence and Scandinavia." In *Crossing the River: Essays in Honour of Margaret Laurence*. Ed. Kristjana Gunners. Winnipeg: Turnstone, 1988, 207–13.

Silverman, Kaja. *The Acoustic Mirror: The Female Voice in Psychoanalysis and Cinema*. Bloomington: Indiana University Press, 1988.

Smith, Donald C. *Passive Obedience and Prophetic Protest: Social Criticism in the Scottish Church, 1830–1945*. New York: Peter Lang, 1987.

Smythe, Karen E. *Figuring Grief: Gallant, Munro, and the Poetics of Elegy*. Montreal and Kingston: McGill-Queen's University Press, 1992.

Sparrow, Fiona. *Into Africa With Margaret Laurence*. Toronto: ECW Press, 1992.

Spencer, Metta. "The Peacemaking of a Radical: Margaret Laurence." *Canadian Woman Studies/les cahiers de la femme* 8.3 (1987): 20–22.

Spender, Stephen. "Confessions and Autobiography." In *Autobiography: Essays Theoretical and Critical.* Ed. James Olney. Princeton: Princeton University Press, 1980, 115–22.

Spriet, Pierre. "A Retrospective Reading of *The Stone Angel* in the Light of *The Diviners."* World Literature Written in English* 24.2 (Autumn 1984): 312–27.

———. "Narrative and Thematic Patterns in *The Stone Angel." Etudes Canadiennes/Canadian Studies,* no. 11 (1981): 105–19.

Stegner, Wallace. *Angle of Repose.* Fawcett: Greenwich, 1972.

———. "History, Myth, and the Western Writer." In *The Sound of Mountain Water.* Garden City: Doubleday, 1969, 186–201.

Stegner, Wallace and Richard Etulain. *Conversations with Wallace Stegner on Western History and Literature.* Salt Lake City: University of Utah Press, 1983.

Steinem, Gloria. "Marilyn Monroe: The Women Who Died Too Soon." *The Broadview Reader.* 2nd ed. Eds. Herbert Rosengarten and Jane Flick. Peterborough: Broadview, 1987, 491–96.

Stelzig, Eugene. "Poetry and/or Truth: An Essay on the Confessional Imagination." *University of Toronto Quarterly* 54.1 (Fall 1984): 17–37.

Stepanek, Sally. *John Calvin.* New York: Chelsea House Publishers, 1987.

Sternberg, Meir. *Expositional Modes and Temporal Ordering in Fiction.* Baltimore: Johns Hopkins University Press, 1978.

Stovel, Bruce. "Coherence in Margaret Laurence's *A Bird in the House." Anglo-American Studies* 9.2 (1989): 129–44.

Stovel, Nora Foster. *Rachel's Children: Margaret Laurence's* A Jest of God. Toronto: ECW Press, 1992.

———. *Stacey's Choice: Margaret Laurence's* The Fire-Dwellers. Toronto: ECW Press, 1993.

Stratton, Florence. *Contemporary African Literature and the Politics of Gender.* New York and London: Routledge, 1994.

Suleri, Sara. "Amorphous India: Questions of Geography." *Southwest Review* 71.3 (Summer 1989).

Sullivan, Rosemary. "An Interview With Margaret Laurence." In *A Place To Stand On: Essays By and About Margaret Laurence.* Ed. George Woodcock. Edmonton: NeWest, 1983, 61–79.

Swayze, Walter E. "Introduction: Knowing through Writing: The Pilgrimage of Margaret Laurence." In *Crossing the River: Essays in Honour of Margaret Laurence.* Ed. Kristjana Gunnars. Winnipeg: Turnstone, 1988, 3–23.

Tapping, Craig. "Margaret Laurence and Africa." In *Crossing the River: Essays in Honour of Margaret Laurence.* Ed. Kristjana Gunnars. Winnipeg: Turnstone, 1988, 65–80.

Thieme, John. "Acknowledging Myths: The Image of Europe in Margaret Laurence's *The Diviners* and Jack Hodgins's *The Invention of the World.*" In *Critical Approaches to the Fiction of Margaret Laurence.* Ed. Colin Nicholson. Vancouver: UBC Press, 1990, 152–61.

Thomas, Clara. "A Conversation About Literature: An Interview With Margaret Laurence and Irving Layton." *Journal of Canadian Fiction* 1.1 (1972): 65–68.

———. Afterword. *The Prophet's Camel Bell.* New Canadian Library. Toronto: McClelland and Stewart, 1963, rpt. 1991, 265–68.

———. Introduction. *The Tomorrow-Tamer*. By Margaret Laurence. Toronto: McClelland and Stewart, 1970, xi–xvii.

———. *Margaret Laurence*. Toronto: McClelland and Stewart, 1969.

———. "Morning Yet on Creation Day: A Study of This Side Jordan." In *A Place To Stand On: Essays By and About Margaret Laurence*. Ed. George Woodcock. Edmonton: NeWest, 1983, 93–105.

———. "Pilgrim's Progress: Margaret Laurence and Hagar Shipley." In *Margaret Laurence: An Appreciation*. Ed. Christl Verduyn. Peterborough: Broadview Press, 1988, 58–69.

Todd, Loreto. *Modern Englishes: Pidgins and Creoles*. Oxford: Blackwell, 1984.

Toon, Peter. *The Emergence of Hyper-Calvinism in English Nonconformity, 1689–1765*. London: The Olive Tree, 1967.

Turner, Alan R. "Scottish Settlement in the West." *The Scottish Tradition in Canada*. Ed. W. Stanford Reid. Toronto: McClelland and Stewart and The Multicultural Program, Department of the Secretary of State of Canada and the Publishing Centre, Supply and Services Canada, 1976.

van Herk, Aritha. "The Eulalias of Spinsters and Undertakers." In *Crossing the River: Essays in Honour of Margaret Laurence*. Ed. Kristjana Gunnars. Winnipeg: Turnstone Press, 1988, 133–46.

Vaudry, Richard W. *The Free Church in Victorian Canada, 1844–1861*. Waterloo: Wilfrid Laurier University Press, 1989.

Verduyn, Christl, ed. *Margaret Laurence: An Appreciation*. Peterborough: Journal of Canadian Studies and Broadview Press, 1988.

———. "Language, Body and Identity in Margaret Laurence's *The Fire-Dwellers*." In *Margaret Laurence: An Appreciation*. Ed. Christl Verduyn. Peterborough: Broadview Press, 1988, 128–40.

Wainwright, J.A. *A Very Large Soul: Selected Letters From Margaret Laurence to Canadian Writers*. Dunvegan: Cormorant, 1995.

———. Introduction. *A Very Large Soul: Selected Letters From Margaret Laurence to Canadian Writers*. Dunvegan: Cormorant, 1995, vii–xviii.

———. Preface. *A Very Large Soul: Selected Letters From Margaret Laurence to Canadian Writers*. Dunvegan: Cormorant, 1995, i–v.

Wali, Obiajunwa. "The Dead End of African Literature." *Transition* 3.10 (1963): 13–15.

Walsh, Mary Ellen Williams. "*Angle of Repose* and the Writings of Mary Hallock Foote: A Source Study." *Critical Essays on Wallace Stegner*. Ed. Anthony Arthur. Boston: G.K. Hall, 1982, 184–209.

Walzer, Michael. *The Revelation of the Saints: A Study in the Origins of Radical Politics*. New York: Atheneum, 1972.

Warwick, Susan. *The River of Now and Then: The Diviners*. Toronto: ECW, 1993.

Watt, F.W. Review of *The Fire-Dwellers*. *The Canadian Forum* (July 1969): 87.

Whitenack, Judith. "A New Look at Autobiography and Confession." *Ball State University Forum* 23.3 (Summer 1982): 40–47.

Wigmore, Donnalu. "Margaret Laurence: The Woman Behind the Writing." *Chatelaine* (February 1971): 28.

Williams, David. "Jacob and the Demon: Hagar as Storyteller in *The Stone Angel.*" In *Crossing the River: Essays in Honour of Margaret Laurence.* Ed. Kristjana Gunnars. Winnipeg: Turnstone, 1988, 81–98.

Williams, Patrick, and Laura Chrisman. Introduction. In *Colonial Discourse and Post-Colonial Theory: A Reader.* Eds., Patrick Williams and Laura Chrisman. New York: Columbia University Press, 1994, 1–20.

Wilson, Elizabeth. "Tell It Like It Is: Women and Confessional Writing." In *Sweet Dreams: Sexuality, Gender and Popular Fiction.* Ed. Susannah Radstone. London: Lawrence and Wishart, 1988.

Wilson, Ethel. *Swamp Angel.* Toronto: McClelland and Stewart, 1954.

Wilson, Lois. Personal conversation. 30 April 1994.

Wiseman, Adele. Interview with Donez Xiques, October 1991.

Woodcock, George. *A Place To Stand On: Essays By and About Margaret Laurence.* Western Canada Literary Documents Series 4. Edmonton: NeWest, 1983.

Woodsworth, James S. *Strangers Within Our Gates or Coming Canadians.* Rpt. 1909; Toronto: The University of Toronto Press, 1972.

Wyile, Herb and Jeanette Lynes. "Regionalism and Ambivalence in Canadian Literary History." *Open Letter* 9.4 (1995): 117–27.

Xiques, Donez. Introduction. *A Tree For Poverty: Somali Prose and Poetry.* Hamilton: McMaster University Library Press and Toronto: ECW Press, 1993, 7–17.

Yeats, W.B. "The Second Coming." *Collected Poems of W.B. Yeats.* London: Macmillan, 1967, 210–11.

INDEX

245

Presbyterianism, 181
    British influence on, 181
psyche, xi
self-knowledge, xi
Canadian Arts scene, 189
Canadian Pacific Railway, 196, 203
The Canadian Settler's Guide, 85
Canadian women, value of, 46
Canadian writing, Laurence's response
    to, 193
catharsis
    in reconstruction of the past, 60
    in tragedy, 69
Catholicism, 170–71, 176–77
Caute, David, 26
CBC (Canadian Broadcasting
    Corporation), 192–93, 197–200,
    203, 207
cemeteries, 128–29
censorship, effect on Laurence, 206, 212,
    215–17, 227
Cheyne, A.C., 174
childbirth, 13–14, 30, 41, 44–45, 73–74, 84,
    131–32, 136
childhood, 113, 132, 144, 154–55, 159
children, 54, 60, 110–11, 124, 144, 146
    as representative of new Africa, 41
    helplessness of, 160
    loss of, 191
    role of in relation to parents, 126–27
    school children, 128
    possible abandonment of, 136
    possible birth of, 131–32
Chora, psychoanalysis, 84
Christ, 91, 169–71, 175
Christianity, 33–34, 40, 82, 102–3, 108, 157, 164,
    181–82
chronology, narratology, 56
Chunn, Margaret, 191
church, 7, 123
Cixous, Helene, 87
Clarke, Nelson, 192
class difference, 140
clergy, 76
code-switching, 3

Coetzee, J.M., 7
Cohan, Steven and Linda M. Shires, 61, 65
colonial
    condition, 144
    discursive tradition, 25–26
    oppression, 39
    position, 37–38
    society, 5
colonialism, xiv, 13, 24, 39–40, 43, 46
colonialists, resistance to, 44
colonies, 41
colonization, 20
    myths of, 144
    resistance to, 13
coming-of-age, 23, 68
communication, 127, 220
    as manipulation, 41
    barriers to, 99
    failure of, 44, 76, 110–11, 125–26
    inability to communicate, 12
    lack of, 4, 105
    problems of, 4
    role of language in, 3, 7
    semiotic, 93–94
Communist politics, 187, 206
community, 120, 165
compassion, role of love in expressing, 120
conception, 83. *See also* childbirth
Confederation, 181
confession, 47–48, 61
    religious, 52
confessional
    form, 49
    literature, 49–50
    memoir, 70
    narrator, 50
    novel, 47, 50
Conrad, Joseph, 19, 25–26, 30
consolation, 69, 74, 76
construction of self, 81–82
contemporary women's fiction, parody
    in, 101
convergence of object and subject, 90
Co-operative Commonwealth
    Federation (CCF), 192

co-operatives, 187

corpses, 90–91, 123, 189

counter-culture, 149–50

Covenant, the, 166, 173

Covenanters, the, 181

creativity
    as sign of subjectivity, 81
    loss of, 159
    of narrator, 67–69
    role of language in, 157–58
    tenuous nature of, 115
    unacknowledged, 92

critical response to African writing, xiv

Crombruach, Scotland, 114–15

cross cultural
    observation and responsibility, 16
    understanding, 41

crucifixion, 83, 170

Culloden, Scotland, 89–90

cultural difference, 20, 22, 127, 140
    acknowledgement of, 43
    awareness of, 36
    in heritage, 147–48, 200
    in Manawaka, 124
    in Manitoba, 124, 203, 207–8
    in North Winnipeg, 107–8

cultural fictions, 144
    semiotics, importance of, 65
    signifier, 5
    traditions informing narrative, 157
    upheaval in Africa, 36

culture, 33, 87, 141–42, 146
    African, 44
    and the body, 83
    complexity of, 125
    critique of, 101
    fragmentation of, 121
    ideologically defined, 157
    inherited, 143
    of American West, 140
    of Canadian West, 140
    patriarchal Western, 108
    places outside of, 92

Dante, Alleghieri, 103

Darling, Michael, 69, 74

daughterhood
    as contributing to identity, 84
    and motherhood, 125

Davidon, Ann Morrissett, 224

Davidson, Arnold, 67

Davies, Alan, 182

death, 9, 14, 29, 35, 43, 45, 47, 51, 53–54, 56, 58,
        61–64, 67, 73–79, 82–83, 87–90, 104,
        121–23, 128–32, 135, 146, 179, 190–91

Declatory Act, 175

defiance of colonized, 13

democracy, 192

Depression, 190

desire, 83–84

Desoudry, Mauri, 199

dialect, use of, 201

dialogue in narrative, 58

diaries, role of in *The Prophet's Camel Bell*, 37

didacticism
    criticism of Laurence for, 212
    in African writing, 45–46
    in Laurence's writing, 214–15, 228

dignity, search for, 36–37

Diop, David, 25

disarmament, 214

discourse, xii, 3–4, 7, 22, 82, 84–87, 89, 93, 102,
        108, 113, 126–29, 146, 201, 225–26

dispossessed males, 94

Doctorow, E.L., 160

Dombrowski, Theo, 156, 160

Donne, John, 86–87, 111, 189

doppelganger, 123

Doppler Effect, 140–41, 151, 156, 160

Dostoyevsky, Fyodor, 62

Douglas, J.D., 163

Douglass, Jane Dempsey, 167

Draine, John, 199

dreams, 105, 110, 112, 122, 125, 127, 135, 150–51

Dugald, Manitoba, 191

Dumas, Alex, 189

duration, narratology, 58–59

Easingwood, Peter, 215

eastern Canada, 203

Ecclesiastes, 76

economic independence in Africa, 45

Eden, 145

education, Laurence's, 37

Egejuru, 6

elegy, 68–69

Eliot, T.S., 102–3, 189

embedded fictions, 81

empathy when relating to Other, 20, 28

empowerment of women, 110

Engel, Marian, 33

England, 5, 28, 44, 163, 206, 213

English
adapting, 3
as second language, 5
language, 6

Enlightenment, 175

environmental issues and Laurence, 214

essentialism in Kristeva, 84

ethics appropriate to women, 83

ethnic difference in *A Jest of God* and *The Fire-Dwellers*, 124

ethnic minorities in Manawaka, 182

ethnocentricity, Anglo-Saxon, 181

ethnocentrism and Laurence, 183

Europe, 94, 175, 188, 192

exile from Africa and England, 44

expatriate, Laurence's role as, 1

Fabre, Michel, 156, 166, 217

faith, 115
as part of Laurence's conception of fiction, 223
of Somalis, 38,
religious, 104, 166, 173–74, 176

family, influence of, 68, 139, 141

fantasies
deconstruction of, 112
imaginative, 134
science fiction, 127

fatalism, Somalis sense of, 38

father-daughter relationships, 85

fatherhood, 112, 114

father-infant relationship, 84

fathers, 73, 84, 94, 105, 119, 134, 136, 146, 170

Federalism, religious movement, 173–76

female
narrators, 202
perception, 109
role models, 107

feminine acoustic, 87
discourse, 83
geneaology, 81
voice, 62

femininity, 82

feminism, 33, 39, 42, 45, 64, 99, 102–3, 123, 213, 216, 219, 224
assertion of, 116
Laurence and, 214
progression of, 108

feminist consciousness, 102

feminists, French, 82, 93

fetishism, 45

fiction
concept of, 223
creation of, 92, 157, 187
Laurence's reputation and, 187

fictionality, 71

fictionalizing, 35, 88, 143, 152, 195, 205

fiction-elegy, 68

Fifeshire, Scotland, 165

figuring death, 76, 122

films, 168, 193, 205. *See also* media

fire, 90–91, 133–34, 189–91

Fleet, Brenda, 225–26

focalization, narratology, 57

Fontaine, Robert, 204

Foote, Mary Hallock, 153

Forster, E.M., 19, 30

Foucault, Michel, 85

Fraser, Brian, 181, 183

Free Church, 165, 175, 181, 183

freedom of speech, 206–7

freedom, 35–37, 40, 120
as American, 142
as autonomous woman, 64
as theme in newspaper writing, 207

Highlands, Scotland, 165

Hinz, Evelyn, 178

historical knowledge of Africa, 5

history, xvi, 40, 83, 85, 113, 140–43, 145, 148,
    151–52, 156–57, 164–65, 170, 175, 181,
    205–6, 215, 219

Hjartarson, Paul, 86

Hollywood, 198

Hopkins, Gerard Manley, 87

host-text, psychoanalysis, 81

housewives, role of, 35, 191

Hudson's Bay Company, 165

Hughes, Kenneth, 217

human condition, the, 214

humanism, 215, 219–20, 228

humanity, xi, 40

Hume, David, 163

humility, character's sense of, 20

humour, Laurence's review of, 204

Hurtig, Mel, 218

Hutcheon, Linda, 87, 101

hymns, 53, 75, 77, 135–36, 177

iconography, 87, 93

identity, xii, xiv, 51, 62, 68, 70, 82–83, 91, 106,
    111, 112, 116, 120–21, 125, 127, 139, 143,
    144–46, 148

ideology, 49, 65

Ignatieff, George, 213

illiteracy, 42

imagination
    and caring, 225
    living in, 123
    role of listener and, 197–98
    vibrant literary, 207

immigration to Canada, 181–82

immortality, 83

imperialism, 37, 40, 220
    Anglo-American, 181
    Laurence's opposition to, 183

implied author, 52

independence, 1, 36, 38–40, 42, 45, 141, 144,
    146–47, 160

individuation, 86, 100

influence, Laurence's on other writers,
    199

Ingrese, 2

inner
    change and identity, 49
    voice, 102, 104, 106–7, 113–14, 116, 122, 125,
        154
    world, 123, 127

interior monologues, 100, 109, 123, 153
    conversations, 106

internal
    conflict, 151
    worlds, 120

intertextuality, 85

interviews, 188–89

irony, 99, 101, 103, 106–7, 109, 146, 216

Isaiah, 124

Islam, 38

Italian colonies, 38

James, Henry, 199–200

Jesus, 183

Jesuits, 205

Job, 132

Jonah, 35, 121, 129–30, 132

Jordan, river, 40–42

journalism, 188

Joyce, James, 87, 101

Jung, Carl, 166

justice, themes of social, 222

juvenilia, 35, 206

Keith, W.J., xv, 69

Kellogg, Robert, 49

Kendall, R.T., 164

Kertzer, J.M., 61, 69, 70

Kildonan, Manitoba, 165

Killam, G.D., xvi, 122

Kipling, Rudyard, 25

Kirzner, Ellie, 227–28

Klemper, William, 174

Kolodny, Annette, 25

Kristeva, Julia, 82–85, 90, 93

Kristevan subject, 85
Kroetsch, Robert, 141, 145, 149, 157, 165

labour issues, as reported in Laurence's
    newspaper writing, 188, 191–94
Lacan, Jacques, 84
Laing, R.D., 122
Lamar, Howard, 146
language, 3–5, 7, 12, 15, 22, 69, 76, 84, 89, 91, 93,
    101, 105–6, 144, 146, 156–69, 201, 203,
    219, 225–27
Laurence, Jack, 4, 23, 36–37, 220
Laurence, Margaret
    adult fiction compared to children's
        books, 212
    African books, xii
    and critical heritage, xiii
    and labour issues, 188, 191–94
    and Nigerian writing, xiv
    and oral cultures of Commonwealth,
        xiv
    anti-establishment sentiments, 36
    apprentice writing, xv
    apprenticeship, newspaper, 187
    artistic achievement, xii
    as anti-colonialist, 28
    as colonial writer, xiv
    as feminist, 116
    as journalist, 187
    as postcolonial writer, xiv
    as translator, 37, 220
    as white liberal, 22–23, 38, 41
    as writer, xiv, 81, 99, 106, 143, 146–47, 154,
        157
    attention to voice, 201
    awareness of health issues, 190
    book reviews, 187, 189, 193–97
    books on, xiii
    career as reporter, 187–88
    career, xi
    censorship, effect on, 206, 212, 215–17, 227
    children's books, xii
    college graduation, 189
    college years, 36

    commentary on the British, 220
    contribution of African works, xv
    critique of Greek drama, 200-202
    death of, xiii
    development of voice, 146
    diaries, 37
    effect on Canadians, xi
    faith and fiction, 223
    feminism, 214
    humanity, xi
    in postcolonial context, xiv
    influence on other writers, 199
    letters, xii
    opposition to imperialism, 183
    popular magazines, 213
    posthumous publication, xii
    public's love for, xii
    publishing history, xii
    reaction to death by others, xiii
    recognition of Canadian culture, 198,
        202–8
    reputation, xi–xiii, 187
    response to Canadian writing, 193
    review of humour, 204
    role as expatriate, 1
    role of politics in writing, 215–17
    technical development, xv
Laurence's books
    A Bird in the House, xii, 34–35, 67–80, 129,
        167–68, 212, 222
    The Christmas Birthday Story, xii
    Dance on the Earth, xii, 16–17, 34–35, 188,
        196, 206, 212–13, 224
    The Diviners, xii, 3, 35, 81–97, 99–101, 105–9,
        111–16, 119, 127, 139–61, 165–71, 173,
        177, 179–83, 189, 206, 211–12, 217–18,
        222, 224, 227
    The Fire-Dwellers, xii, 35, 41, 42, 99–101,
        103–4, 106–13, 116, 119–22, 125–9,
        132–37, 167, 168, 172–73, 179, 222
    Heart of a Stranger, xii, 2–3, 5, 44
    Jason's Quest, xii
    A Jest of God, xii, 34–35, 41, 44, 81, 99–100,
        101–5, 108–13, 116, 119–25, 127–32,
        135–37, 167, 171–73, 177, 217, 222

Marxism, 193, 217

masculinity, 145, 150, 160

masochism, 83

maternal, 81–83, 94
    function, 82
    loss, 87

maternity, 82, 84

matriarchal models, 34

matrilinearity, 81, 87

McCance, Dawn, 83

McGann, Jerome, xvi–xvii

McKillop, A.B., 175

media, 85, 126, 151–52

Mellor, David, 68

Melville, Herman, 129

memoirs, 37, 70, 188–89, 206, 212–13, 215–16, 220–21, 228

memories, 90
    and censorship, 206
    and happiness, 135
    invented, 151, 154–55
    role of in narrative, 47, 67, 70–71, 77–78, 87, 127, 164–65

memory
    and ancestors, 164–65
    in self-understanding, 51
    role of in lifestory, 55
    site of, 83
    tenuous nature of, 189

metafiction, 140–41, 143, 152–54

Methodist Church, 177–78

Métis. *See also* Louis Riel
    and creativity, 111, 205–6
    and fiction, 205–6
    and fire, 90–91, 133
    and identity, 115, 146–48
    denial of human rights to, 212
    marginalization of, 85, 223
    silencing of, 90–91
    tales, 143
    Tonnerre family, 85, 90–91, 113–14, 133, 143, 146
    military, the, 225

Milton, John, 87

mimesis, 52, 55, 207

miscegenation, 26, 30

missionaries
    criticism of, 24
    in Canada, 165, 182

Mitchell, W.O., 193–96

monoglossia, 3

Montreal, 135

Moodie, Susanna, 145, 147

morality, 159, 166–67, 172, 174, 176, 193, 212–13

moral vision, 213

Morley, Patricia, xv, 213

mortality, 51, 73

Moses, 36, 41

mother-child relationships, 83, 126–27

mother-daughter relationships, 84, 86–87, 115, 125, 134, 147, 149, 158, 160

motherhood, 54, 82, 99, 104, 107, 110, 214, 223

mothers, 41, 73–74, 81–82, 84, 86, 94, 105, 119–20, 123, 125, 127–28, 191, 223, 226

mourning, 41, 67–69, 82, 124, 128, 130, 135–36
    practice, 71
    ritual, 77
    work, 69

movies, 122

multiplicity, elision of, xv

Munro, Alice, 33

music
    and narrative technique, 85, 127–28
    and sliding of genre, 85
    hymns, 53, 75, 77, 135–36, 177
    Laurence's discussion of, 188, 199
    songs, 53, 75, 77–78, 85, 92, 127–28, 135–36, 147, 153, 177
        as means of fictionalizing, 88
        for the purpose of narrative, 92

myth of empire, 141

mythology, 35, 56, 83, 85, 88, 114, 141, 143–44, 147, 157–58, 165

myths of origin, 56

Naipaul, V.S., 19, 21, 25–27, 30

narcissism, 82, 86

narration, 44, 47–49, 55, 64, 67, 85, 106, 125, 153–54, 156, 158, 201–2

Reformed Protestants, 183
reformed religious tradition, 163–64
regionalism, xii, xiv, 139, 193–96, 203
relationships, quest for, 36
religion, 52, 75–76, 103, 115–16, 123, 163, 166, 169
Renaissance painting, 92–93
reporter, Laurence's career as, 187–88
representation, 20, 67–68, 71, 82, 89–93
reproduction, 82
reputation, 187
resistance, 160
retrospective narration, 47, 67
revelation in confession, 52
Richards, David, 3, 217
Riel, Louis, 87, 189, 205–6
Rimmon-Kenan, Schlometh, 56–57, 59
rivers, 14, 75–76, 92, 140, 151, 160, 179
Robbins, Tom, 160
Robertson, James, 165
role of politics in Laurence's writing,
    215–17
Rolston, Holmes, III, 166
Ross, Scotland, 165
Rousseau, Jean-Jacques, 62
Russell, Kenneth, 169

Sacks, Peter, 69
Sago, Mitch, 189
Said, Edward, 21
Saint Augustine of Hippo, 49, 62
Saint Boniface, Manitoba, 197, 203
Sandburg, Carl, 121, 129, 133
Saskatchewan, 139
Sayers, Dorothy, 189
schizophrenia, 40, 122, 126
Scholes, Robert, 49
Schull, Joseph, 192, 198, 200–201, 205
Scotland, 89–90, 94, 114–15, 143, 146, 163,
    165–66, 175
Scots-Presbyterianism, 34, 119–20, 124,
    165–66, 172, 176, 178–79, 183
Scott, F.R., 207
Scott, Jamie S., 48
Scott, Robert, 201

Scott, Walter, 163
Scottish church history, 164
Scottish highlanders, 56
Seelye, John, 160
self, 54, 122, 132, 172, 176–77
    affirmation, 50
    analysis, 50
    assertion, 114
    awareness, 47, 49, 51, 100, 102, 112, 115,
        124–25
    consciousness, 103
    definition, 113
    determination, 67
    disclosure, 52–53
    discovery, 64, 70
    justification, 52
    knowledge, 62
    perception, 53
    reflexivity, 50, 67, 69, 85–86, 140–41,
        152–54, 215–16, 221
Selkirk, Lord, 165
semiotics, 65
Senghor, Leopold, 25
sexual violence, 12, 27, 30, 40, 110, 126
sexuality, 52, 99, 100, 108–11, 126, 130, 132, 150,
    167
Shakespeare, William, 42, 87, 129, 200
Shaw, Irwin, 189
Shoub, Max, 200
sibling rivalry, 120
signification, 48, 62, 64–65, 82–83, 88
silence
    construction of, 90
    of mother, 88
silencing of African women, 26
Silverman, Kaja, 84, 90
Sinclair, Lister, 198, 204
The 60th Canadian Field Artillery Book, 85
Smith, Donald, 179–80, 206
Smythe, Karen E., 68, 70
social
    commentary, 218
    issues, 190
    order, 180
    roles, 99, 119–20

sphere, 49, 63, 79, 163, 166, 179, 181, 188, 190, 223–24

socialist politics, 36, 182, 187, 206

societal standards, resistance to, 100

society, 35

Somali nomads, 39

Somalia, 2, 16, 21–23, 36–38, 41, 221

Somalis, 2, 220–21

songs, 53, 75, 77–78, 85, 88, 92, 127–28, 135–36, 147, 153, 177. *See also* music

South Wachakwa river, 92, 179

Soyinka, Wole, 25

Sparrow, Fiona, 8

speaker, subjective location of, 21

speech, 3–4, 7, 22, 89, 124

    acts, 85

    patterns, 201

Spencer, Metta, 213

Spender, Stephen, 51, 55

spinsterhood, 124, 131

spirituality, 36, 38, 115, 159, 167

Spivak, Gayatri, 21

split discourse, 82

Spriet, Pierre, 57, 62–63

Sri Lanka, 27

stage drama, 197–98

Stark, James, 226–27

Stelzig, Eugene, 54–55

Stepanek, Sally, 176

Sternberg, Meir, 53, 55

Stevenson, R.C., 163

stoicism, 73

stories

    in *A Bird in the House*, 72

    multiplicity of, 157

    telling, 85–86

story, 156

storytelling, 69–70, 74–75, 86, 88, 90

story-time, 58–59

stranger, figure in African writing, 16, 35

Strathcona, Lord, 206

Stratton, Florence, 25–26

subjectivity, 42, 48, 64, 81–82, 84–87, 92, 121, 143

subject-position, 26, 30–31

suffering

human, 39

    of old age, 50

suicide, 131–36

Suleri, Sara, 19

Sullivan, Rosemary, 165, 178, 217

superstition, 42

survival, theme of, xi, 36, 46

Sutherland, Scotland, 94, 143, 146

Swan, Susan, 34

Swayze, Walter, xiii–xiv, 218

symbolic order, the, 84

Synode of Dort, 176

Tarzan, 87

teleology, 83

temporality, 49, 55–57

testimony, 52

    in confession, 51

thematic coherence, 61

theology, 163, 166, 173–75

Third World, 19

Thomas, Audrey, 33

Thomas, Clara, xiii, 14, 121, 165–67, 188, 212

Thurlow, James, 227

time, narrative, 49, 55–56, 140, 155–56

Togoland, 9

tombs, 124, 128

Toon, Peter, 166

topoi, 100

Toronto, 145

tradition, 77, 79, 93, 139, 142

tragedy, 69

Traill, Catharine Parr, 81, 87, 107–8, 147, 152, 168–69, 211, 224

translator, Laurence as, 37, 220

Trauerarbeit, 68

travelogue, 37

tribal past, 42

tribalism, 40

truth, the, 52–53, 64, 85–86, 115, 141, 143, 152–53, 156–57, 165, 177, 189, 219, 228

Tuomi, Bill, 189

Turner, Alan R., 165

Turner, Frederick Jackson, 142

Twi, 5–9, 24
twins, 123

Ukrainians, 124, 203
unions, 194, 199
Unitarian Church, 174
United Church, 77, 174, 178, 191
United College, 187
University of Manitoba, 193
urban issues, 191, 207

Vancouver, 94, 102–3, 105, 119, 146, 167–68, 174
Varga, Eugene, 192
Vaudry, Richard, 166
Verduyn, Christl, xiii
verisimilitude, loss of in *The Stone Angel*, 57
Verne, Jules, 201
victimization of African women, 26, 36, 39
victims, 212, 219
    blaming, 27
    communicating with, 13
    irony and, 113
    Jesus as, 170
    women as, 36, 39, 212, 219
Vietnam War, 222
violence
    act of, 124
    against women, 212, 218, 223–25
    men's, 216, 222–24, 227
    sexual, 12, 27, 30, 110
    sexual/colonial, 30
Virgin Mary, 83
virginity, 82–84, 109
voice
    adopted from other, 105
    alternating of colonizer and colonized, 217
    articulation of a expression of liberation, 100
    attention to by young Laurence, 201
    development of as writer, 146
    liberation of, 160

of mourners, 132
of strength, 116
polyphony of, 153
straining to make heard, 17

Wainwright, Andrew, xi–xii
Walsh, Mary Ellen Williams, 153
war, 73, 134, 188, 207, 222, 228
Warwick, Susan, 88
water imagery in *The Fire-Dwellers*, 135–36
Wayne and Schuster, 204
Wesleyans, the, 177
West, the, 139–40, 144, 157, 160, 194–96
    development of, 144
Western civilization, 39
    culture, 108
    literary tradition, 49
    ways, 45
Westernization of Africa, 28
Westminster Confession, 166–67, 175–76
white liberal, Laurence's position as, 22–23, 38, 41
Wigmore, Donnali, 216
Whitenack, Judith, 49
Williams, Patrick and Laura Chrisma, xiv
Wilson, Elizabeth, 64
Wilson, Ethel, 136
Winnipeg, 36, 77, 94, 124, 187, 191, 207
Wiseman, Adele, 193
Wister, Owen, 145
woman as symbol, 25, 30, 82
womanhood on three continents, 35
womb, the, 84
women
    and confession, 63
    as metaphor, 12, 25
    as threat, 150
    experience, 48
    groups, 213
    issues, 223–25
    movement, 228
    roles, 42
    writing, 34
Woodcock, George, xv